# Practical MongoDB Aggregations

The official guide to developing optimal
aggregation pipelines with MongoDB 7.0

Paul Done

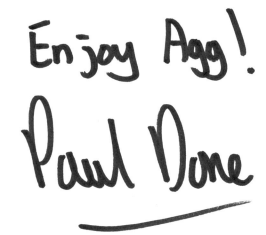

Enjoy Agg!

Paul Done

BIRMINGHAM—MUMBAI

# Practical MongoDB Aggregations

## First edition

**Acquisition Editor**: Sathya Mohan

**Lead Development Editor**: Siddhant Jain

**Development Editor**: Afzal Shaikh

**Content Development Editor**: Rhea Gangavkar

**Project Coordinator**: Yash Basil

**Copy Editor**: Safis Editing

**Proofreader**: Safis Editing

**Production Designer**: Deepak Chavan

**Production reference**: 1050923

Published by Packt Publishing Ltd.

Grosvenor House, 11 St Paul's Square, Birmingham, B3 1RB, UK.

ISBN 978-1-83508-064-1

www.packtpub.com

# Contributors

## About the author

**Paul Done** is one of two distinguished solutions architects at MongoDB, Inc., having been at MongoDB for 10 years. He has previously held roles in various software disciplines, including engineering, consulting, and pre-sales, at companies such as Oracle, Novell, and BEA Systems. Paul specializes in databases and middleware, focusing on resiliency, scalability, transactions, event processing, and applying evolvable data model approaches. He spent most of the early 2000s building **Java EE (J2EE)** transactional systems on WebLogic, integrated with relational databases such as Oracle RAC and messaging systems such as MQSeries.

## About the reviewers

**Rachelle Palmer** is the Product Leader for Developer Database Experience and Developer Education at MongoDB, overseeing the driver client libraries, documentation, framework integrations, and MongoDB University. She is passionate about being hands-on and has built sample applications for MongoDB in Java, PHP, Rust, Python, Node.js, and Ruby. She joined MongoDB in 2013 and was previously director of the technical services engineering team, creating and managing the team that provided support and CloudOps to MongoDB Atlas. She is also passionate about education for all, and runs a family scholarship fund for youth interested in STEM majors.

**Nicholas Cottrell** has used MongoDB as the data layer for dozens of software development projects since version 2.0, long before joining the company as a consulting engineer in 2017. He now helps technical services engineers learn about all aspects of MongoDB to support an ever-growing range of customer use cases. He holds dual Australian and Swedish citizenship and lives in Normandy, France.

# Acknowledgements

Creating this book has been a labor of love for me over the last few years. Writing a book is hard, but the process is much easier when the book's subject (MongoDB software) is a joy to use. With that said, this book only exists due to the valuable input and feedback from many of my colleagues at MongoDB, Inc.

Two of these colleagues are the reviewers of this book—Rachelle Palmer and Nicholas Cottrell. Thank you for your tireless work of catching errors and poor phrasing.

Earlier incarnations of the book's content also benefitted from insight and advice from other colleagues, who I will be eternally grateful to: Jake McInteer, John Page, Asya Kamsky, Mat Keep, Brian Leonard, Marcus Eagan, Elle Shwer, Ethan Steininger, and Andrew Morgan.

In particular, I would like to single out Asya Kamsky (who also wrote the Foreword for this book). I often refer to Asya as *MongoDB Aggregations Royalty*. Whatever Asya doesn't know about aggregations isn't worth knowing and being able to lean on her knowledge helped improve this book immensely.

There was also a whole team of people at Packt involved in the production who went above and beyond with a razor-sharp focus on quality, which I greatly appreciated—thank you.

Finally, I'd like to thank my wife, Helen, and my daughters, Caitlin and Elsie. They will have zero interest in reading this book, but they've put up with me being 'zoned out' for too long while I was creating it. Thank you for just being you and making me laugh every day!

# Foreword

I've been involved with databases since I joined a small database company in the early 1990s. For the next two decades, I believed databases were synonymous with SQL until someone asked me what I thought about the new *NoSQL* databases, and MongoDB—in particular. This led me to try MongoDB for a small side project I was working on. The rest, as they say, is history.

When I joined *10gen*—the company that created *MongoDB*, in early 2012, the query language was simple and straightforward. There weren't options for easy data aggregation because the general advice was, "*Store the data the way you expect to access the data,*" which was a fantastic approach for fast point queries.

However, as time went on, it became clear that there are times when you must answer questions you never expected when you were first designing the application and database schema. The options for this type of analytical data aggregation within MongoDB were limited. MongoDB's initial pass at data aggregation was the `mapReduce` command. However, map-reduce was hard to understand and get right. Plus, it required writing and running inefficient JavaScript.

Developers needed a new way to aggregate data natively on the server that was both intuitive and efficient. We called what we came up with the *aggregation framework*. Since the stages of data processing in the aggregation framework were organized as a pipeline (familiarly evoking processing files on the Unix command line, for those of us who did such things a lot), we also referred to it as the *aggregation pipeline*. Very quickly, *agg* became my favorite feature of MongoDB because of its flexibility, power, and ease of debugging.

We've come a long way in the intervening years. We started with just seven stages and three dozen expressions operating on a single collection. Today, there are over 30 stages, more than 150 expressions, and the ability to run aggregations across multiple collections.

The nature of data is such that it never reveals up front all the questions we might have about it in the future. Being able to construct complex aggregations on that data as it evolves is critical for successfully using it, while complex data processing can be performed in any programming language you are comfortable with. The ability to analyze your data without having to move it from the database where it is stored provides a tremendous advantage over exporting and loading the data elsewhere.

For years, I've given talks about the power of *aggregation pipelines*, answered questions from users about how to do complex analysis, and frequently fielded requests for a comprehensive *Aggregation Cookbook*. Of course, it would be great to have a repository of *recipes* with which to solve common data tasks that involve more than a single stage or expression combination, but it's hard to find the time to sit down and write something like that. This is why I was so stoked to see that my colleague, *Paul Done*, wrote this book, *Practical MongoDB Aggregations*, and laid the foundation for developers around the world—and it's also why this book is the first in the new *MongoDB Press Imprint*.

I hope you find this collection of suggestions, general principles, and specific pipeline examples useful in your own application development. I look forward to seeing how people use this book in the coming years to realize the full power of their data.

**Asya Kamsky**

Principal Engineer

MongoDB, Inc.

# Table of Contents

# Part 2:

## Aggregations by Example                                    93

# 6

## Foundational Examples: Filtering, Grouping, and Unwinding    95

# 7

## Joining Data Examples                                      117

# 8

## Fixing and Generating Data Examples                                129

# 9

## Trend Analysis Examples                                           149

# 10

## Securing Data Examples                                    171

# 11

## Time-Series Examples                                       195

# 12

# Array Manipulation Examples    215

# 13

## Full-Text Search Examples                                                261

## Appendix                                                                   277

## Afterword                                                                  281

## Index                                                                      283

## Other books you may enjoy                                                  288

# Preface

This book is about the MongoDB aggregation framework. It provides a set of practical, easy-to-digest principles and approaches for increasing your effectiveness in developing aggregation pipelines, supported by examples for building pipelines to solve various data manipulation and analysis tasks.

The aggregation framework is a runtime component of MongoDB with an API for client applications. By using the aggregation framework, developers can invoke queries to perform sophisticated transformations, analytics, and computations on the data held directly within the database. MongoDB aggregations help with tasks such as filtering, grouping, sorting, and calculating aggregated values from large datasets without needing to extract and process the data externally.

## How will this book help you?

Mastering the MongoDB aggregation framework can seem overwhelming. The focus of this book is to streamline your learning process for aggregations and make difficult concepts and steps simpler to understand. You'll be able to craft aggregation pipelines that exhibit increased performance and scalability by using the guidance and practical examples shared in this book. Instead of inefficiently extracting vast amounts of data for external processing, you'll learn how to shift more of your data processing tasks directly to the database. Furthermore, your developed pipelines will be more robust and adaptable, ready to evolve in response to changing business requirements.

## Who this book is for

This book is for developers, architects, data analysts, data engineers, and data scientists who have a foundational grasp of MongoDB and preliminary experience with its aggregation framework; that is, a working knowledge of MongoDB is assumed. This book is not for beginners who want to learn about aggregation pipelines from the ground up.

Given the programming-centric approach of MongoDB aggregations, this book is for readers with some coding experience. While knowledge of JavaScript is advantageous, proficiency in any modern programming language is sufficient.

This book will empower readers to elevate their capabilities regarding the richness, agility, performance, and scalability of the pipelines they develop.

# What this book covers

*Chapter 1, MongoDB Aggregations Explained*, provides a level-set of what aggregations are and how to use them.

*Chapter 2, Optimizing Pipelines for Productivity*, helps you to develop composable and adaptable pipelines.

*Chapter 3, Optimizing Pipelines for Performance*, informs you how to reduce the latency of your aggregations.

*Chapter 4, Harnessing the Power of Expressions*, helps you leverage the power of expressions for transforming data, especially arrays.

*Chapter 5, Optimizing Pipelines for Sharded Clusters*, provides considerations for executing your pipelines against large volumes of data.

*Chapter 6, Foundational Examples: Filtering, Grouping, and Unwinding*, provides examples of common data manipulation patterns used in many aggregation pipelines, which are relatively straightforward to understand and adapt.

*Chapter 7, Joining Data Examples*, offers guidance on joining together data from different collections.

*Chapter 8, Fixing and Generating Data Examples*, provides tools and techniques to clean data within a dataset.

*Chapter 9, Trend Analysis Examples*, showcases the capabilities of the MongoDB aggregation framework in performing advanced data analytics.

*Chapter 10, Securing Data Examples*, helps you discover ways to use aggregation pipelines to secure the data in a MongoDB database and reduce the risk of a data breach.

*Chapter 11, Time-Series Examples*, shows examples of how you can use aggregation pipelines to extract insight from time-series data.

*Chapter 12, Array Manipulation Examples*, shows how to break down array manipulation problems into manageable pieces, streamlining your assembly of solutions.

*Chapter 13, Full-Text Search Examples*, demonstrates how to build aggregation pipelines that leverage full-text search capabilities in MongoDB Atlas.

# To get the most out of this book

You will require the following software:

| Software covered in the book | Operating system requirements |
|---|---|
| MongoDB version 4.4 or newer | Windows, macOS, or Linux |
| MongoDB Atlas Search | Windows, macOS, or Linux |
| MongoDB Shell | Windows, macOS, or Linux |

After reading this book, we encourage you to check out some of the other resources available at `https://www.mongodb.com/developer` or `https://learn.mongodb.com/`

# Download the example code files

You can download the example code files for this book from GitHub at `https://github.com/PacktPublishing/Practical-MongoDB-Aggregations`. If there's an update to the code, it will be updated in the GitHub repository.

We also have other code bundles from our rich catalog of books and videos available at `https://github.com/PacktPublishing/`. Check them out!

# Conventions used

There are a number of text conventions used throughout this book.

`Code in text`: Indicates code words in text, database collection names, folder names, filenames, file extensions, pathnames, dummy URLs, and user input. Here is an example: "When considering the `$sort` and `$group` stages, it becomes evident why they have to block."

A block of code is set as follows:

```
db.persons.find(
    {"vocation": "ENGINEER"},
    {"_id": 0, "vocation": 0, "address": 0},
).sort(
    {"dateofbirth": -1}
).limit(3);
```

**Bold**: Indicates a new term, an important word, or words that you see onscreen. For instance, words in menus or dialog boxes appear in **bold**. Here is an example: "A **MongoDB database, version 4.2 or greater**, that is network accessible from your workstation."

> Tips or important notes
> Appear like this.

## Get in touch

Feedback from our readers is always welcome.

**General feedback**: If you have questions about any aspect of this book, email us at customercare@packtpub.com and mention the book title in the subject of your message.

**Errata**: Although we have taken every care to ensure the accuracy of our content, mistakes do happen. If you have found a mistake in this book, we would be grateful if you would report this to us. Please visit www.packtpub.com/support/errata and fill in the form.

**Piracy**: If you come across any illegal copies of our works in any form on the internet, we would be grateful if you would provide us with the location address or website name. Please contact us at copyright@packt.com with a link to the material.

**If you are interested in becoming an author**: If there is a topic that you have expertise in and you are interested in either writing or contributing to a book, please visit authors.packtpub.com.

# Download a free PDF copy of this book

Thanks for purchasing this book!

Do you like to read on the go but are unable to carry your print books everywhere? Is your eBook purchase not compatible with the device of your choice?

Don't worry, now with every Packt book you get a DRM-free PDF version of that book at no cost.

Read anywhere, any place, on any device. Search, copy, and paste code from your favorite technical books directly into your application.

The perks don't stop there, you can get exclusive access to discounts, newsletters, and great free content in your inbox daily

Follow these simple steps to get the benefits:

1.  Scan the QR code or visit the link below

https://packt.link/free-ebook/9781835080641

2.  Submit your proof of purchase
3.  That's it! We'll send your free PDF and other benefits to your email directly

# 1

# MongoDB Aggregations Explained

Getting insights from data stored in a database can be challenging, especially when there are millions or even billions of records to process.

In this chapter, you will learn how the MongoDB aggregation framework is designed to make mass data processing, analysis, and reporting intuitive and performant. Even though you may already be familiar with building basic aggregation pipelines, this chapter will lay a solid foundation to help you understand the mindset required for building more powerful, optimized aggregations for the real world.

By the end of this chapter, you will have a grasp of the following:

- The purpose and design of the MongoDB aggregation framework
- The MongoDB aggregation language's approach for building aggregation pipelines
- Relevant use cases for the MongoDB aggregation framework
- Suggestions for tools to use to run aggregation pipelines and how to get help if you get stuck

# What is the MongoDB aggregation framework?

The MongoDB aggregation framework enables you to perform data processing and manipulation on the documents in one or more MongoDB collections. It allows you to perform data transformations and gather summary data using various operators for filtering, grouping, sorting, and reshaping documents. You construct a pipeline consisting of one or more stages, each applying a specific transformation operation on the documents as they pass through the pipeline. One of the common uses of an aggregation pipeline is to calculate sums and averages, similar to using SQL's GROUP BY clause in a relational database but tailored to the MongoDB document-oriented structure.

The MongoDB aggregation framework enables users to send an analytics or data processing workload—written using an aggregation language—to the database to execute the workload against the data it holds. The MongoDB aggregation framework has two parts:

- An aggregation API provided by the MongoDB driver that you embed in your application. You define an aggregation pipeline in your application's code and send it to the database for processing.

- The aggregation runtime in the database that receives the pipeline request from the application and executes the pipeline against the persisted data.

*Figure 1.1* illustrates these two elements and their relationship:

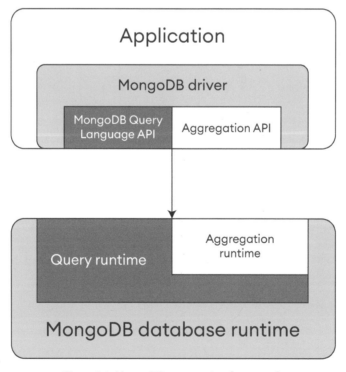

Figure 1.1: MongoDB aggregation framework

Each driver provides APIs to enable an application to use both the **MongoDB Query Language** (**MQL**) and the aggregation framework. In the database, the aggregation runtime reuses the query runtime to efficiently execute the query part of an aggregation workload that typically appears at the start of an aggregation pipeline.

# What is the MongoDB aggregation language?

MongoDB's aggregation pipeline language is somewhat of a paradox. It can appear daunting, yet it is straightforward. It can seem verbose, yet it is lean and to the point. It is Turing complete and able to solve any business problem. Conversely, it is a strongly opinionated **domain-specific language** (**DSL**); if you attempt to veer away from its core purpose of mass data manipulation, it will try its best to resist you.

Invariably, for beginners, the aggregation framework seems difficult to understand and comes with an initially steep learning curve that you must overcome to become productive. In some programming languages, you only need to master a small set of the language's aspects to be largely effective. With MongoDB aggregations, the initial effort you must invest is slightly greater. However, once mastered, users find it provides an elegant, natural, and efficient solution to breaking down a complex set of data manipulations into a series of simple, easy-to-understand steps.

The MongoDB aggregation pipeline language is focused on data-oriented problem-solving rather than business process problem-solving. It can be regarded as a functional programming language rather than a procedural programming language. Since an aggregation pipeline is an ordered series of statements, called stages, the entire output of one stage forms the entire input of the next stage, with no side effects. This functional nature is why many users regard the aggregation framework as having a steeper learning curve than many languages—not because it is inherently more difficult to understand but because most developers come from a procedural programming background and not a functional one. Most developers also have to learn how to think like a functional programmer to learn the aggregation framework.

The functional characteristics of the aggregation framework ultimately make it especially powerful for processing massive datasets. Users focus more on defining the *what* in terms of the required outcome and less on the *how* of specifying the exact logic to apply to achieve each transformation. You provide one specific and clearly advertised purpose for each stage in the pipeline. At runtime, the database engine can then understand the exact intent of each stage. For example, the database engine can obtain clear answers to the questions it asks, such as, *"Is this stage for performing a filter or is this stage for grouping on some fields?"* With this knowledge, the database engine has the opportunity to optimize the pipeline at runtime. *Figure 1.2* shows an example of the database performing a pipeline optimization. It may decide to reorder stages to optimally use an index while ensuring that the output hasn't changed. Alternatively, it may choose to execute some steps in parallel against subsets of the data in different shards, reducing the response time while again ensuring the output hasn't changed.

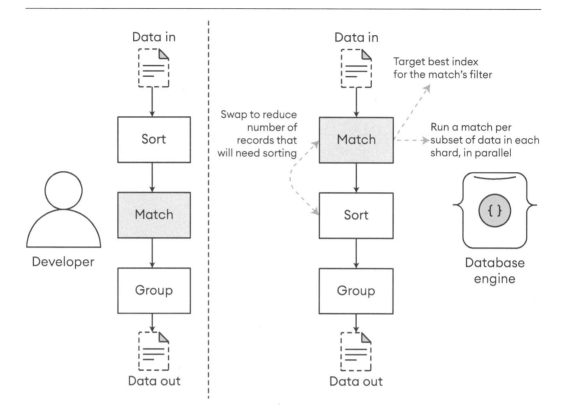

Figure 1.2: Database performing a pipeline optimization

Last and least in terms of importance is the syntax. So far, MongoDB aggregations have been described here as a programming language. However, what syntax *do* you use to construct a MongoDB aggregation pipeline? The answer is it *depends*, and the answer is mostly irrelevant.

This book will highlight pipeline examples using MongoDB Shell and the JavaScript interpreter it runs in. The book will express aggregation pipelines using a JSON-based syntax. However, if you are using one of the many programming language drivers that MongoDB offers, you will be using that language to construct an aggregation pipeline, not JSON. To learn more about MongoDB drivers, see `https://docs.mongodb.com/drivers/`. An aggregation is specified as an array of objects, regardless of how the programming language may facilitate it. This programmatic rather than textual format has a couple of advantages compared to querying with a string. It has a low vulnerability to injection attacks, and it is highly composable.

# What do developers use the aggregation framework for?

The aggregation framework is versatile and used for many different data processing and manipulation tasks. Some typical use cases include the following:

- Generating business reports, which include roll-ups, sums, and averages

- Performing real-time analytics to generate insight and actions for end users

- Presenting real-time business dashboards with an up-to-date summary status

- Performing data masking to securely obfuscate and redact sensitive data ready to expose to consumers via views

- Joining data together from different collections on the *server side* rather than in the client application for improved performance

- Conducting data science activities such as data discovery and data wrangling

- Performing mass data analysis at scale (i.e., *big data*) as a faster and more intuitive alternative to technologies such as Hadoop

- Executing real-time queries where deeper *server-side* data post-processing is required than what is available via default MongoDB Query Language

- Navigating a graph of relationships between records, looking for patterns

- Performing the transform part of an **extract, load, transform** (**ELT**) workload to transform data landed in MongoDB into a more appropriate shape for consuming applications to use

- Enabling data engineers to report on the quality of data in the database and perform data-cleansing activities

- Updating a materialized view with the results of the most recent source data changes so that real-time applications don't have to wait for long-running analytics jobs to complete

- Performing full-text search and fuzzy search on data using MongoDB Atlas Search, see `https://www.mongodb.com/atlas/search`

- Exposing MongoDB data to analytics tools that don't *natively* integrate with MongoDB via SQL, ODBC, or JDBC (using MongoDB BI Connector, see `https://www.mongodb.com/docs/bi-connector/current/`, or Atlas SQL, `https://www.mongodb.com/atlas/sql`)

- Supporting machine learning frameworks for efficient data analysis (e.g., via MongoDB Spark Connector, see `https://docs.mongodb.com/spark-connector`)

# A short history of MongoDB aggregations

MongoDB released the first major version of the database (version 1.0) in early 2009. Back then, users and the predominant company behind the database, *MongoDB, Inc.* (then called *10gen*), were still establishing the sort of use cases the database would excel at and where the critical gaps were. Within half a year of this first major release, the engineering team at MongoDB identified an essential requirement to generate materialized views on demand. Users needed this capability to maintain counts, sums, and averages for their real-time client applications to query. By the end of 2009, in time for the following major release (1.2), the database engineers introduced a quick tactical solution to address this gap. This solution involved embedding a JavaScript engine in the database and allowing client applications to submit and execute *server-side* logic using a simple *map-reduce*-style API. Although from a functional perspective, the MongoDB map-reduce capability provided a solution to the typical data processing requirements of users, it came with some drawbacks:

- The database used an inherently slow JavaScript engine to execute the user's code.

- Users had to provide two sets of JavaScript logic: a *map* (or matching) function and a *reduce* (or grouping) function. Both were unintuitive to develop and lacked a solid data-oriented bias.

- At runtime, the database could not determine the specific intent of an arbitrary piece of logic. The database engine had no opportunity to identify and apply optimizations. It couldn't easily target indexes or reorder logic for more efficient processing. The database had to be conservative, executing the workload with minimal concurrency and employing locks at various times to prevent race conditions.

- If returning the response to the client application, rather than sending the output to a collection, the response payload had to be less than 16 MB.

Over the subsequent two years, MongoDB engineers envisioned a better solution as user behavior with the map-reduce capability became more understood. Given the ability to hold large datasets in MongoDB, users increasingly tried to use map-reduce to perform mass data processing. They were hitting the same map-reduce limitations. Users desired a more targeted capability leveraging a data-oriented DSL. The engineers saw how to deliver a framework enabling developers to define data manipulation steps with valuable composability characteristics. Each step would have a clearly advertised intent, allowing the database engine to apply optimizations at runtime. The engineers could also design a framework that would execute *natively* in the database and not require a JavaScript engine. In mid-2012, the database introduced the aggregation framework solution in the 2.2 version of MongoDB, which provided a far more powerful, efficient, scalable, and easy-to-use replacement to map-reduce.

Within its first year, the aggregation framework rapidly became the go-to tool for processing large volumes of data in MongoDB. Now, over a decade on, it is as if the aggregation framework has always been part of MongoDB. It feels like part of the database's core DNA. The old map-reduce capability in MongoDB is deprecated and offers no value nowadays. A MongoDB aggregation pipeline is always the correct answer for processing data in the database!

## Aggregation capabilities in MongoDB server releases

The following is a summary of the evolution of the aggregation framework in terms of significant capabilities added in each major release of MongoDB from when the framework debuted in MongoDB 2.2:

- **MongoDB 2.2 (August 2012)**: Marked the initial release of the MongoDB aggregation framework

- **MongoDB 2.4 (March 2013)**: Focused predominantly on aggregation performance improvements, especially for sorting data, but also included a new string concatenation operator

- **MongoDB 2.6 (April 2014)**: Enabled unlimited-size result sets to be generated, explain plans to be viewed, the ability to spill aggregations to disk for large sorting operations, the ability to output aggregation results to a new collection, and the ability to redact data flagged as sensitive

- **MongoDB 3.0 (March 2015)**: Added nothing significant to aggregations apart from some new date-to-string operators

- **MongoDB 3.2 (December 2015)**: Incorporated many sharded cluster optimizations, added the ability to join data between collections, introduced the ability to sample data, and added many new arithmetic and array operators

- **MongoDB 3.4 (November 2016)**: Enabled graph relationships in data to be traversed, provided new bucketing and facet capabilities, and added many new array and string operators

- **MongoDB 3.6 (November 2017)**: Added the ability to convert arrays into objects and vice versa, introduced extensive date string conversion operators, and added the ability to remove a field conditionally

- **MongoDB 4.0 (July 2018)**: Included new number to conversion operators and the ability to trim strings

- **MongoDB 4.2 (August 2019)**: Introduced the ability to merge aggregation results into existing collections, added new set and unset stages to address the verbosity and rigidity of project stages, added support for Atlas Search, and included new trigonometry and regular expression operators

- **MongoDB 4.4 (July 2020)**: Added the ability to union data from multiple collections and define JavaScript functions and accumulator expressions, plus provided many new operators for string replacements, random number generation, and accessing the first and last elements of an array

- **MongoDB 5.0 (July 2021)**: Introduced the ability to perform operations across a sliding window of documents and added new date manipulation capabilities

- **MongoDB 6.0 (July 2022)**: Improved support for aggregations performing joining and graph traversing activities in sharded clusters, and added many new stages and operators for filling in missing records and fields, sorting array elements, and accessing subsets of arrays

- **MongoDB 7.0 (August 2023)**: Introduced a system variable to enable a pipeline to determine the identity of the calling user and their roles as well as providing new median and percentile operators

# Getting going

You probably have a preferred tool for prototyping aggregation pipelines, having already explored the MongoDB aggregation framework before reaching for this book. However, suppose you are looking for alternatives. In that case, in the following section, you will find suggestions to get a MongoDB database and client tool up and running, ready to execute the example aggregations presented in this book.

## Setting up your environment

To develop aggregation pipelines effectively, and to try the examples in *Part 2: Aggregations by Example*, you will need:

- A **MongoDB database, version 4.2 or greater**, that is network accessible from your workstation

- A **MongoDB client tool** running on your workstation to submit aggregation pipeline execution requests and view the results

> **Note**
>
> In *Part 2: Aggregations by Example*, most example aggregation pipelines are compatible with MongoDB version 4.2 and above. However, some examples utilize aggregation features introduced after version 4.2. For these, the book specifies the minimum MongoDB version required.

## Database

The MongoDB database deployment for you to connect to can be a single server, a replica set, or a sharded cluster. You can run this deployment locally on your workstation, remotely on-premises, or in the cloud. You will need the MongoDB URL to connect to the database and, if authentication is enabled, the credentials required for full read and write access.

If you don't have access to a MongoDB database, the two most accessible options for running a database are as follows:

1. Provision a free-tier MongoDB cluster (see `https://www.mongodb.com/docs/atlas/tutorial/deploy-free-tier-cluster/`) in MongoDB Atlas, which is a MongoDB cloud-based database as a service (once it's deployed, in the Atlas console, there is a button you can click to copy the URL of the cluster)

2. Install and run a single MongoDB server (see `https://docs.mongodb.com/guides/server/install/`) locally on your workstation

> **Note**
>
> Aggregation pipelines in *Chapter 13, Full-Text Search Examples*, use Atlas Search. Consequently, you must use Atlas for your database deployment if you want to run the few Atlas Search-based examples.

## Client tool

There are various options for the client tool, some of which are:

- **MongoDB Shell**: Install the MongoDB command-line tool, MongoDB Shell, *mongosh* (see `https://www.mongodb.com/try/download/shell`)

- **MongoDB for Visual Studio (VS) Code**: Install *MongoDB for VS Code* (see `https://www.mongodb.com/docs/mongodb-vscode/install/`) and use the *Playgrounds* feature (see `https://www.mongodb.com/docs/mongodb-vscode/playgrounds/`)

- **MongoDB Compass**: Install the *official* MongoDB-provided **graphical user interface (GUI)** tool, *MongoDB Compass* (see `https://www.mongodb.com/products/compass`)

- **Studio 3T**: Install the *third-party* 3T Software Labs–provided GUI tool, *Studio 3T* (see `https://studio3t.com/download/`)

All examples in this book present code that is easy to copy and paste into MongoDB Shell, i.e., `mongosh`, to execute. All subsequent instructions in this book assume you are using the shell. However, you will find it straightforward to use one of the mentioned GUI tools instead, to execute the code examples.

### *MongoDB Shell with Atlas database*

Here is how you can connect MongoDB Shell to an Atlas free-tier MongoDB cluster:

```
mongosh "mongodb+srv://mycluster.a123b.mongodb.net/test" --username myuser
```

Before running the command, ensure:

- You *add your workstation's IP address* (see `https://www.mongodb.com/docs/atlas/security/add-ip-address-to-list/`) to the Atlas access list

- You *create a database user* (see `https://www.mongodb.com/docs/atlas/government/tutorial/create-mongodb-user-for-cluster/`) for the deployed Atlas cluster, with rights to create, read, and write to any database

- You *change the dummy URL and username text*, shown in the preceding example command, to match your real cluster's details (these details are accessible via the cluster's `Connect` button in the Atlas console)

## MongoDB Shell with local database

Here is the command for starting MongoDB Shell and connecting it to a MongoDB single-server database if you've installed MongoDB locally on your workstation:

```
mongosh "mongodb://localhost:27017"
```

## MongoDB for VS Code

By using the *MongoDB Playground* tool in VS Code, you can quickly prototype queries and aggregation pipelines and execute them against a MongoDB database with the results shown in an output tab. *Figure 1.3* shows the Playground tool in action:

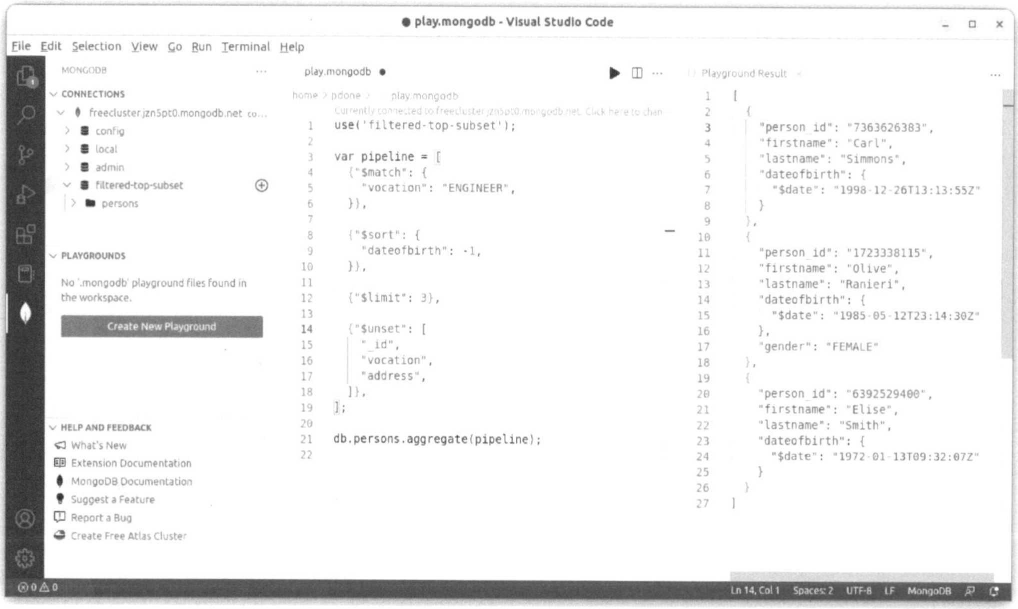

Figure 1.3: MongoDB Playground tool in Microsoft Visual Studio Code

## MongoDB Compass GUI

MongoDB Compass provides an *Aggregation Pipeline Builder* tool to assist users in prototyping and debugging aggregation pipelines and exporting them to different programming languages. You can see the aggregation tool in MongoDB Compass in *Figure 1.4*:

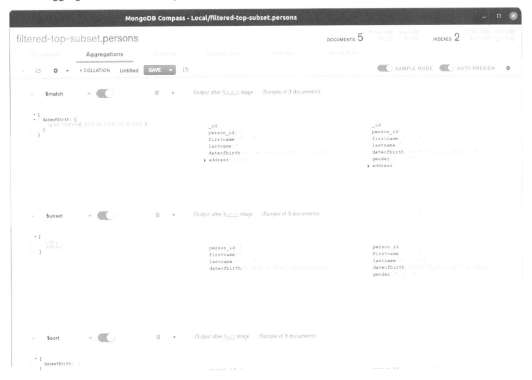

Figure 1.4: MongoDB Compass

## Studio 3T GUI

Studio 3T provides an *Aggregation Editor* tool to help you prototype and debug aggregation pipelines and translate them to different programming languages. You can see the aggregation tool in Studio 3T in *Figure 1.5*:

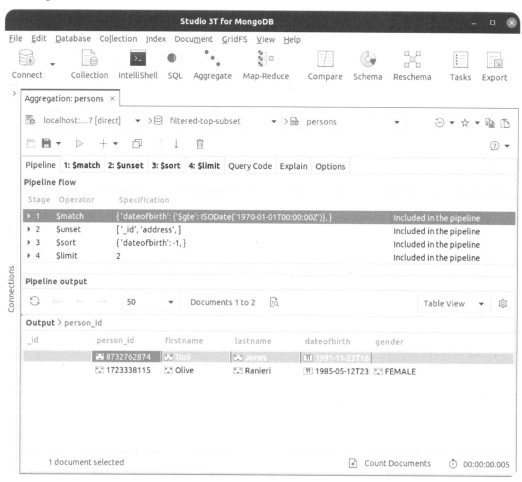

Figure 1.5: Studio 3T

# Getting further help

This book does not aim to document every possible option and parameter for the stages and operators that can constitute a MongoDB aggregation pipeline. That's what the MongoDB online documentation is for. Specifically, you should consult the following for help on the syntax of aggregation stages and operators:

- MongoDB aggregation pipeline stages (see `https://docs.mongodb.com/manual/reference/operator/aggregation-pipeline/`)

- MongoDB aggregation pipeline operators (see `https://www.mongodb.com/docs/manual/reference/operator/aggregation/`)

If you are getting stuck with an aggregation pipeline and want some help, an active online community will almost always have the answer. So, pose your questions here:

- The MongoDB Community Forums (see `https://www.mongodb.com/community/forums/`)

- Stack Overflow – MongoDB Questions (see `https://stackoverflow.com/questions/tagged/mongodb`)

You may be asking for just general advice. However, suppose you want to ask for help on a specific aggregation pipeline under development. In that case, you should provide a sample input document, a copy of your current pipeline code (in its JSON syntax format and not a programming language-specific format), and an example of the output that you are trying to achieve. If you provide this extra information, you will have a far greater chance of receiving a timely and optimal response.

# Summary

This chapter explored the purpose and composition of the MongoDB aggregation framework and the pipeline language you use to express data processing tasks. The chapter provided insight into how MongoDB engineers designed and implemented the aggregation framework to process data at a large scale, laying the foundations for subsequent chapters where you will learn how to build richer and more optimal aggregations than you may have done before. You also learned how to find help if you get stuck and to set up your environment to run the aggregation pipelines this book provides.

In the next chapter, you will learn about the best way to construct your aggregation pipelines for composability and robustness, which is especially important when your data structures and aggregation pipelines evolve over time, which is the nature of all modern data-centric applications.

# Part 1:
# Guiding Tips and Principles

The following set of chapters will provide practical, easy-to-digest principles and approaches for increasing your effectiveness in developing aggregation pipelines.

This part of the book includes the following chapters:

- *Chapter 2, Optimizing Pipelines for Productivity*
- *Chapter 3, Optimizing Pipelines for Performance*
- *Chapter 4, Harnessing the Power of Expressions*
- *Chapter 5, Optimizing Pipelines for Sharded Clusters*

# 2

# Optimizing Pipelines for Productivity

In this chapter, you will learn the principles of composability to help you become more productive in building pipelines. You will discover strategies to structure your aggregation pipelines and optimize them for reusability and maintainability, enabling you to build effective pipelines rapidly. This chapter will guide you and help you avoid potential pitfalls, such as needing to revisit and refactor your existing aggregation pipelines whenever your data model evolves.

This chapter covers the following topics:

- Understanding and applying the principles of composability
- Tips and best practices for increasing productivity
- Better alternatives for using a project stage

# Embrace composability for increased productivity

An aggregation pipeline is an ordered series of instructions, called stages. The entire output of one stage forms the whole input of the next stage, and so on—without any side effects. Pipelines exhibit high composability, where stages are stateless, self-contained components selected and assembled in various combinations (pipelines) to satisfy specific requirements. This property of aggregation pipelines makes iterative prototyping possible, with straightforward testing after each increment.

With MongoDB aggregations, you can take a complex problem, requiring a complex aggregation pipeline, and break it down into straightforward individual stages, where each step can be developed and tested in isolation. To better comprehend composability, it may be helpful to memorize the following visual model, in *Figure 2.1*:

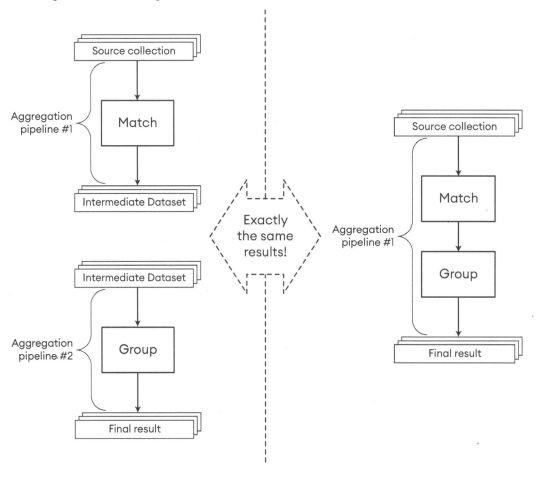

Figure 2.1: Aggregation pipeline model

Suppose you have two pipelines with each pipeline containing a single stage. After saving the intermediate results by running the first pipeline, you can run the second pipeline against the saved intermediate dataset. The final result is the same as running a single pipeline containing both stages in a serial order. There is no difference between the two. As a developer, you can reduce the cognitive load by understanding how a problem can be broken down when building aggregation pipelines. Aggregation pipelines enable you to decompose a big challenge into lots of minor challenges. By embracing this approach of first developing each stage separately, you will find that even the most complex challenges become surmountable.

## Guiding principles to promote composability

Once most developers become adept at using the aggregation framework, they tend not to rely on temporary intermediate datasets while prototyping each stage. Of course, having intermediate datasets is still a reasonable development approach. Seasoned aggregation pipeline developers typically comment out one or more stages of an aggregation pipeline when using MongoDB Shell (or they use the *disable stage* capability provided by the GUI tools for MongoDB).

To encourage composability and hence productivity, you can strive for the following:

- Easy disabling of subsets of stages, while prototyping or debugging

- Easy addition of new fields to a stage or new stages to a pipeline by performing a copy, a paste, and then a modification without hitting cryptic error messages resulting from issues such as missing a comma before the added element

- Easy appreciation of each distinct stage's purpose at a glance

With these principles in mind, let's have a look at some conventions for textually crafting your pipelines in JavaScript to improve your pipeline development pace:

1. Don't start or end a stage on the same line as another stage.

2. For every field in a stage, and stage in a pipeline, include a trailing comma even if it is currently the last item.

3. Include an empty newline between every stage.

4. For complex stages, include a // comment with an explanation on a newline before the stage.

5. To *disable* some stages of a pipeline while prototyping or debugging another stage, use the multi-line comment /* prefix and */ suffix.

The following is an example of a poor pipeline layout if you have followed none of the guiding principles:

```
// BAD

var pipeline = [
  {"$unset": [
    "_id",
    "address"
  ]}, {"$match": {
    "dateofbirth": {"$gte": ISODate("1970-01-01T00:00:00Z")}
  }}//, {"$sort": {
  //  "dateofbirth": -1
  //}}, {"$limit": 2}
];
```

Whereas the following is an example of a far better pipeline layout, where you meet all of the guiding principles:

```
// GOOD

var pipeline = [
  {"$unset": [
    "_id",
    "address",
  ]},

  // Only match people born on or after 1st January 1970
  {"$match": {
    "dateofbirth": {"$gte": ISODate("1970-01-01T00:00:00Z")},
  }},

  /*
  {"$sort": {
    "dateofbirth": -1,
  }},

  {"$limit": 2},
  */
];
```

In the preceding example, you will notice trailing commas are included in the code snippet, both at the end of the stage level and at the end of the field level.

It is worth mentioning that some (but not all) developers take an alternative but equally valid approach to constructing a pipeline. They decompose each stage in the pipeline into different JavaScript variables, where each variable in a stage is defined separately, as shown in the following example:

```
// GOOD

var unsetStage = {
  "$unset": [
    "_id",
    "address",
  ]};

var matchStage = {
  "$match": {
    "dateofbirth": {"$gte": ISODate("1970-01-01T00:00:00Z")},
  }};

var sortStage = {
   "$sort": {
    "dateofbirth": -1,
  }};


var limitStage = {"$limit": 2};

var pipeline = [
  unsetStage,
  matchStage,
  sortStage,
  limitStage,
];
```

Some developers may take additional steps if they don't intend to transfer the prototyped pipeline to a different programming language. They may choose to decompose elements inside a stage into additional JavaScript variables to avoid code *typos* (for instance, to prevent one part of a pipeline from incorrectly referencing a field computed earlier in the pipeline due to a misspelling).

## Using macro functions

For very complex aggregations, some developers choose to factor out the generation of some boilerplate code, representing a complex set of expressions, from part of a pipeline into a separate JavaScript function. This new function is essentially a *macro*. For example, let's say the documents in the collection have address fields represented as objects, as follows:

```
"address": {
    "number": 1,
    "street": "Rue du Moulin",
    "city": "Leonaulle"
}
```

You might want to build a pipeline similar to the following to create a comma-separated text version of the address as a single string:

```
var pipeline = [
  {"$match" : {
    "birth_country": "UK",
  }},

  {"$set" : {
    "flattennedAddress": {
      "$concat": [
        {"$toString": "$address.number"},
        ", ",
        "$address.street",
        ", ",
        "$address.city"
      ]
    },
  }},
];
```

Instead, you may choose to factor out part of this pipeline to be generated by a macro function, taking the text separator as an argument, as follows:

```
function getFlattenedAddresssMacro(separator) {
  return {
    "$concat": [
      {"$toString": "$address.number"},
      separator,
      "$address.street",
      separator,
      "$address.city"
    ]
  };
}

var pipeline = [
  {"$match" : {
    "birth_country": "UK",
  }},

  {"$set" : {
    "flattennedAddress": getFlattenedAddresssMacro(", "),
  }},
];
```

The macro function executes on the client side, for example, in MongoDB Shell or your application, and the pipeline simply embeds the function's returned boilerplate code before the shell ever submits the expanded pipeline to MongoDB. The MongoDB aggregation runtime has no idea that you had initially split the pipeline code out this way. It just receives a single large pipeline to execute. You can prove this by typing the text `pipeline` into the shell and pressing *Enter*. It will show you the expanded pipeline contents the shell gives to the `aggregate(pipeline)` command.

A developer can reuse the same macro function from multiple places within the main pipeline's code. Whenever the pipeline invokes this function, the pipeline's body directly embeds the same returned boilerplate code. Later in this book, in *Chapter 12, Array Manipulation Examples*, you will explore practical examples of this macro approach.

## So, what's the best way of factoring out code?

Ultimately, it comes down to personal preference based on individual comfort and productivity to choose between a multi-variable and a single-variable approach or to factor out pieces of code into macro functions. All of these options are highly composable for defining a pipeline. You will also need to consider the code reuse conventions related to the programming language you use, such as Java or C#, to construct your application's aggregations.

# Better alternatives for a projection stage

The typical method for specifying fields to include or exclude in the MongoDB aggregation framework has been the $project stage. This was the only way to define which fields to keep or omit for many earlier versions of MongoDB. However, $project comes with a few usability challenges:

- $project **can be confusing and non-intuitive**. You can only choose to include fields or exclude fields in a single stage, but not both. However, there is one exception, where you can exclude the _id field and still define other fields to include. This only applies to the _id field and this ambiguity makes $project unintuitive to apply.

- $project **can be verbose and inflexible**. If you want to define one new field or revise one field, you will have to name all other fields in the projection to include. If each input record has 100 fields and the pipeline needs to employ a $project stage for the first time, defining these files can become time consuming. To include a new 101st field, you'll have to name all the original 100 fields in this new $project stage again. It becomes even more difficult when you have an evolving data model, where additional new fields appear in some records over time. Because you use $project for inclusion, each time a new field appears in the dataset, you must go back to the old aggregation pipeline to modify it to name the new field explicitly for inclusion in the results. This is the antithesis of flexibility and agility.

In MongoDB version 4.2, the $set and $unset stages were introduced, which, in most cases, are preferable to using $project for declaring field inclusion and exclusion. They make the code's intent much clearer, lead to less verbose pipelines, and, critically, reduce the need to refactor a pipeline whenever the data model evolves. How this works and guidance on when to use the $set and $unset stages are explained in the next section.

Despite the challenges, there are some specific situations where using $project is advantageous over $set and $unset. You will learn more about this in the *When to use $project* section.

> **Note**
>
> MongoDB version 3.4 addressed some of the disadvantages of $project by introducing a new $addFields stage, which has the same behavior as $set. $set was released after $addFields and is actually just an alias for $addFields. Both the $set and $unset stages are available in modern versions of MongoDB, and their counter purposes are obvious to deduce by their names. The name $addFields doesn't fully reflect that you can modify existing fields rather than just adding new fields. This book prefers $set over $addFields to help promote consistency and avoid any confusion of intent, but there is no behavioral difference between the two.

## When to use $set and $unset

You should use the $set and $unset stages when you need to retain most of the fields in the input records, and you want to add, modify, or remove a minority subset of fields. This is the case for most uses of aggregation pipelines.

For example, let's consider a collection of credit card payment documents similar to the following:

```
// INPUT (record from source collection to be operated on by an agg)
{
  _id: ObjectId("6044faa70b2c21f8705d8954"),
  card_name: "Mrs. Jane A. Doe",
  card_num: "1234567890123456",
  card_expiry: "2023-08-31T23:59:59.736Z",
  card_sec_code: "123",
  card_provider_name: "Credit MasterCard Gold",
  transaction_id: "eb1bd77836e8713656d9bf2debba8900",
  transaction_date: ISODate("2021-01-13T09:32:07.000Z"),
  transaction_curncy_code: "GBP",
  transaction_amount: NumberDecimal("501.98"),
  reported: true
}
```

You want an aggregation pipeline to produce modified versions of these documents, as shown:

```
// OUTPUT  (a record in the results of the executed aggregation)
{
  card_name: "Mrs. Jane A. Doe",
  card_num: "1234567890123456",
  card_expiry: ISODate("2023-08-31T23:59:59.736Z"), // converted
  card_sec_code: "123",
  card_provider_name: "Credit MasterCard Gold",
  transaction_id: "eb1bd77836e8713656d9bf2debba8900",
  transaction_date: ISODate("2021-01-13T09:32:07.000Z"),
  transaction_curncy_code: "GBP",
  transaction_amount: NumberDecimal("501.98"),
  reported: true,
  card_type: "CREDIT"                              // added
}
```

Here, shown by the // comments, there was a requirement to modify each document's structure slightly, to convert the card_expiry text field into a proper date field, and add a new card_type field, set to the value CREDIT, for every record.

Naively, you might decide to build an aggregation pipeline using a $project stage to achieve this transformation, which might look similar to the following:

```
// BAD
[
  {"$project": {
    // Modify a field + add a new field
    "card_expiry": {"$dateFromString": {"dateString": "$card_expiry"}},
    "card_type": "CREDIT",

    // Must now name all the other fields for those fields to be retained
    "card_name": 1,
    "card_num": 1,
    "card_sec_code": 1,
    "card_provider_name": 1,
    "transaction_id": 1,
    "transaction_date": 1,
    "transaction_curncy_code": 1,
    "transaction_amount": 1,
    "reported": 1,

    // Remove _id field
    "_id": 0,
  }},
]
```

As you can see, the pipeline stage is quite lengthy, and because you use a $project stage to modify/add two fields, you must also explicitly name each other existing field from the source records for inclusion. Otherwise, you will lose those fields during the transformation. Imagine if each payment document had hundreds of possible fields, rather than just ten!

A more efficient approach to building the aggregation pipeline, to achieve the same results, would be to use $set and $unset instead, as shown:

```
// GOOD
[
  {"$set": {
    // Modified + new field
    "card_expiry": {"$dateFromString": {"dateString": "$card_expiry"}},
    "card_type": "CREDIT",
  }},
```

```
{"$unset": [
  // Remove _id field
  "_id",
]},
]
```

This time, when you need to add new documents to the collection of existing payments, which include additional new fields, for example, `settlement_date` and `settlement_curncy_code`, no changes are required. The existing aggregation pipeline allows these new fields to appear in the results automatically. However, when using `$project`, each time the possibility of a new field arises, a developer must first refactor the pipeline to incorporate an additional inclusion declaration (e.g., `"settlement_date": 1`, or `"settlement_curncy_code": 1`).

## When to use $project

It is best to use a `$project` stage when the required shape of output documents is very different from the input documents' shape. This situation often arises when you do not need to include most of the original fields.

This time, for the same input payments collection, let's consider that you require a new aggregation pipeline to produce result documents. You need each output document's structure to be very different from the input structure, and you need to retain far fewer original fields, similar to the following:

```
// OUTPUT  (a record in the results of the executed aggregation)
{
  transaction_info: {
    date: ISODate("2021-01-13T09:32:07.000Z"),
    amount: NumberDecimal("501.98")
  },
  status: "REPORTED"
}
```

Using $set/$unset in the pipeline to achieve this output structure would be verbose and require naming all the fields (for exclusion this time), as shown:

```
// BAD
[
  {"$set": {
    // Add some fields
    "transaction_info.date": "$transaction_date",
    "transaction_info.amount": "$transaction_amount",
    "status": {
      "$cond": {
        "if": "$reported",
        "then": "REPORTED",
        "else": "UNREPORTED"
      }
    },
  }},

  {"$unset": [
    // Remove _id field
    "_id",

    // Must name all other existing fields to be omitted
    "card_name",
    "card_num",
    "card_expiry",
    "card_sec_code",
    "card_provider_name",
    "transaction_id",
    "transaction_date",
    "transaction_curncy_code",
    "transaction_amount",
    "reported",
  ]},
]
```

By using $project for this specific aggregation, as shown below, to achieve the same result, the pipeline will be less verbose. The pipeline will have the flexibility of not requiring modification if you ever make subsequent additions to the data model, with new, previously unknown fields:

```
// GOOD
[
  {"$project": {
    // Add some fields
    "transaction_info.date": "$transaction_date",
    "transaction_info.amount": "$transaction_amount",
    "status": {
      "$cond": {
        "if": "$reported",
        "then": "REPORTED",
        "else": "UNREPORTED"
      }
    },

    // Remove _id field
    "_id": 0,
  }},
]
```

## The hidden danger of $project

Another potential downside can occur when using $project to define field inclusion, rather than using $set (or $addFields). When using $project to declare all required fields for inclusion, it can lead to carelessly specifying more fields from the source data than intended. Later on, if the pipeline contains something like a $group stage, this will cover up your mistake. The final aggregation's output will not include the erroneous field in the output. You might ask, "*Why is this a problem?*" when using the $group stage here will mean the erroneous fields don't appear in the output. Suppose you wanted the aggregation to take advantage of a covered query for optimized performance. A covered query is a query that can be satisfied entirely using an index, and the query engine does not have to pull the matched documents from slow storage to get the remaining fields. In most cases, the MongoDB aggregation engine can track fields' dependencies throughout a pipeline and, left to its own devices, can understand which fields are not required. However, you would be overriding this capability by explicitly asking for the extra field. A common error is forgetting to exclude the _id field in the projection inclusion stage, and so it will be included by default. This mistake will silently kill the potential optimization. If you must use a $project stage, try to use it as late as possible in the pipeline because it is then clear to you precisely what you are asking for as the aggregation's final output. Also, unnecessary fields such as _id may already have been identified by the aggregation engine as no longer required, due to the occurrence of an earlier $group stage, for example.

## Key projection takeaways

You should always use $set (or $addFields) and $unset for field inclusion and exclusion, rather than $project. The main exception is if you have an obvious requirement for a very different structure for result documents, where you only need to retain a small subset of the input fields.

# Summary

In this chapter, you learned about the concept of composability, equipping you with the knowledge to create efficient and flexible aggregation pipelines. Throughout the chapter, you discovered practical approaches to optimize the pipelines you build for simplicity, reusability, and maintainability.

In the next chapter, you will learn about considerations for optimizing pipeline performance, understanding explain plans, and applying various recommendations that will enable your aggregation pipelines to execute and complete in the minimum amount of time possible.

# 3

# Optimizing Pipelines for Performance

This chapter will teach you how to measure aggregation performance and identify bottlenecks. Then, you will learn essential techniques to apply to suboptimal pipeline parts to reduce the aggregation's total response time. Adopting these principles may mean the difference between aggregations completing in a few seconds versus minutes, hours, or even longer for sizeable datasets.

The chapter will cover the following:

- What an explain plan is and how to use it
- How blocking stages can significantly impede performance
- How to refactor your pipelines to remove bottlenecks

# Using explain plans to identify performance bottlenecks

When you're using the MongoDB Query Language to develop queries, it is essential to view the explain plan for a query to determine whether you've used the appropriate index and determine whether you need to optimize other aspects of the query or the data model. An explain plan allows you to fully understand the performance implications of the query you have created.

The same applies to aggregation pipelines. However, an explain plan tends to be even more critical with aggregations because considerably more complex logic can be assembled and run inside the database. There are far more opportunities for performance bottlenecks to occur, thus requiring optimization.

The MongoDB database engine will do its best to apply its own aggregation pipeline optimizations at runtime. Nevertheless, there could be some optimizations that only you can make. A database engine should never optimize a pipeline in such a way as to risk changing the functional behavior and outcome of the pipeline. The database engine doesn't always have the extra context that your brain has relating to the actual business problem to solve. It may not be able to make some types of judgment calls about what pipeline changes to apply that would make it run faster. The availability of an explain plan for aggregations enables you to bridge this gap. It allows you to understand the database engine's applied optimizations and detect further potential optimizations that you can then manually implement in the pipeline.

## Viewing an explain plan

To view the explain plan for an aggregation pipeline, you can execute the following command:

```
db.coll.explain().aggregate([{"$match": {"name": "Jo"}}]);
```

In this book, you have already seen the convention used to first define a separate variable for the pipeline, followed by the call to the `aggregate()` function, passing in the pipeline argument, as shown here:

```
db.coll.aggregate(pipeline);
```

By adopting this approach, it's easier for you to use the same pipeline definition interchangeably with different commands. While prototyping and debugging a pipeline, it is handy for you to be able to quickly switch from executing the pipeline to instead generating the explain plan for the same defined pipeline, as follows:

```
db.coll.explain().aggregate(pipeline);
```

As with the MongoDB Query Language, there are three different verbosity modes that you can generate an explain plan with, as shown:

```
// QueryPlanner verbosity (default if no verbosity parameter provided)
db.coll.explain("queryPlanner").aggregate(pipeline);
```

```
// ExecutionStats verbosity
db.coll.explain("executionStats").aggregate(pipeline);



// AllPlansExecution verbosity
db.coll.explain("allPlansExecution").aggregate(pipeline);
```

In most cases, you will find that running the `executionStats` variant is the most informative mode. Rather than showing just the query planner's thought process, it also provides actual statistics on the *winning* execution plan (e.g., the total keys examined, the total docs examined, etc.). However, this isn't the default because it actually executes the aggregation in addition to formulating the query plan. If the source collection is large or the pipeline is suboptimal, it will take a while to return the explain plan result.

> **Note**
>
> The `aggregate()` function also provides a vestigial `explain` optional parameter to ask for an explain plan to be generated and returned. Nonetheless, this is more limited and cumbersome to use, so you should avoid it.

## Understanding the explain plan

As an example, let's consider a shop's dataset that includes information on each customer and what retail orders the customer has made over the years. The *customer orders* collection contains documents similar to the following example:

```
{
  "customer_id": "elise_smith@myemail.com",
  "orders": [
    {
      "orderdate": ISODate("2020-01-13T09:32:07Z"),
      "product_type": "GARDEN",
      "value": NumberDecimal("99.99")
    },
    {
      "orderdate": ISODate("2020-05-30T08:35:52Z"),
      "product_type": "ELECTRONICS",
      "value": NumberDecimal("231.43")
    }
  ]
}
```

You've defined an index on the customer_id field. You create the following aggregation pipeline to show the three most expensive orders made by a customer whose ID is tonijones@myemail.com, as shown:

```
var pipeline = [
  // Unpack each order from customer orders array as a new separate record
  {"$unwind": {
    "path": "$orders",
  }},

  // Match on only one customer
  {"$match": {
    "customer_id": "tonijones@myemail.com",
  }},

  // Sort customer's purchases by most expensive first
  {"$sort" : {
    "orders.value" : -1,
  }},

  // Show only the top 3 most expensive purchases
  {"$limit" : 3},

  // Use the order's value as a top level field
  {"$set": {
    "order_value": "$orders.value",
  }},

  // Drop the document's id and orders sub-document from the results
  {"$unset" : [
    "_id",
    "orders",
  ]},
];
```

Upon executing this aggregation against an extensive sample dataset, you receive the following result:

```
[
  {
    customer_id: 'tonijones@myemail.com',
    order_value: NumberDecimal("1024.89")
  },
  {
    customer_id: 'tonijones@myemail.com',
    order_value: NumberDecimal("187.99")
  },
  {
    customer_id: 'tonijones@myemail.com',
    order_value: NumberDecimal("4.59")
  }
]
```

You then request the *query planner* part of the explain plan:

```
db.customer_orders.explain("queryPlanner").aggregate(pipeline);
```

The query plan output for this pipeline shows the following (excluding some information for brevity):

```
stages: [
  {
    '$cursor': {
      queryPlanner: {
        parsedQuery: { customer_id: { '$eq': 'tonijones@myemail.com' } },
        winningPlan: {
          stage: 'FETCH',
          inputStage: {
            stage: 'IXSCAN',
            keyPattern: { customer_id: 1 },
            indexName: 'customer_id_1',
            direction: 'forward',
            indexBounds: {
              customer_id: [
                '["tonijones@myemail.com", "tonijones@myemail.com"]'
              ]
            }
          }
        }
      },
    }
  }
}
```

```
  },

  { '$unwind': { path: '$orders' } },

  { '$sort': { sortKey: { 'orders.value': -1 }, limit: 3 } },

  { '$set': { order_value: '$orders.value' } },

  { '$project': { _id: false, orders: false } }
]
```

You can deduce some illuminating insights from this query plan:

- To optimize the aggregation, the database engine has reordered the pipeline, positioning the filter belonging to $match at the top of the pipeline. The database engine moves the content of $match ahead of the $unwind stage without changing the aggregation's functional behavior or outcome.

- The first stage of the database-optimized version of the pipeline is an *internal* $cursor stage, regardless of the order you placed the pipeline stages in. The $cursor *runtime* stage is always the first action executed for any aggregation. Under the covers, the aggregation engine reuses the MongoDB Query Language query engine to perform a *regular* query against the collection, with a filter based on the aggregation's $match contents (where possible). The aggregation runtime uses the resulting query cursor to pull batches of records. This is similar to how a client application with a MongoDB driver uses a query cursor when remotely invoking a MongoDB Query Language query to pull batches. As with a normal MongoDB Query Language query, the regular database query engine will try to use an index if it makes sense. In this case, an index is indeed leveraged, as is visible in the embedded $queryPlanner metadata, showing the "stage" : "IXSCAN" element and the index used, "indexName" : "customer_id_1".

- To further optimize the aggregation, the database engine has collapsed $sort and $limit into a single *special internal sort stage*, which can perform both actions in one go. In this situation, during the sorting process, the aggregation engine only has to track the current three most expensive orders in memory. It does not have to hold the whole dataset in memory when sorting, which may otherwise be resource prohibitive in many scenarios, requiring more RAM than is available.

You might also want to see the execution stats part of the explain plan. The specific new information shown in executionStats, versus the default of queryPlanner, is identical to the normal MongoDB Query Language explain plan returned for a regular find() operation. Consequently, for aggregations, similar principles to the MongoDB Query Language apply to answer questions such as *"Have I used the optimal index?"* and *"Does my data model lend itself to efficiently processing this query?"*

Consider what happens when you ask for the execution stats part of the explain plan:

```
db.customer_orders.explain("executionStats").aggregate(pipeline);
```

The following is a redacted example of the output you will see, highlighting some of the most relevant metadata elements you should generally focus on:

```
executionStats: {
  nReturned: 1,
  totalKeysExamined: 1,
  totalDocsExamined: 1,
  executionStages: {
    stage: 'FETCH',
    nReturned: 1,
    works: 2,
    advanced: 1,
    docsExamined: 1,
    inputStage: {
      stage: 'IXSCAN',
      nReturned: 1,
      works: 2,
      advanced: 1,
      keyPattern: { customer_id: 1 },
      indexName: 'customer_id_1',
      direction: 'forward',
      indexBounds: {
        customer_id: [
          '["tonijones@myemail.com", "tonijones@myemail.com"]'
        ]
      },
      keysExamined: 1,
    }
  }
}
```

Here, this part of the plan also shows that the aggregation uses the existing index. Because totalKeysExamined and totalDocsExamined match, the aggregation fully leverages this index to identify the required records, which is good news. Nevertheless, the targeted index doesn't necessarily mean the aggregation's query part is fully optimized. For example, if there is the need to reduce latency further, you can do an analysis to determine whether the index can completely cover the query. Suppose the *cursor query* part of the aggregation is satisfied entirely using the index and does not have to examine any raw documents. In that case, you will see totalDocsExamined: 0 in the explain plan.

# Guidance for optimizing pipeline performance

Similar to any programming language, there is a downside if you prematurely optimize an aggregation pipeline. You risk producing an over-complicated solution that doesn't address the performance challenges that will manifest. As described in the previous section, the tool you should use to identify performance bottlenecks and opportunities for optimization is the *explain plan*. You will typically use the explain plan during the *final* stages of your pipeline's development once it is functionally correct.

With all that said, it can still help you to be aware of some guiding principles regarding performance while you are prototyping a pipeline. Critically, such guiding principles will be invaluable to you once the aggregation's explain plan is analyzed and if it shows that the current pipeline is suboptimal.

## Be cognizant of streaming vs blocking stages ordering

When executing an aggregation pipeline, the database engine pulls batches of records from the initial query cursor generated against the source collection. The database engine then attempts to stream each batch through the aggregation pipeline stages. For most types of stages, referred to as streaming stages, the database engine will take the processed batch from one stage and immediately stream it into the next part of the pipeline. It will do this without waiting for all the other batches to arrive at the prior stage. However, two types of stages must block and wait for all batches to arrive and accumulate together at that stage. These two stages are referred to as blocking stages; specifically, the two types of stages that block are the following:

- `$sort`
- `$group`

> **Note**
>
> Actually, when referring to `$group` here, we are also referring to the other less frequently used grouping stages. This includes the `$bucket`, `$bucketAuto`, `$count`, `$sortByCount`, and `$facet` stages. It might be a stretch to refer to `$facet` as a group stage, but in the context of this topic, it's best to think of it that way.

*Figure 3.1* highlights the nature of the streaming and blocking stages. Streaming stages allow batches to be processed and then passed through without waiting. Blocking stages wait for the whole of the input dataset to arrive at that stage and accumulate before processing all this data together.

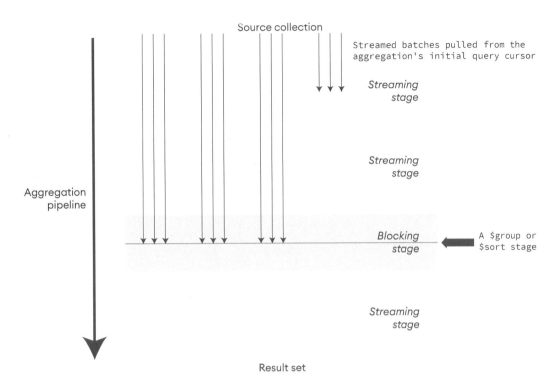

Figure 3.1: Nature of streaming and blocking stages

When considering the $sort and $group stages, it becomes evident why they have to block. The following examples illustrate why this is the case:

- $sort **blocking example**: A pipeline must sort *people* in ascending order of age. If the stage only sorts each batch's content before passing the batch on to the pipeline's result, only individual batches of output records are sorted by age but not the whole result set.

- $group **blocking example**: A pipeline must group employees by one of two work departments (either the *sales* or *manufacturing* department). If the stage only groups employees for a batch, before passing it on, the final result contains the work departments repeated multiple times. Each duplicate department consists of some but not all of its employees.

These often unavoidable blocking stages don't just increase aggregation execution time by reducing concurrency. If used without careful forethought, the throughput and latency of a pipeline will slow dramatically due to significantly increased memory consumption. The following subsections explore why this occurs and tactics to mitigate this.

## *$sort memory consumption and mitigation*

Used naïvely, a $sort stage will need to see all the input records at once, and so the host server must have enough capacity to hold all the input data in memory. The amount of memory required depends heavily on the initial data size and the degree to which the prior stages reduced the size. Also, multiple instances of the aggregation pipeline may be in flight at any one time, in addition to other database workloads. These all compete for the same finite memory. Suppose the source dataset is many gigabytes or even terabytes in size, and earlier pipeline stages have not reduced this size significantly. It will be unlikely that the host machine has sufficient memory to support the pipeline's blocking $sort stage. Therefore, MongoDB enforces that every blocking stage is limited to 100 MB of consumed RAM. The database throws an error if it exceeds this limit.

To avoid the memory limit obstacle, you can set the allowDiskUse:true option for the overall aggregation for handling large result datasets. Consequently, the pipeline's sort operation spills to disk if required, and the 100 MB limit no longer constrains the pipeline. However, the sacrifice here is significantly higher latency, and the execution time is likely to increase by orders of magnitude.

To circumvent the aggregation needing to manifest the whole dataset in memory or overspill to disk, attempt to refactor your pipeline to incorporate one of the following approaches (in the order of effectiveness):

1.  **Use an index to sort**: If the $sort stage does not depend on an $unwind, $group, or $project stage preceding it, move the $sort stage to near the start of your pipeline to target an index for the sort (also ensure the relevant index already exists). The aggregation runtime does not need to perform an expensive in-memory sort operation as a result. The $sort stage won't necessarily be the first stage in your pipeline because there may also be a $match stage that takes advantage of the same index. Always inspect the explain plan to ensure you are inducing the intended behavior and correctly targeting an index.

2.  **Apply a limit to sorting**: If you only need the first subset of records from the sorted dataset, add a $limit stage directly after the $sort stage, limiting the results to the fixed amount you require (e.g., 10). At runtime, the aggregation engine will collapse $sort and $limit into a single special internal sort stage, which performs both actions together. The in-flight sort process only has to track the 10 records in memory, which currently satisfy the executing sort/limit rule. It does not have to hold the whole dataset in memory to execute the sort successfully.

3.  **Reduce the number of records to sort**: If options 1 and 2 are not possible, move the $sort stage to as late as possible in your pipeline and ensure earlier stages significantly reduce the number of records streaming into this late blocking $sort stage. This blocking stage will have fewer records to process, thus reducing its need for RAM.

### $group memory consumption and mitigation

Like the $sort stage, the $group stage has the potential to consume a large amount of memory. The aggregation pipeline's 100 MB RAM limit for blocking stages applies equally to the $group stage because it will potentially pressure the host's memory capacity. As with sorting, you can use the pipeline's allowDiskUse:true option to avoid this limit for heavyweight grouping operations, but with the same performance downsides.

In reality, most grouping scenarios focus on accumulating summary data such as totals, counts, averages, and highs and lows, and not itemized data. In these situations, considerably reduced result data sets are produced, requiring far less processing memory than a $sort stage. Contrary to many sorting scenarios, grouping operations will typically demand a fraction of the host's RAM.

To ensure you avoid excessive memory consumption when you are looking to use a $group stage, adopt the following principles:

- **Avoid unnecessary grouping**: The next section, *Avoid unwinding and regrouping documents just to process each array's elements*, covers this recommendation in far greater detail.

- **Group summary data only**: If the use case permits it, use the group stage to accumulate things such as totals, counts, and summary roll-ups only, rather than holding all the raw data of each record belonging to a group. The aggregation framework provides a robust set of *accumulator operators* (for example, $addToSet, $first, $last, $max, and $count) to help you achieve this inside a $group stage.

## Avoid unwinding and regrouping documents just to process each array's elements

Sometimes, you need an aggregation pipeline to mutate or reduce an array field's content for each record. Take the following examples:

- You may need to add together all the values in the array into a total field

- You may need to retain the first and last elements of the array only

- You may need to retain only one recurring field for each subdocument in the array or apply numerous other array *reduction* scenarios

To bring this to life, imagine a retail *orders* collection where each document contains an array of products purchased as part of the order, as shown in the following example:

```
[
  {
    _id: 1197372932325,
    products: [
      {
        prod_id: 'abc12345',
        name: 'Asus Laptop',
        price: NumberDecimal('429.99')
      }
    ]
  },
  {
    _id: 4433997244387,
    products: [
      {
        prod_id: 'def45678',
        name: 'Karcher Hose Set',
        price: NumberDecimal('23.43')
      },
      {
        prod_id: 'jkl77336',
        name: 'Picky Pencil Sharpener',
        price: NumberDecimal('0.67')
      },
      {
        prod_id: 'xyz11228',
        name: 'Russell Hobbs Chrome Kettle',
        price: NumberDecimal('15.76')
      }
    ]
  }
]
```

The retailer wants to see a report of all the orders but only containing the expensive products purchased by customers (e.g., having just products priced greater than 15 dollars). Consequently, an aggregation is required to filter out the inexpensive product items of each order's array. The desired aggregation output might be as follows:

```
[
  {
    _id: 1197372932325,
    products: [
      {
        prod_id: 'abc12345',
        name: 'Asus Laptop',
        price: NumberDecimal('429.99')
      }
    ]
  },
  {
    _id: 4433997244387,
    products: [
      {
        prod_id: 'def45678',
        name: 'Karcher Hose Set',
        price: NumberDecimal('23.43')
      },
      {
        prod_id: 'xyz11228',
        name: 'Russell Hobbs Chrome Kettle',
        price: NumberDecimal('15.76')
      }
    ]
  }
]
```

Notice order 4433997244387 now only shows two products and is missing the inexpensive product.

One naïve way of achieving this transformation is to *unwind* the `products` array of each order document to produce an intermediate set of individual product records. These records can then be *matched* to retain products priced greater than 15 dollars. Finally, the products can be *grouped* back together again by each order's `_id` field. The required pipeline to achieve this is as follows:

```
// SUBOPTIMAL

var pipeline = [
  // Unpack each product from each order to a new separate record
  {"$unwind": {
    "path": "$products",
  }},

  // Match only products valued over 15.00
  {"$match": {
    "products.price": {
      "$gt": NumberDecimal("15.00"),
    },
  }},

  // Group by product type
  {"$group": {
    "_id": "$_id",
    "products": {"$push": "$products"},
  }},
];
```

This pipeline is suboptimal because a `$group` stage has been introduced, which is a blocking stage, as outlined earlier in this chapter. Both memory consumption and execution time will increase significantly, which could be fatal for a large input dataset. There is a far better alternative by using one of the *array operators* instead. Array operators are sometimes less intuitive to code, but they avoid introducing a blocking stage into the pipeline. Consequently, they are significantly more efficient, especially for large data sets. The following is a far more economical pipeline, using the `$filter` array operator, rather than the `$unwind`/`$match`/`$group` combination, to produce the same outcome:

```
// OPTIMAL

var pipeline = [
  // Filter out products valued 15.00 or less
  {"$set": {
    "products": {
      "$filter": {
        "input": "$products",
        "as": "product",
        "cond": {"$gt": ["$$product.price", NumberDecimal("15.00")]},
      }
    },
  }},
];
```

> **Note**
>
> Unlike the suboptimal pipeline, the optimal pipeline will include *empty orders* in the results for those orders that contained only inexpensive items. If this is a problem, you can include a simple $match stage at the start of the optimal pipeline with the same content as the $match stage shown in the suboptimal example.

To reiterate, there should never be the need to use an $unwind/$group combination in an aggregation pipeline to transform an array field's elements for each document in isolation. One way to recognize this anti-pattern is if your pipeline contains a $group on a $_id field. Instead, use array operators to avoid introducing a blocking stage. Otherwise, you will suffer a magnitude increase in execution time when the blocking group stage in your pipeline handles more than 100 MB of in-flight data. Adopting this best practice may mean the difference between achieving the required business outcome and abandoning the whole task as unachievable.

> **Note**
>
> The primary use of an $unwind/$group combination is to correlate patterns across many records' arrays rather than transforming the content within each input record's array only. For an illustration of the appropriate use of $unwind/$group, refer to *Chapter 6, Foundational Examples: Filtering, Grouping, and Unwinding*, the *Unpack arrays and group differently* section.

## Encourage match filters to appear early in the pipeline

As discussed, the database engine will do its best to optimize the aggregation pipeline at runtime, with a particular focus on attempting to move the $match stages to the top of the pipeline. Top-level $match content will form part of the filter that the engine first executes as the initial query. The aggregation then has the best chance of leveraging an index. However, it may not always be possible to promote $match filters in such a way without changing the meaning and resulting output of an aggregation.

### *Explore whether bringing forward a full match is possible*

Sometimes, a $match stage is defined later in a pipeline to perform a filter on a field that the pipeline computed in an earlier stage. The computed field isn't present in the pipeline's original input collection. Some examples include the following:

- A pipeline where a $group stage creates a new total field based on an accumulator operator. Later in the pipeline, a $match stage filters groups where each group's total is greater than 1000.

- A pipeline where a $set stage computes a new total field value based on adding up all the elements of an array field in each document. Later in the pipeline, a $match stage filters documents where the total is less than 50.

At first glance, it may seem like the match on the computed field is irreversibly trapped behind an earlier stage that computed the field's value. Indeed, the aggregation engine cannot automatically optimize this further. In some situations, though, there may be a missed opportunity where beneficial refactoring is possible by you, the developer.

Take the following trivial example of a collection of customer order documents:

```
[
  {
    customer_id: 'elise_smith@myemail.com',
    orderdate: ISODate('2020-05-30T08:35:52.000Z'),
    value: NumberDecimal('9999')
  }
  {
    customer_id: 'elise_smith@myemail.com',
    orderdate: ISODate('2020-01-13T09:32:07.000Z'),
    value: NumberDecimal('10101')
  }
]
```

Let's assume the orders are in dollar currency, and each `value` field shows the order's value in cents. You may have built a pipeline to display all orders where the value is greater than 100 dollars, as follows:

```
// SUBOPTIMAL

var pipeline = [
  {"$set": {
    "value_dollars": {"$multiply": [0.01, "$value"]}, // Convert to dollars
  }},

  {"$unset": [
    "_id",
    "value",
  ]},

  {"$match": {
    "value_dollars": {"$gte": 100},  // Performs a dollar check
  }},
];
```

The collection has an index defined for the `value` field (in cents). However, the `$match` filter uses a computed field, `value_dollars`. When you view the explain plan, you will see the pipeline does not leverage the index. `$match` is trapped behind the `$set` stage (which computes the field) and cannot be moved to the start of the pipeline. MongoDB's aggregation engine tracks a field's dependencies across multiple stages in a pipeline. It can establish how far up the pipeline it can promote fields without risking a change in the aggregation's behavior. In this case, it knows that if it moves the `$match` stage ahead of the `$set` stage it depends on, things will not work correctly.

In this example, as a developer, you can easily make a pipeline modification that will enable this pipeline to be more optimal without changing the pipeline's intended outcome. Change the $match filter to be based on the value source field instead (greater than 10000 cents), rather than the computed field (greater than 100 dollars). Also, ensure the $match stage appears before the $unset stage (which removes the value field). This change is enough to allow the pipeline to run efficiently. The following is how the pipeline looks after you have made this change:

```
// OPTIMAL

var pipeline = [
  {"$set": {
    "value_dollars": {"$multiply": [0.01, "$value"]},
  }},

  {"$match": {                    // Moved to before the $unset
    "value": {"$gte": 10000},   // Changed to perform a cents check
  }},

  {"$unset": [
    "_id",
    "value",
  ]},
];
```

This pipeline produces the same data output. However, when you look at its explain plan, it shows the database engine has pushed the $match filter to the top of the pipeline and applied an index for the value field. The aggregation is now optimal because the $match stage is no longer "blocked" by its dependency on the computed field.

### Explore whether bringing forward a partial match is possible

There may be some cases where you can't unravel a computed value in such a manner. However, it may still be possible for you to include an additional $match stage, to perform a *partial match* targeting the aggregation's query cursor. Suppose you have a pipeline that masks the values of sensitive date_of_birth fields (replaced with computed masked_date fields). The computed field adds a random number of days (one to seven) to each current date. The pipeline already contains a $match stage with the masked_date > 01-Jan 2020 filter. The runtime cannot optimize this to the top of the pipeline due to the dependency on a computed value. Nevertheless, you can manually add an extra $match stage at the top of the pipeline, with the date_of_birth > 25-Dec-2019 filter. This new $match leverages an index and filters records seven days earlier than the existing $match, but the aggregation's final output is the same. The new $match may pass on a few more records than intended. However, later on, the pipeline applies the existing filter, masked_date > 01-Jan-2020, which will naturally remove surviving surplus records before the pipeline completes.

In conclusion, if you have a pipeline leveraging a `$match` stage and the explain plan shows this is not moving to the start of the pipeline, explore whether manually refactoring will help. If the `$match` filter depends on a computed value, examine whether you can alter this or add an extra `$match` to yield a more efficient pipeline.

## Summary

In this chapter, you learned valuable techniques for identifying and addressing performance bottlenecks in aggregation pipelines. These techniques will help you to deliver the most optimal, performance-efficient aggregations possible to your users.

In the next chapter, you will learn about aggregation expressions and how expressions can enable you to apply sophisticated data transformation rules to your data, especially when dealing with document arrays.

# 4

# Harnessing the Power of Expressions

In this chapter, you will learn about the different types of aggregation expressions, how to combine them, and how they can help you enhance your aggregation pipelines. Using nested expressions can be highly effective for solving complex problems, particularly those involving arrays. Since nesting introduces added complexity, this chapter devotes significant attention to guiding you through the intricacies of crafting composite expressions for array processing.

To summarize, you will learn the following key concepts in this chapter:

- Types of aggregation expressions
- How to chain expressions together
- The power array operators
- Conditional comparisons
- Techniques for looping through and processing array elements

Let's begin by exploring the various types of aggregation expressions.

# Aggregation expressions explained

Aggregation expressions provide syntax and a library of commands to allow you to perform sophisticated data operations within many of the stages you include in your aggregation pipelines. You can use expressions within the pipeline to perform tasks such as the following:

- Compute values (e.g., calculate the average value of an array of numbers)

- Convert an input field's value (e.g., a string) into an output field's value (e.g., a date)

- Extract the specific reoccurring field's value from an array of sub-documents into a new list of values

- Transform the shape of an input object into an entirely differently structured output object

In many cases, you can nest expressions within other expressions, enabling a high degree of sophistication in your pipelines, albeit sometimes at the cost of making your pipelines appear complex.

You can think of an aggregation expression as being one of three possible types:

- **Operators**: Similar to library functions provided by regular programming languages, where the function (operator) can take arguments and return a value. You access an operator as an object with a $ prefix followed by the operator function name. The *dollar-operator-name* is used as the main key for the object. Examples include: {$arrayElemAt: ...}, {$cond: ...}, {$dateToString: ...}.

- **Field paths**: Similar to references to objects in regular programming languages, you can access a field path as a string with a $ prefix followed by the field's path in each record being processed. Examples include "$account.sortcode" and "$addresses.address.city".

- **Variables**: Similar to variables in regular programming languages, you can access the variable as a string with a $$ prefix followed by the fixed name. Variables fall into three sub-categories:

  - **Context system variables**: Similar to environment variables and constants in regular programming languages, the aggregation runtime provides these values dynamically as *system-wide* variables rather than as part of each input record an aggregation stage is processing. Examples include "$$NOW" and "$$CLUSTER_TIME".

  - **Marker flag system variables**: Similar to flags in regular programming languages, these variables allow you to indicate a specific action or behavior that the aggregation runtime should infer. Examples include "$$ROOT", "$$REMOVE", and "$$PRUNE".

  - **Bind user variables**: Similar to a variable holding a value in a regular programming language, you can store values in the variables you declare with a $let operator (or with the let option of a $lookup stage, or as an option of a $map or $filter stage). Examples include "$$product_name_var" and "$$orderIdVal".

You can combine these three categories of aggregation expressions when operating on input records, enabling you to perform complex comparisons and transformations of data. To highlight this, the following code snippet is an excerpt from the *Mask sensitive fields* section of *Chapter 10, Securing Data Examples*, which combines all three expression types:

```
"customer_info": {"$cond": {
                    "if":   {"$eq": ["$customer_info.category", "SENSITIVE"]},
                    "then": "$$REMOVE",
                    "else": "$customer_info",
                 }}
```

The pipeline retains an embedded sub-document (customer_info) in each resulting record unless a field in the original sub-document has a specific value (category=SENSITIVE). {$cond: ...} is one of the operator expressions used in the excerpt (a **conditional** operator expression that takes three arguments: if, then, and else). {$eq: ...} is another operator expression (a **comparison** operator expression). "$$REMOVE" is a **marker flag** variable expression instructing the pipeline to exclude the field. The "$customer_info.category" and "$customer_info" elements are field path expressions referencing fields from each incoming record.

# What do expressions produce?

An expression can be an operator (e.g., {$concat: ...}), a variable (e.g., "$$ROOT"), or a field path (e.g., "$address"). In all these cases, an expression is just something that dynamically populates and returns a new element, which can be one of the following types:

- Number (including integer, long, float, double, and decimal128)
- String (UTF-8)
- Boolean
- DateTime (UTC)
- Array
- Object

However, a specific expression can restrict you to returning just one or a few of these types. For example, the {$concat: ...} operator, which combines multiple strings, can only produce a *string* data type (or null). The "$$ROOT" variable can only return an *object* that refers to the root document currently being processed in the pipeline stage.

A field path (e.g., "$address") is different and can return an element of any data type, depending on what the field refers to in the current input document. For example, suppose "$address" references a sub-document. In this case, it will return an *object*. However, if it references a list of elements, it will return an *array*. As a human, you can guess that the field path "$address" won't return a *DateTime*, but the aggregation runtime does not know this ahead of time. There could be even more dynamics at play. Due to MongoDB's flexible data model, "$address" could yield a different type for each record processed in a pipeline stage. The first record's address may be an *object* sub-document with street name and city fields. The second record's address might represent the full address as a single *string*.

Lastly, the return data type of a variable depends on its category. A context system variable or marker flag variable has a fixed return type specific to that variable, so you must consult the MongoDB Manual to determine its return type. Bind user variables are similar to field paths in that they are dynamic and can reference and return any data type.

## Chaining operator expressions together

The parameters for operator expressions can nearly always take another expression of any type as an argument. The ability to nest operator expressions makes them highly composable. Suppose you need to determine the day of the week for a given date:

```
{"$dayOfWeek": ISODate("2021-04-24T00:00:00Z")}
```

Here, the $dayOfWeek operator expression can only return an element of the *number* type and takes a single parameter, an element of the *DateTime* type. However, you could have provided an expression rather than using a hardcoded *DateTime* for the parameter. This could be a *field path* expression:

```
{"$dayOfWeek": "$person_details.data_of_birth"}
```

Alternatively, you could have defined the parameter using a *context system variable* expression:

```
{"$dayOfWeek": "$$NOW"}
```

Or you could even have defined the parameter using yet another operator expression:

```
{"$dayOfWeek": {"$dateFromParts": {"year" : 2021, "month" : 4, "day": 24}}}
```

Furthermore, you could have defined year, month, and day parameters for $dateFromParts to be dynamically generated using expressions rather than literal values. The ability to chain expressions together in this way gives your pipelines a lot of power and flexibility when you need it.

# Can all stages use expressions?

There are many types of stages in the aggregation framework that don't allow expressions to be embedded. Here are some examples of some of the most popular of these stages:

- $match
- $limit
- $skip
- $sort
- $count
- $lookup
- $out

Some of these stages may be a surprise to you if you've never really thought about it before. You might consider $match to be the most surprising item in this list. The content of a $match stage is just a set of query conditions with the same syntax as MongoDB Query Language rather than an aggregation expression. There is a good reason for this. The aggregation engine reuses the MongoDB Query Language query engine to perform a *regular* query against the collection, enabling the query engine to use all its usual optimizations. The query conditions are taken as-is from the $match stage at the top of the pipeline. Therefore, the $match filter must use the same syntax as MongoDB Query Language.

In most of the stages that are unable to use expressions, it doesn't usually make sense for their behavior to be dynamic and based on the pipeline data entering the stage. For a client application that paginates results, you might define a value of 20 for the $limit stage. However, maybe you want to dynamically bind a value to the $limit stage, sourced by a $lookup stage earlier in the pipeline. The lookup operation might pull in the user's preferred *page list size* value from a *user preferences* collection. Nonetheless, the aggregation framework does not support this today for the listed stage types to avoid the overhead of the extra checks it would need to perform for what are essentially rare cases.

In most cases, only one of the listed stages needs to be more expressive—the $match stage. However, this stage is already flexible because it is based on expressive MongoDB Query Language query conditions. Sometimes, even MongoDB Query Language isn't expressive enough to sufficiently define a rule to identify records to retain in an aggregation. The next section explores this potential challenge and how it can be solved.

## What is using $expr inside $match all about?

Version 3.6 of MongoDB introduced the $expr operator, which you can embed within a $match stage (or in a MongoDB Query Language filter) to leverage aggregation expressions when filtering records. Essentially, this enables MongoDB's query runtime (which executes an aggregation's $match) to reuse expressions provided by MongoDB's aggregation runtime.

Inside an $expr operator, you can include any composite expression fashioned from $ operator functions, $ field paths, and $$ variables. A few situations demand having to use $expr from inside a $match stage:

- A requirement to compare two fields from the same record to determine whether to keep the record based on the comparison's outcome

- A requirement to perform a calculation based on values from multiple existing fields in each record and then compare the calculation to a constant

These are impossible to implement in an aggregation (or MongoDB Query Language find()) if you use regular $match query conditions.

Take the example of a collection holding information on different instances of rectangles (capturing their width and height), like the following:

```
[
  { _id: 1, width: 2, height: 8 },
  { _id: 2, width: 3, height: 4 },
  { _id: 3, width: 20, height: 1 }
]
```

What if you wanted to run an aggregation pipeline to only return rectangles with an area value greater than 12? This comparison isn't possible in a conventional aggregation when using a single $match query condition. However, with $expr, you can analyze a combination of fields in-situ using expressions. You can implement the requirement with the following pipeline:

```
var pipeline = [
  {"$match": {
    "$expr": {"$gt": [{"$multiply": ["$width", "$height"]}, 12]},
  }},
];
```

The result of executing an aggregation with this pipeline is as follows:

```
[
  { _id: 1, width: 2, height: 8 },
  { _id: 3, width: 20, height: 1 }
]
```

As you can see, the second of the three shapes is not output because its area is exactly 12 ( 3 x 4), not *greater than 12.*

## Restrictions when using expressions within $match

There are restrictions regarding when the runtime can benefit from an index when using a $expr operator inside a $match stage. This partly depends on the version of MongoDB you are running. Using $expr, you can leverage a $eq comparison operator with some constraints, including an inability to use a *multi-key index*. For MongoDB versions before 5.0, if you use a *range* comparison operator ( $gt, $gte, $lt, and $lte), an index cannot be employed to match the field using $expr, but this works fine in version 5.0 and greater.

There are also subtle differences when ordering values for a specific field across multiple documents when some values have different types. MongoDB's query runtime (which executes regular MongoDB Query Language and $match filters) and MongoDB's aggregation runtime (which implements $expr) can apply different ordering rules when filtering, referred to as *type bracketing*. Consequently, a range query may not yield the same result with $expr as it does with MongoDB Query Language if some values have different types.

Due to the potential challenges outlined, only use a $expr operator in a $match stage if there is no other way of assembling the filter criteria using regular MongoDB Query Language syntax.

Now that you have a good understanding of aggregation expressions and how they are implemented, let's take the next step to work on array expressions.

# Advanced use of expressions for array processing

One of the most compelling aspects of MongoDB is the ability to embed arrays within documents. Unlike relational databases, this characteristic allows each entity's entire data structure to exist in one place as a document.

The aggregation framework provides a rich set of aggregation *operator expressions* for analyzing and manipulating arrays. When optimizing for performance, array expressions are critical because they prevent the unwinding and regrouping of documents when you only need to process each document's array in isolation. For most situations when you need to manipulate an array, there is usually a single *array operator expression* that you can utilize for your requirements.

Occasionally, you won't be able to use a single *out-of-the-box* array operator expression to solve an array processing challenge. Consequently, you must assemble a composite of nested lower-level expressions to handle the challenging array manipulation task. These situations are the most demanding aspects for anyone using the aggregation framework.

Like aggregation pipelines in general, a large part of the challenge relates to adapting your mindset to the *functional programming* paradigm rather than the *procedural* one. Comparing with procedural approaches can provide clarity when describing array manipulation pipeline logic. Thus, the first few explanations in the remaining part of the chapter include examples of equivalent JavaScript code snippets you would use to achieve comparable outcomes in regular client-side applications.

## if-else conditional comparison

Performing conditional comparisons is a broad concept and not exclusive to array manipulation. Nevertheless, the application of conditional comparisons is crucial for handling arrays. Therefore, it's valuable to address this as an introductory pathway into the complex subject of advanced expressions for arrays.

Consider the trivial scenario of a retailer wanting to calculate the total cost of a customer's shopping order. The customer might order multiples of the same product, and the vendor applies a discount if more than five of the product items are in the order. In a procedural style of JavaScript, you might write the following code to calculate the total order cost:

```
let order = {"product" : "WizzyWidget", "price": 25.99, "qty": 8};

// Procedural style JavaScript
if (order.qty > 5) {
  order.cost = order.price * order.qty * 0.9;
} else {
  order.cost = order.price * order.qty;
}
```

This code modifies the customer's order to the following to include the total cost:

```
{product: 'WizzyWidget', qty: 8, price: 25.99, cost: 187.128}
```

To achieve a similar outcome in an aggregation pipeline, you might use the following:

```
db.customer_orders.insertOne(order);

var pipeline = [
  {"$set": {
    "cost": {
      "$cond": {
        "if":   {"$gte": ["$qty", 5]},
        "then": {"$multiply": ["$price", "$qty", 0.9]},
        "else": {"$multiply": ["$price", "$qty"]},
      }
    },
  }},
];

db.customer_orders.aggregate(pipeline);
```

This pipeline produces the following output with the customer order document transformed:

```
{product: 'WizzyWidget', price: 25.99, qty: 8, cost: 187.128}
```

If you were going to use a functional programming approach in JavaScript, the code would be more like the following to achieve the same outcome:

```
// Functional style JavaScript
order.cost = (
                (order.qty > 5) ?
                (order.price * order.qty * 0.9) :
                (order.price * order.qty)
             );
```

Here, you can see that the JavaScript code's construction in a functional style closely resembles the aggregation pipeline's structure. This comparison highlights why some people may find composing aggregation expressions foreboding. The challenge is predominantly due to the less familiar paradigm of *functional programming* rather than the intricacies of MongoDB's aggregation language per se.

The other difference between this comparison and the rest of the comparisons in this chapter is the pipeline will work unchanged when run against a collection of many records, which could feasibly be many billions. The sample JavaScript code only works against one document at a time and would need to be modified to loop through a list of records. This JavaScript code would need to fetch each document from the database back to a client, apply the modifications, and then write the result back to the database. Instead, the aggregation pipeline's logic operates against each document in-situ within the database for far superior performance and efficiency.

## The power array operators

When you want to transform or extract data from an array field, and a single high-level array operator (e.g., $avg, $max, and $filter) does not give you what you need, the tools to turn to are the $map and $reduce array operators. These two *power* operators enable you to iterate through an array, perform whatever complexity of logic you need against each array element, and collect the result for inclusion in a stage's output.

The $map and $reduce operators are the *Swiss army knives* of the aggregation framework, but do not confuse these two array operators with MongoDB's old map-reduce functionality. The old map-reduce functionality forced you to combine a map() function and a reduce() function to generate a result, and the map-reduce functionality is now redundant and deprecated.

In the aggregation framework, the $map and $reduce operators are independent of each other. Depending on your specific requirements, you would use one or the other to process an array's field, but not necessarily both together. Here's an explanation of these two *power* operators:

- $map: Allows you to specify some logic to perform against each element in the array that the operator iterates, returning an array as the final result. Typically, you use $map to mutate each array member and then return this transformed array. The $map operator exposes the current array element's content to your logic via a special variable, with the default name of $$this.

- $reduce: Similarly, you can specify some logic to execute for each element in an array that the operator iterates, but instead returning a single value (rather than an array) as the result. You typically use $reduce to compute a summary having analyzed each array element. For example, you might want to return a number by multiplying together a specific field value from each element in the array. Like the $map operator, the $reduce operator provides your logic with access to the current array element via the $$this variable. The operator also provides a second variable, called $$value, for your logic to update when accumulating the single result (for example, storing the multiplication result).

The rest of this chapter explores how these two *power* operators are used to manipulate arrays.

## for-each looping to transform an array

Imagine you want to process a list of the products ordered by a customer and convert the array of product names to uppercase. In the procedural style of JavaScript, you might write the following code to loop through each product in the array and convert its name to uppercase:

```
let order = {
  "orderId": "AB12345",
  "products": ["Laptop", "Kettle", "Phone", "Microwave"]
};

// Procedural style JavaScript
for (let pos in order.products) {
  order.products[pos] = order.products[pos].toUpperCase();
}
```

This code modifies the order's product names to the following, with the product names now in uppercase:

```
{orderId: 'AB12345', products: ['LAPTOP', 'KETTLE', 'PHONE', 'MICROWAVE']}
```

To achieve a similar outcome in an aggregation pipeline, you might use the following:

```
db.orders.insertOne(order);

var pipeline = [
  {"$set": {
    "products": {
      "$map": {
        "input": "$products",
        "as": "product",
        "in": {"$toUpper": "$$product"}
      }
    }
  }}
];


db.orders.aggregate(pipeline);
```

Here, a $map operator expression is applied to loop through each product name in the input products array and add the uppercase version of the product name to the replacement output array.

This pipeline produces the following output with the order document transformed to the following:

```
{orderId: 'AB12345', products: ['LAPTOP', 'KETTLE', 'PHONE', 'MICROWAVE']}
```

Using the functional style of JavaScript, your looping code would more closely resemble the following to achieve the same outcome:

```
// Functional style JavaScript
order.products = order.products.map(
  product => {
    return product.toUpperCase();
  }
);
```

Comparing an aggregation $map operator expression to a JavaScript map() array function is far more illuminating to help illustrate how the operator works.

## for-each looping to compute a summary value from an array

Suppose you want to process a list of the products ordered by a customer but produce a single summary string field from this array by concatenating all the product names from the array. In a procedural JavaScript style, you could code the following to produce the product names summary field:

```
let order = {
  "orderId": "AB12345",
  "products": ["Laptop", "Kettle", "Phone", "Microwave"]
};

order.productList = "";

// Procedural style JavaScript
for (const pos in order.products) {
  order.productList += order.products[pos] + "; ";
}
```

This code yields the following output with a new `productList` string field produced, which contains the names of all the products in the order, delimited by semicolons:

```
{
  orderId: 'AB12345',
  products: [ 'Laptop', 'Kettle', 'Phone', 'Microwave' ],
  productList: 'Laptop; Kettle; Phone; Microwave; '
}
```

You can use the following pipeline to achieve a similar outcome:

```
db.orders.insertOne(order);

var pipeline = [
  {"$set": {
    "productList": {
      "$reduce": {
        "input": "$products",
        "initialValue": "",
        "in": {
          "$concat": ["$$value", "$$this", "; "]
        }
      }
    }
  }}
];
```

```
db.orders.aggregate(pipeline);
```

Here, the $reduce operator expression loops through each product in the input array and concatenates each product's name into an accumulating string. You use the $$this expression to access the current array element's value during each iteration. For each iteration, you employ the $$value expression with reference to the final output value, to which you append the current product string (and delimiter).

This pipeline produces the following output, where it transforms the order document to the following:

```
{
  orderId: 'AB12345',
  products: [ 'Laptop', 'Kettle', 'Phone', 'Microwave' ],
  productList: 'Laptop; Kettle; Phone; Microwave; '
}
```

Using the functional approach in JavaScript, you could have used the following code to achieve the same result:

```
// Functional style JavaScript
order.productList = order.products.reduce(
  (previousValue, currentValue) => {
    return previousValue + currentValue + "; ";
  },
  ""
);
```

Once more, by comparing the use of the aggregation operator expression ( $reduce) to the equivalent JavaScript array function ( reduce()), the similarity is more pronounced.

## for-each looping to locate an array element

Imagine storing data about buildings on a campus where each building document contains an array of rooms along with their respective size (width and length). A room reservation system may require finding the first room in the building with sufficient floor space for a particular number of meeting attendees. Here is an example of one building's data that you might load into the database, with an array of rooms and their dimensions in meters:

```
db.buildings.insertOne({
  "building": "WestAnnex-1",
  "room_sizes": [
    {"width": 9, "length": 5},
    {"width": 8, "length": 7},
    {"width": 7, "length": 9},
    {"width": 9, "length": 8},
  ]
});
```

You want to create a pipeline to locate an appropriate meeting room that produces an output such as the following. The result should contain a newly added field, firstLargeEnoughRoomArrayIndex, to indicate the array position of the first room found to have enough capacity:

```
{
  building: 'WestAnnex-1',
  room_sizes: [
    { width: 9, length: 5 },
    { width: 8, length: 7 },
    { width: 7, length: 9 },
    { width: 9, length: 8 }
  ],
  firstLargeEnoughRoomArrayIndex: 2
}
```

Here is a suitable pipeline that iterates through the room array elements, capturing the position of the first one with a calculated area greater than 60 m²:

```
var pipeline = [
  {"$set": {
    "firstLargeEnoughRoomArrayIndex": {
      "$reduce": {
        "input": {"$range": [0, {"$size": "$room_sizes"}]},
        "initialValue": -1,
        "in": {
          "$cond": {
            "if": {
              "$and": [
                // IF ALREADY FOUND DON'T CONSIDER SUBSEQUENT ELEMENTS
                {"$lt": ["$$value", 0]},
                // IF WIDTH x LENGTH > 60
                {"$gt": [
                  {"$multiply": [
                    {"$getField": {
                      "input": {"$arrayElemAt": ["$room_sizes", "$$this"]},
                      "field": "width"
                    }},
                    {"$getField": {
                      "input": {"$arrayElemAt": ["$room_sizes", "$$this"]},
                      "field": "length"
                    }},
                  ]},
                  60
                ]}
              ]
            },
            // IF ROOM SIZE IS BIG ENOUGH CAPTURE ITS ARRAY POSITION
            "then": "$$this",
            // IF ROOM SIZE NOT BIG ENOUGH RETAIN EXISTING VALUE (-1)
            "else": "$$value"
          }
        }
      }
    }
  }}
];
```

Here, the $reduce operator is again used to loop and eventually return a single value. However, the pipeline uses a generated sequence of incrementing numbers for its input rather than the existing array field in each source document. The $range operator is used to create this sequence, which has the same size as the rooms array field of each document. The pipeline uses this approach to track the array position of the matching room using the $$this variable. For each iteration, the pipeline calculates the room array element's area. If the size is greater than 60, the pipeline assigns the current array position (represented by $$this) to the final result (represented by $$value).

The *iterator* array expressions have no concept of the *break* command that procedural programming languages typically provide. Therefore, even though the executing logic may have already located a room of sufficient size, the looping process will continue through the remaining array elements. Consequently, the pipeline logic must include a check during each iteration to avoid overriding the final value (the $$value variable) if it already has a value. Naturally, for massive arrays containing a few hundred or more elements, an aggregation pipeline will incur a noticeable latency impact when iterating over the remaining array members even though the logic has already identified the required element.

Suppose you just wanted to return the first matching array element for a room with sufficient floor space, not its index. In that case, the pipeline can be more straightforward, that is, using $filter to trim the array elements to only those with sufficient space and then the $first operator to grab just the first element from the filter. You would use a pipeline similar to the following:

```
var pipeline = [
  {"$set": {
    "firstLargeEnoughRoom": {
      "$first": {
        "$filter": {
          "input": "$room_sizes",
          "as": "room",
          "cond": {
            "$gt": [
              {"$multiply": ["$$room.width", "$$room.length"]},
              60
            ]
          }
        }
      }
    }
  }}
];

db.buildings.aggregate(pipeline);
```

This pipeline produces the following output:

```
[
  {
    _id: ObjectId("637b4b8a86fac07908ef98b3"),
    building: 'WestAnnex-1',
    room_sizes: [
      { width: 9, length: 5 },
      { width: 8, length: 7 },
      { width: 7, length: 9 },
      { width: 9, length: 8 }
    ],
    firstLargeEnoughRoom: { width: 7, length: 9 }
  }
]
```

The array of rooms would be likely to also include an ID for each building's room:

```
"room_sizes": [
  {"roomId": "Mercury", "width": 9, "length": 5},
  {"roomId": "Venus", "width": 8, "length": 7},
  {"roomId": "Jupiter", "width": 7, "length": 9},
  {"roomId": "Saturn", "width": 9, "length": 8},
]
```

Consequently, `firstLargeEnoughRoom: { roomId: "Jupiter", width: 7, length: 9 }` would be the first element returned from the filtering pipeline stage, giving you the room's ID, so there would be no need to obtain the array's index for this particular use case. However, the previous example, using the $reduce-based pipeline, is helpful for more complicated situations where you do need the index of the matching array element.

## Reproducing $map behavior using $reduce

It is possible to implement the $map behavior using $reduce to transform an array. This method is more complex, but you may need to use it in some rare circumstances. Before looking at an example to explain why, let's first compare a more basic example of using $map and then $reduce to achieve the same thing.

Suppose you have captured some sensor readings for a device:

```
db.deviceReadings.insertOne({
  "device": "A1",
  "readings": [27, 282, 38, -1, 187]
});
```

Imagine you want to produce a transformed version of the readings array, with the device's ID concatenated with each reading in the array. You want the pipeline to produce an output similar to the following, with the newly included array field:

```
{
  device: 'A1',
  readings: [ 27, 282, 38, -1, 187 ],
  deviceReadings: [ 'A1:27', 'A1:282', 'A1:38', 'A1:-1', 'A1:187' ]
}
```

You can achieve this using the $map operator expression in the following pipeline:

```
var pipeline = [
  {"$set": {
    "deviceReadings": {
      "$map": {
        "input": "$readings",
        "as": "reading",
        "in": {
          "$concat": ["$device", ":", {"$toString": "$$reading"}]
        }
      }
    }
  }}
];


db.deviceReadings.aggregate(pipeline);
```

You can also accomplish the same with the $reduce operator expression in the following pipeline:

```
var pipeline = [
  {"$set": {
    "deviceReadings": {
      "$reduce": {
        "input": "$readings",
        "initialValue": [],
        "in": {
          "$concatArrays": [
            "$$value",
            [{"$concat": ["$device", ":", {"$toString": "$$this"}]}]
          ]
        }
      }
```

```
      }
    }}
  ];
```

```
db.deviceReadings.aggregate(pipeline);
```

You will see the pipeline has to do more work here, such as holding the transformed element in a new array and then concatenating it with the *final value* array that the logic is accumulating in the $$value variable.

So, why would you ever want to use $reduce for this requirement and take on this extra complexity?

Suppose the mapping code in the stage needs to include a condition to omit outlier readings that signify a device sensor faulty reading (i.e., a −1 reading value). The challenge here when using $map is that for five input array elements, five array elements will need to be output. However, using $reduce, for an input of five array elements, four array elements can be output using a pipeline such as the following:

```
var pipeline = [
  {"$set": {
    "deviceReadings": {
      "$reduce": {
        "input": "$readings",
        "initialValue": [],
        "in": {
          "$concatArrays": [
            "$$value",
            {"$cond": {
              "if": {"$gte": ["$$this", 0]},
              "then": [
                {"$concat": [
                  "$device",
                  ":",
                  {"$toString":"$$this"}
                ]}
              ],
              "else": []
            }}
          ]
        }
      }
    }
  }}
];
```

This time, the output does not include the faulty device reading ($-1$):

```
[
  {
    device: 'A1',
    readings: [ 27, 282, 38, -1, 187 ],
    deviceReadings: [ 'A1:27', 'A1:282', 'A1:38', 'A1:187' ]
  }
]
```

Of course, this being the aggregation framework, multiple ways exist to solve the same problem. Another approach could be to continue with the $map-based pipeline and, using the $cond operator, return an empty string ( ' ' ) for each faulty reading. You would then need to wrap the $map stage in a $filter stage with logic to filter out elements where the element's string length is zero.

In summary, you typically use a $map stage when the ratio of input elements to output elements is the same (i.e., many-to-many or *M:M*). You employ a $reduce stage when the ratio of input elements to output elements is many-to-one (i.e., *M:1*). For situations where the ratio of input elements is many-to-few (i.e., *M:N*), instead of $map, you would invariably reach for $reduce with its *null array concatenation* trick when $filter does not suffice.

## Adding new fields to existing objects in an array

One of the primary uses of the $map operator expression is to add more data to each existing object in an array. Suppose you've persisted a set of retail orders, where each order document contains an array of order items. Each order item in the array captures the product's *name, unit price,* and *quantity purchased,* as shown in the following example:

```
db.orders.insertOne({
    "custid": "jdoe@acme.com",
    "items": [
      {
        "product" : "WizzyWidget",
        "unitPrice": 25.99,
        "qty": 8,
      },
      {
        "product" : "HighEndGizmo",
        "unitPrice": 33.24,
        "qty": 3,
      }
    ]
});
```

You now need to calculate the total cost for each product item (quantity x unitPrice) and add that cost to the corresponding order item in the array. You can use a pipeline such as the following to achieve this:

```
var pipeline = [
  {"$set": {
    "items": {
      "$map": {
        "input": "$items",
        "as": "item",
        "in": {
          "product": "$$item.product",
          "unitPrice": "$$item.unitPrice",
          "qty": "$$item.qty",
          "cost": {"$multiply": ["$$item.unitPrice", "$$item.qty"]}},
        }
      }
    }
  }
];


db.orders.aggregate(pipeline);
```

Here, for each element in the source array, the pipeline creates an element in the new array by explicitly pulling in the three fields from the old element (product, unitPrice, and quantity) and adding one new computed field (cost). The pipeline produces the following output:

```
{
  custid: 'jdoe@acme.com',
  items: [
    {
      product: 'WizzyWidget',
      unitPrice: 25.99,
      qty: 8,
      cost: 187.128
    },
    {
      product: 'HighEndGizmo',
      unitPrice: 33.24,
      qty: 3,
      cost: 99.72
    }
  ]
}
```

Similar to the disadvantages of using a $project stage in a pipeline, outlined in *Chapter 2, Optimizing Pipelines for Productivity*, the $map code is burdened by explicitly naming every field in the array element to retain. You will find this tiresome if each array element has lots of fields. In addition, if your data model evolves and new types of fields appear in the array's items over time, you will be forced to return to your pipeline and refactor it each time to include these newly introduced fields.

Just like using $set instead of $project for a pipeline stage, there is a better solution to allow you to retain all existing array item fields and add new ones when you process arrays. A good solution is to employ the $mergeObjects operator expression to combine all existing fields plus the newly computed fields into each new array element. $mergeObjects takes an array of objects and combines the fields from all the array's objects into one single object. To use $mergeObjects in this situation, you provide the current array element as the first parameter to $mergeObjects. The second parameter you provide is a new object containing each computed field. In the following example, the code adds only one generated field, but if you require it, you can include multiple generated fields in this new object:

```
var pipeline = [
  {"$set": {
    "items": {
      "$map": {
        "input": "$items",
        "as": "item",
        "in": {
          "$mergeObjects": [
            "$$item",
            {"cost": {"$multiply": ["$$item.unitPrice", "$$item.qty"]}},
          ]
        }
      }
    }
  }}
];


db.orders.aggregate(pipeline);
```

This pipeline produces the same output as the previous *hardcoded field names* pipeline, but with the advantage of being sympathetic to new types of fields appearing in the source array in the future.

Instead of using $mergeObjects, there is an alternative and slightly more verbose combination of three different array operator expressions that you can similarly employ to retain all existing array item fields and add new ones. These three operators are as follows:

- $objectToArray: This converts an object containing different field key/value pairs into an array of objects where each object has two fields: k, holding the field's name, and v, holding the field's value. For example, {height: 170, weight: 60} becomes [{k: 'height', v: 170}, {k: 'weight', v: 60}].

- $concatArrays: This combines the contents of multiple arrays into one single array result.

- $arrayToObject: This converts an array into an object by performing the reverse of the $objectToArray operator. For example, {k: 'height', v: 170}, {k: 'weight', v: 60}, {k: 'shoeSize', v: 10}] becomes {height: 170, weight: 60, shoeSize: 10}.

The following pipeline shows the combination in action for the same retail orders dataset as before, adding the newly computed total cost for each product:

```
var pipeline = [
  {"$set": {
    "items": {
      "$map": {
        "input": "$items",
        "as": "item",
        "in": {
          "$arrayToObject": {
            "$concatArrays": [
              {"$objectToArray": "$$item"},
              [{
                "k": "cost",
                "v": {"$multiply": ["$$item.unitPrice", "$$item.qty"]},
              }]
            ]
          }
        }
      }
    }
  }}
];

db.orders.aggregate(pipeline);
```

If this achieves the same as using $mergeObjects but is more verbose, why use this pattern? Well, in most cases, you wouldn't. One situation where you will use the more verbose combination is if you need to dynamically set the name of an array item's field, in addition to its value. Rather than naming the computed total field as cost, suppose you want the field's name also to reflect the product's name (e.g., costForWizzyWidget and costForHighEndGizmo). You can achieve this by using the $arrayToObject/$concatArrays/$objectToArray approach rather than the $mergeObjects method, as follows:

```
var pipeline = [
  {"$set": {
    "items": {
      "$map": {
        "input": "$items",
        "as": "item",
        "in": {
          "$arrayToObject": {
            "$concatArrays": [
              {"$objectToArray": "$$item"},
              [{
                "k": {"$concat": ["costFor", "$$item.product"]},
                "v": {"$multiply": ["$$item.unitPrice", "$$item.qty"]},
              }]
            ]
          }
        }
      }
    }}
  }
];

db.orders.aggregate(pipeline);
```

Here, you can see the new pipeline's output. The pipeline has retained all the existing array item's fields and added a new field to each item with a dynamically generated name:

```
{
  custid: 'jdoe@acme.com',
  items: [
    {
      product: 'WizzyWidget',
      unitPrice: 25.99,
      qty: 8,
      costForWizzyWidget: 207.92
    },
    {
      product: 'HighEndGizmo',
      unitPrice: 33.24,
      qty: 3,
      costForHighEndGizmo: 99.72
    }
  ]
}
```

When retaining existing items from an array, plus adding new fields, you can use either approach to override an existing item's field with a new value. For example, you may want to modify the current unitPrice field to incorporate a discount. For both $mergeObjects and $arrayToObject expressions, to achieve this, you provide a redefinition of the field as a subsequent parameter after first providing the reference to the source array item. This tactic works because the last definition wins if the same field is defined more than once with different values.

## Rudimentary schema reflection using arrays

As our final example, let's see how to employ an $objectToArray operator expression to use *reflection* to analyze the shape of a collection of documents as part of a custom schema analysis tool. Such reflection capabilities are vital in databases that provide a flexible data model, such as MongoDB, where the included fields may vary from document to document.

Imagine you have a collection of customer documents, similar to the following:

```
db.customers.insertMany([
  {
    "_id": ObjectId('6064381b7aa89666258201fd'),
    "email": 'elsie_smith@myemail.com',
    "dateOfBirth": ISODate('1991-05-30T08:35:52.000Z'),
    "accNnumber": 123456,
    "balance": NumberDecimal("9.99"),
    "address": {
      "firstLine": "1 High Street",
      "city": "Newtown",
      "postcode": "NW1 1AB",
    },
    "telNums": ["07664883721", "01027483028"],
    "optedOutOfMarketing": true,
  },
  {
    "_id": ObjectId('734947394bb73732923293ed'),
    "email": 'jon.jones@coolemail.com',
    "dateOfBirth": ISODate('1993-07-11T22:01:47.000Z'),
    "accNnumber": 567890,
    "balance": NumberDecimal("299.22"),
    "telNums": "07836226281",
    "contactPrefernece": "email",
  },
]);
```

In your schema analysis pipeline, you use $objectToArray to capture the name and type of each top-level field in the document as follows:

```
var pipeline = [
  {"$project": {
    "_id": 0,
    "schema": {
      "$map": {
        "input": {"$objectToArray": "$$ROOT"},
        "as": "field",
        "in": {
          "fieldname": "$$field.k",
          "type": {"$type": "$$field.v"},
```

```
                }
              }
            }
         }}
];

db.customers.aggregate(pipeline);
```

For the two example documents in the collection, the pipeline outputs the following:

```
{
  schema: [
    {fieldname: '_id', type: 'objectId'},
    {fieldname: 'email', type: 'string'},
    {fieldname: 'dateOfBirth', type: 'date'},
    {fieldname: 'accNnumber', type: 'int'},
    {fieldname: 'balance', type: 'decimal'},
    {fieldname: 'address', type: 'object'},
    {fieldname: 'telNums', type: 'array'},
    {fieldname: 'optedOutOfMarketing', type: 'bool'}
  ]
},
{
  schema: [
    {fieldname: '_id', type: 'objectId'},
    {fieldname: 'email', type: 'string'},
    {fieldname: 'dateOfBirth', type: 'date'},
    {fieldname: 'accNnumber', type: 'int'},
    {fieldname: 'balance', type: 'decimal'},
    {fieldname: 'telNums', type: 'string'},
    {fieldname: 'contactPrefernece', type: 'string'}
  ]
}
```

The difficulty with this basic pipeline approach is once there are many documents in the collection, the output will be too lengthy and complex for you to detect common schema patterns. Instead, you will want to add an $unwind and $group stage combination to accumulate recurring fields that match. The generated result should also highlight if the same field name appears in multiple documents but with different data types. Here is the improved pipeline:

```
var pipeline = [
  {"$project": {
    "_id": 0,
    "schema": {
      "$map": {
        "input": {"$objectToArray": "$$ROOT"},
        "as": "field",
        "in": {
          "fieldname": "$$field.k",
          "type": {"$type": "$$field.v"},
        }
      }
    }
  }},

  {"$unwind": "$schema"},

  {"$group": {
    "_id": "$schema.fieldname",
    "types": {"$addToSet": "$schema.type"},
  }},

  {"$set": {
    "fieldname": "$_id",
    "_id": "$$REMOVE",
  }},
];

db.customers.aggregate(pipeline);
```

This pipeline's output now provides a far more comprehensible summary, as shown here:

```
{fieldname: '_id', types: ['objectId']},
{fieldname: 'address', types: ['object']},
{fieldname: 'email', types: ['string']},
{fieldname: 'telNums', types: ['string', 'array']},
{fieldname: 'contactPrefernece', types: ['string']},
{fieldname: 'accNnumber', types: ['int']},
{fieldname: 'balance', types: ['decimal']},
{fieldname: 'dateOfBirth', types: ['date']},
{fieldname: 'optedOutOfMarketing', types: ['bool']}
```

This result highlights that the telNums field can have one of two different data types within documents. The main drawback of this rudimentary schema analysis pipeline is its inability to descend through layers of arrays and sub-documents hanging off each top-level document. This challenge is indeed solvable using a pure aggregation pipeline, but the code involved is far more complex and beyond the scope of this chapter. If you are interested in exploring this further, the *mongo-agg-schema-analyzer* GitHub project (see `https://github.com/pkdone/mongo-agg-schema-analyzer`) solves this problem. This project shows you how to traverse hierarchically structured documents using a single aggregation pipeline to infer the schema.

## Summary

In this chapter, you started your journey with basic aggregation expressions. You explored the different types of expressions and how to combine them using nesting to solve complex data transformations. Then you moved on to bootstrapping this knowledge to undertake typically complicated tasks related to mutating arrays and extracting detail from the contents of arrays. There was a particular focus on techniques for looping through array elements efficiently without necessarily having to resort to unwinding and regrouping documents, where you only need to process each document's array in isolation.

The next chapter will enable you to understand the impact of sharding on aggregation pipelines and how to ensure your pipelines run efficiently when your database is sharded.

# 5

# Optimizing Pipelines for Sharded Clusters

In this chapter, you will learn about the potential impacts on performance when your aggregation pipelines run in a sharded cluster. You will discover how the aggregation runtime distributes aggregation stages across the cluster and where potential bottlenecks can occur. Finally, you will learn the recommended steps to ensure your pipeline's performance scales efficiently in a sharded cluster.

This chapter will cover the following:

- What sharded clusters are
- Sharded aggregation constraints
- The sharded distribution of pipeline stages
- Performance tips for achieving efficient sharded aggregations

Let's start with a summary of the concept of sharding in MongoDB.

# A brief summary of MongoDB sharded clusters

In a sharded cluster, you partition a collection of data across multiple shards, where each shard runs on a separate set of host machines. You control how the system distributes the data by defining a shard key rule. Based on the shard key of each document, the system groups subsets of documents together into *chunks*, where a range of shard key values identifies each chunk. The cluster balances these chunks across its shards.

In addition to holding sharded collections in a database, you may also be storing unsharded collections in the same database. All a database's unsharded collections live on one specific shard in the cluster, designated as the *primary shard* for the database (not to be confused with a replica set's *primary replica*). *Figure 5.1* shows the relationship between a database's collections and the shards in the cluster.

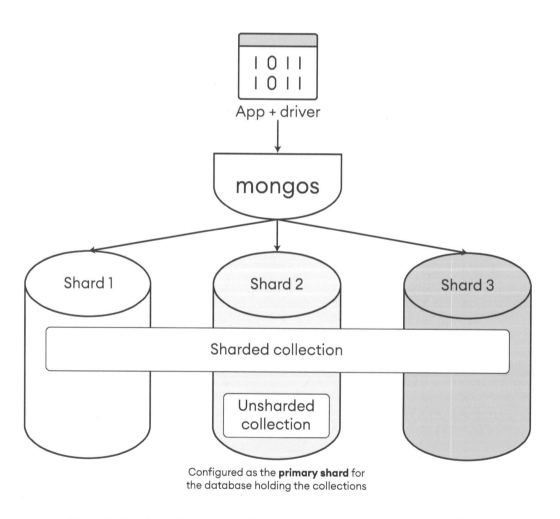

Figure 5.1: Correlation between a database's collections and the shards within a cluster

One or more deployed *mongos* processes act as a reverse proxy, routing read and write operations from the client application to the appropriate shards. For document write operations (i.e., create, update, and delete), a mongos router knows which shard the document lives on and routes the operation to that specific shard. For read operations, if the query includes the shard key, the mongos router knows which shards hold the required documents to route the query to (called *targeting*). If the query does not include the shard key, it sends the query to all shards using a *scatter/gather* pattern (called *broadcasting*). These are the rules for sharded reads and writes, but the approach for sharded aggregations requires a deeper explanation. Consequently, the rest of this chapter outlines how a sharded cluster handles the routing and execution of aggregations.

## Sharding implications for pipelines

*MongoDB sharding* isn't just an effective way to scale out your database to hold more data and support higher transactional throughput. Sharding also helps you scale out your analytical workloads, potentially enabling aggregations to be completed far quicker. Depending on the nature of your aggregation and some adherence to best practices, the cluster may execute parts of the aggregation in parallel over multiple shards for faster completion.

There is no difference between a replica set and a sharded cluster regarding the functional capabilities of the aggregations you build, except for a minimal set of constraints. The *sharded aggregation constraints* section in this chapter will outline these constraints. When it comes to optimizing your aggregations, in most cases, there will be little to no difference in the structure of a pipeline when refactoring for performance on a sharded cluster compared to a simple replica set.

You should always adhere to the advice outlined in *Chapter 3, Optimizing Pipelines for Performance*. The aggregation runtime takes care of distributing the appropriate parts of your pipeline to each shard that holds the required data. The runtime then transparently and optimally combines the results from these shards. Even though the aggregation runtime handles most of the sharding complexities for you, if you ever suffer a performance problem and need to dig deeper into why, it is still worth understanding how the aggregation engine distributes work and applies its sharding optimizations.

## Sharded aggregation constraints

As some MongoDB stages only partly support sharded aggregations, depending on which version of MongoDB you are running, there are some constraints to be aware of for your aggregation stages when you are running a sharded cluster environment. These stages all happen to reference a second collection in addition to the pipeline's source input collection. In each case, the pipeline can use a sharded collection as its source, but the second collection referenced must be unsharded (for earlier MongoDB versions, at least). The affected stages and versions are as follows:

- `$lookup`: In MongoDB versions prior to 6.0, the other referenced collection to join with must be unsharded.

- `$graphLookup`: In MongoDB versions prior to 6.0, the other referenced collection to recursively traverse must be unsharded.

- `$out`: In all MongoDB versions, the other referenced collection used as the destination of the aggregation's output must be unsharded. However, you can use a `$merge` stage instead to output the aggregation result to a sharded collection.

# Where does a sharded aggregation run?

Sharded clusters provide the opportunity to reduce the response times of aggregations because in many scenarios, they allow for the aggregation to be run concurrently. For example, there may be an unsharded collection containing billions of documents where it takes 60 seconds for an aggregation pipeline to process all this data. But within a *sharded* cluster of the same data, depending on the nature of the aggregation, it may be possible for the cluster to execute the aggregation's pipeline concurrently on each shard. In effect, on a four-shard cluster, the same aggregation's total data processing time may be closer to 15 seconds. Note that this won't always be the case because certain types of pipelines will demand combining substantial amounts of data from multiple shards for further processing (depending on your data and the complexity of the aggregation, it can take substantially longer than 60 seconds due to the significant network transfer and marshaling overhead).

## Pipeline splitting at runtime

A sharded cluster will attempt to execute as many of a pipeline's stages as possible, in parallel, on each shard containing the required data. However, certain types of stages must operate on all the data in one place. Specifically, these are the sorting and grouping stages, collectively referred to as the *blocking stages* (described in *Chapter 3, Optimizing Pipelines for Performance*). Upon the first occurrence of a blocking stage in the pipeline, the aggregation engine will split the pipeline into two parts at the point where the blocking stage occurs. The aggregation framework refers to the first section of the divided pipeline as the **shards part**, which can run concurrently on multiple shards. The remaining portion of the split pipeline is called the **merger part**, which executes in one location. *Figure 5.2* shows how this pipeline division occurs.

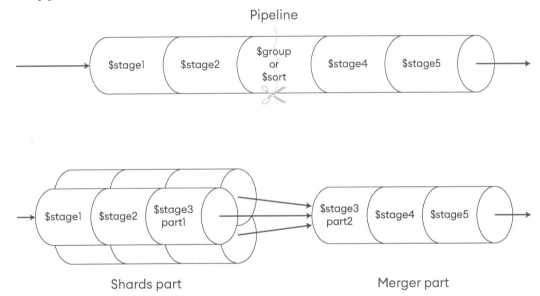

Figure 5.2: Pipeline division

One of the two stages that causes a split, shown as stage 3, is a $group stage. The same behavior actually occurs with all grouping stages, specifically $bucket, $bucketAuto, $count, and $sortByCount. Therefore, any mention of the $group stage in this chapter is synonymous with all these grouping stages.

You can see two examples of aggregation pipeline splitting in action in the MongoDB Shell screenshots that follow, showing each pipeline and its explain plan. The cluster contains four shards (s0, s1, s2, and s3), which hold the distributed collection. The two example aggregations perform the following actions, respectively:

- Sharded sort, matching on shard key values and limiting the number of results

- Sharded group, matching on non-shard key values with allowDiskUse: true and showing the total number of records per group, as shown in *Figure 5.3*:

```
Sharded Sort                              ⊗

> pipeline;
[
  {
    '$match': {
      mykey: {
        '$in': [ 0, 1, 3, 7 ]
      }
    }
  },
  {
    '$sort': { favColour: 1 }
  },
  { '$limit': 5 }
]

> explain;
{
  mergeType: 'mongos',
  splitPipeline: {
    shardsPart: [
      {
        '$match': {
          mykey: {
            '$in': [ 0, 1, 3, 7 ]
          }
        }
      },
      {
        '$sort': {
          sortKey: { favColour: 1 },
          limit: 5
        }
      }
    ],
    mergerPart: [
      {
        '$sort': {
          sortKey: { favColour: 1 },
          mergePresorted: true,
          limit: 5
        }
      }
    ]
  },
  shards: { s0: {}, s2: {}, s3: {} }
}
```

```
Sharded Group (allow-disk)                ⊗

> pipeline;
[
  {
    '$match': {
      randValue: { '$gte': 0.5 }
    }
  },
  {
    '$group': {
      _id: '$favColour',
      total_rcs: { '$sum': 1 }
    }
  }
]

> explain;
{
  mergeType: 'anyShard',
  splitPipeline: {
    shardsPart: [
      {
        '$match': {
          randValue: { '$gte': 0.5 }
        }
      },
      {
        '$group': {
          _id: '$favColour',
          total_rcs: {
            '$sum': { '$const': 1 }
          }
        }
      }
    ],
    mergerPart: [
      {
        '$group': {
          _id: '$$ROOT._id',
          total_rcs: { '$sum': '$$ROOT.total_rcs' },
          '$doingMerge': true
        }
      }
    ]
  },
  shards: { s0: {}, s1: {}, s2: {}, s3: {} }
}
```

Figure 5.3: Aggregation pipeline and its explain plan

You can observe some interesting behaviors from these two explain plans:

- **Shards part of pipeline running in parallel**: In both cases, the pipeline's `shardsPart` executes on multiple shards, as indicated in the `shards` array field at the base of the explain plan. In the first example, the aggregation runtime targets only three shards. However, in the second example, the runtime must broadcast the pipeline's `shardsPart` to run on all shards. The *Execution of the split pipeline shards* section, later in this chapter, discusses why.

- **Optimizations applied in shards part**: For the `$sort` or `$group` blocking stage where the pipeline splits, the blocking stage divides into two. The runtime executes the first phase of the blocking stage as the last stage of the `shardsPart` of the divided pipeline. It then completes the stage's remaining work as the first stage of the `mergerPart`. For a `$sort` stage, this means the cluster conducts a large portion of the sorting work in parallel on all shards, with a remaining *merge sort* occurring at the final location. For a `$group` stage, the cluster performs the grouping in parallel on every shard, accumulating partial sums and totals ahead of its final merge phase. Consequently, the runtime does not have to ship masses of raw ungrouped data from the source shards to where the runtime merges the partially formed groups.

- **Merger part running from a single location**: The specific location where the runtime executes the pipeline's `mergerPart` stages depends on several factors. The explain plan shows the location chosen by the runtime in the `mergeType` field of its output. In these two examples, the locations are `mongos` and `anyShard`, respectively. The *Execution of the merger part of the split pipeline* section, later in this chapter, outlines the rules that the aggregation runtime uses to decide on this location.

- **Final merge sorting when the sort stage is split**: `$sort`'s final phase, shown in the `mergerPart` of the first pipeline, is not a blocking operation, whereas with `$group`, shown in the second pipeline, its final phase is blocking. The *Difference in merging behavior for grouping versus sorting* section, later in this chapter, discusses why.

Unfortunately, if you are running your aggregations in MongoDB versions 4.2 to 5.0, the explain plan generated by the aggregation runtime erroneously neglects to log the final phase of the `$sort` stage in the pipeline's `mergerPart`. This is caused by a now-fixed *explain plan bug*, but rest assured that the final phase of the `$sort` stage (the *merge sort*) does indeed happen in the pipeline's `mergerPart` in all MongoDB versions.

## Execution of the split pipeline shards

When a `mongos` router receives a request to execute an aggregation pipeline, it needs to determine where to target the *shards part* of the pipeline. It will endeavor to run this on the relevant subset of shards rather than broadcasting the work to all shards.

Suppose there is a `$match` stage occurring at the start of the pipeline. If the filter for this `$match` includes the shard key or a prefix of the shard key, the mongos router can perform a targeted operation. It routes the *shards part* of the split pipeline to execute on the applicable shards only.

Furthermore, suppose the runtime establishes that $match's filter contains an exact match on a shard key value for the source collection. In that case, the pipeline can target a single shard only, and doesn't even need to split the pipeline into two. The entire pipeline runs in one place, on the one shard where the data it needs lives. Even if $match's filter only has a partial match on the first part of the shard key (the *prefix*), if this spans a range of documents encapsulated within a single chunk, or multiple chunks on the same shard only, the runtime will just target the single shard.

## Execution of the merger part of the split pipeline

The aggregation runtime applies a set of rules to determine where to execute the merger part of an aggregation pipeline for a sharded cluster and whether a split is even necessary. *Figure 5.4* captures the four different approaches the runtime will choose from.

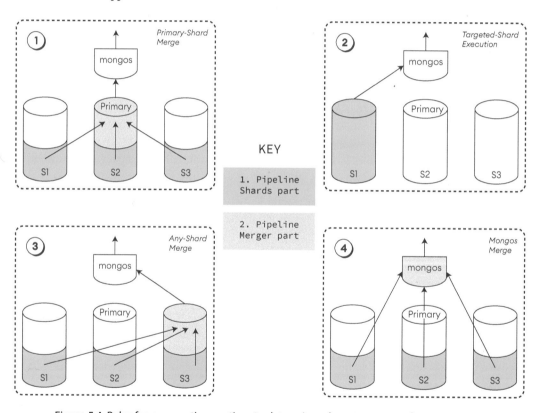

Figure 5.4: Rules for aggregation runtime to determine where to execute the merger part

The aggregation runtime selects the merger part location (if any) by following a decision tree, with four possible outcomes. The following list outlines the ordered decisions the runtime takes. However, it is crucial to understand that this order does not reflect precedence or preference. Achieving either the *Targeted-Shard Execution* (2) or *Mongos Merge* (4) is usually the preferred outcome for optimum performance:

1.  **Primary-Shard Merge**: When the pipeline contains a stage referencing a second unsharded collection, the aggregation runtime will place this stage in the merger part of the split pipeline. It executes this merger part on the designated primary shard, which holds the referenced unsharded collection. This is always the case for the stages that can only reference unsharded collections (i.e., for $out generally or for $lookup and $graphLookup in MongoDB versions before 6.0). This is also the situation if the collection happens to be unsharded and you reference it from a $merge stage or, in MongoDB 6.0 or greater, from a $lookup or $graphLookup stage.

2.  **Targeted-Shard Execution**: As discussed earlier, if the runtime can ensure the pipeline matches the required subset of the source collection data to just one shard, it does not split the pipeline, and there is no merger part. Instead, the runtime executes the entire pipeline on the one matched shard, just like it would for non-sharded deployments. This optimization avoids unnecessarily breaking the pipeline into two parts, where intermediate data then has to move from the shards part(s) to the merger part. The behavior of pinning to a single shard occurs even if the pipeline contains a $merge, $lookup, or $graphLookup stage referencing a second sharded collection containing records dispersed across multiple shards.

3.  **Any-Shard Merge**: Suppose you've configured allowDiskUse: true for the aggregation to avoid the 100 MB memory consumption limit per stage. If one of the following two situations is also true, the aggregation runtime must run the merger part of the split pipeline on a randomly chosen shard (that is, *any shard*):

    - The pipeline contains a grouping stage (which is where the split occurs).

    - The pipeline contains a $sort stage (which is where the split occurs), and a subsequent blocking stage (a grouping or $sort stage) occurs later.

    For these cases, the runtime picks a shard to execute the merger, rather than merging on the mongos router, to maximize the likelihood that the host machine has enough storage space to spill to disk. Invariably, each shard's host machine will have greater storage capacity than the host machine of a mongos router. Consequently, the runtime must take this caution because, with allowDiskUse: true, you are indicating the likelihood that your pipeline will cause memory capacity pressure. Notably, the aggregation runtime does not need to mitigate the same risk by merging on a shard for the other type of blocking stage ($sort) when $sort is the only blocking stage in the pipeline. You can read why a single $sort stage can be treated differently and does not need the same host storage capacity for merging in the *Difference in merging behavior for grouping versus sorting* section, later in this chapter.

4.  **Mongos Merge**: This is the default approach and location. The aggregation runtime will perform the merger part of the split pipeline on the mongos router that instigated the aggregation in all the remaining situations. If the pipeline's merger part only contains streaming stages (described in *Chapter 3, Optimizing Pipelines for Performance*), the runtime assumes it is safe for mongos to run the remaining pipeline. A mongos router has no concept of local storage to hold data. However, it doesn't matter in this situation because the runtime won't need to write to disk as RAM pressure will be minimal. The category of streaming tasks that supports a Mongos Merge also includes the final phase of a split $sort stage, which processes data in a streaming fashion without needing to block to see all the data together. Additionally, suppose you have defined allowDiskUse: false (the default). In that case, you are signaling that even if the pipeline has a $group stage (or a $sort stage followed by another blocking stage), these blocking activities will not need to overspill to disk. Performing the final merge on the mongos router is the default because fewer network data transfer hops are required to fulfill the aggregation, thus reducing latency compared with merging on *any shard*:

Regardless of where the merger part runs, the mongos router is always responsible for streaming the aggregation's final batches of results back to the client application.

It is worth considering when no blocking stages exist in a pipeline. In this case, the runtime executes the entire pipeline in parallel on the relevant shards and the runtime streams each shard's output directly to the mongos router. You can regard this as just another variation of the default behavior (4 – *Mongos Merge*). All the stages in the aggregation constitute just the shards part of the pipeline, and the mongos router *stream merges* the final data through to the client.

## Difference in merging behavior for grouping versus sorting

You read about the $sort and $group stages being blocking stages and potentially consuming copious RAM in *Chapter 3, Optimizing Pipelines for Performance*. Consequently, you may be confused by the statement that, unlike a $group stage, when the pipeline splits, the aggregation runtime will finalize a $sort stage on a mongos router even if you specify allowDiskUse: true. This is because the final phase of a split $sort stage is not a blocking activity, whereas the final phase of a split $group stage is. For $group, the pipeline's merger part must wait for all the data coming out of all the targeted shards. For $sort, the runtime executes a streaming merge sort operation, only waiting for the next batch of records coming out of each shard. As long as it can see the first of the sorted documents in the next batch from every shard, it knows which documents it can immediately process and stream onto the rest of the pipeline. It doesn't have to block waiting to see all of the records to guarantee correct ordering.

This optimization doesn't mean that MongoDB has magically found a way to avoid a $sort stage being a blocking stage in a sharded cluster. It hasn't. The first phase of the $sort stage, run on each shard in parallel, is still blocking, waiting to see all the matched input data for that shard. However, the final phase of the same $sort stage, executed at the merge location, does not need to block.

# Performance tips for sharded aggregations

All the recommended aggregation optimization outlined in *Chapter 3, Optimizing Pipelines for Performance*, equally apply to a sharded cluster. In fact, in most cases, these same recommendations, repeated as follows, become even more important when executing aggregations on sharded clusters:

- **Sorting – use index sort**: When the runtime has to split on a $sort stage, the *shards part* of the split pipeline running on each shard in parallel will avoid an expensive in-memory sort operation.

- **Sorting – use limit with sort**: The runtime has to transfer fewer intermediate records over the network, from each shard performing the shards part of a split pipeline to the location that executes the pipeline's merger part.

- **Sorting – reduce records to sort**: If you cannot adopt point 1 or 2, moving a $sort stage to as late as possible in a pipeline will typically benefit performance in a sharded cluster. Wherever the $sort stage appears in a pipeline, the aggregation runtime will split the pipeline at this point (unless preceded by a $group stage, which would cause the split earlier). By promoting other activities to occur in the pipeline first, the hope is these reduce the number of records entering the blocking $sort stage. This sorting operation, executing in parallel at the end of the shards part of the split pipeline, will exhibit less memory pressure. The runtime will also stream fewer records over the network to the split pipeline's merger part location.

- **Grouping – avoid unnecessary grouping**: Using array operators where possible instead of the $unwind and $group stages will mean that the runtime does not need to split the pipeline due to an unnecessarily introduced $group stage. Consequently, the aggregation can efficiently process and stream data directly to the mongos router rather than flowing through an intermediary shard first.

- **Grouping – group summary data only**: The runtime has to move fewer computed records over the network from each shard performing the shards part of a split pipeline to the merger part's location.

- **Encourage match filters to appear early in the pipeline**: By filtering out a large subset of records on each shard when performing the shards part of the split pipeline, the runtime needs to stream fewer records to the merger part location.

There are two further performance optimizations you should aim to achieve that are specific to sharded clusters:

- **Look for opportunities to target aggregations to one shard only**: If possible, include a $match stage with a filter on a shard key value (or shard key prefix value).

- **Look for opportunities for a split pipeline to Merge on a mongos**: If the pipeline has a $group stage (or a $sort stage followed by a $group/$sort stage) that causes the pipeline to divide, avoid specifying allowDiskUse:true if possible. This eliminates the need to write temporary data to disk and then transfer intermediate data over the network, dramatically reducing latency.

By adhering to these eight performance recommendations, your aggregations will run efficiently and optimally in sharded clusters.

## Summary

In this chapter, you started your journey with an introduction to the concept of sharding and then covered the constraints that apply to aggregations when running in a sharded cluster. You also looked at aggregation performance optimization tips, which are even more critical while executing pipelines in sharded clusters.

Now you know the principles and approaches for increasing your effectiveness in developing aggregation pipelines. The next part of this book will cover practical examples to solve common data manipulation challenges grouped by different data processing requirements.

# Part 2:
# Aggregations by Example

The following set of chapters provides examples to solve common data manipulation challenges grouped by different data processing requirements. The best way to use these examples is to try them out yourself as you read each example (see the *Getting going* section in *Chapter 1, MongoDB Aggregations Explained*, for advice on how to execute these examples). See the *Download the example code files* section in the Preface for how to obtain a copy of the code for these examples.

This part of the book includes the following chapters:

- *Chapter 6, Foundational Examples: Filtering, Grouping, and Unwinding*
- *Chapter 7, Joining Data Examples*
- *Chapter 8, Fixing and Generating Data Examples*
- *Chapter 9, Trend Analysis Examples*
- *Chapter 10, Securing Data Examples*
- *Chapter 11, Time-Series Examples*
- *Chapter 12, Array Manipulation Examples*
- *Chapter 13, Full-Text Search Examples*

# 6

# Foundational Examples: Filtering, Grouping, and Unwinding

This chapter provides examples of common data manipulation patterns used in many aggregation pipelines, which are relatively straightforward to understand and adapt. By getting baseline knowledge with these foundational examples, you will be well positioned to tackle the more advanced examples later in this book.

This chapter will cover the following:

- Finding the most recent subset of data
- Grouping and summarizing data
- Unwinding arrays and grouping them differently
- Capturing a list of unique values

# Filtered top subset

First, you will look at an example that demonstrates how to query a sorted subset of data. As with all subsequent examples, this first example provides the commands you need to populate the dataset in your own MongoDB database and then apply the aggregation pipeline to produce the results shown.

## Scenario

You need to query a collection of people to find the three youngest individuals who have a job in engineering, sorted by the youngest person first.

> **Note**
>
> This example is the only one in the book that you can also achieve entirely using the MongoDB Query Language and serves as a helpful comparison between the MongoDB Query Language and aggregation pipelines.

## Populating the sample data

To start with, drop any old version of the database (if it exists) and then populate a new `persons` collection with six person documents. Each person record will contain the *person's ID, first name, last name, date of birth, vocation,* and *address*:

```
db = db.getSiblingDB("book-filtered-top-subset");
db.dropDatabase();

// Create an index for a persons collection
db.persons.createIndex({"vocation": 1, "dateofbirth": 1});

// Insert records into the persons collection
db.persons.insertMany([
  {
    "person_id": "6392529400",
    "firstname": "Elise",
    "lastname": "Smith",
    "dateofbirth": ISODate("1972-01-13T09:32:07Z"),
    "vocation": "ENGINEER",
    "address": {
        "number": 5625,
        "street": "Tipa Circle",
        "city": "Wojzinmoj",
    },
  },
```

```
{
  "person_id": "1723338115",
  "firstname": "Olive",
  "lastname": "Ranieri",
  "dateofbirth": ISODate("1985-05-12T23:14:30Z"),
  "gender": "FEMALE",
  "vocation": "ENGINEER",
  "address": {
      "number": 9303,
      "street": "Mele Circle",
      "city": "Tobihbo",
  },
},
{
  "person_id": "8732762874",
  "firstname": "Toni",
  "lastname": "Jones",
  "dateofbirth": ISODate("1991-11-23T16:53:56Z"),
  "vocation": "POLITICIAN",
  "address": {
      "number": 1,
      "street": "High Street",
      "city": "Upper Abbeywoodington",
  },
},
{
  "person_id": "7363629563",
  "firstname": "Bert",
  "lastname": "Gooding",
  "dateofbirth": ISODate("1941-04-07T22:11:52Z"),
  "vocation": "FLORIST",
  "address": {
      "number": 13,
      "street": "Upper Bold Road",
      "city": "Redringtonville",
  },
},
```

```
  {
    "person_id": "1029648329",
    "firstname": "Sophie",
    "lastname": "Celements",
    "dateofbirth": ISODate("1959-07-06T17:35:45Z"),
    "vocation": "ENGINEER",
    "address": {
        "number": 5,
        "street": "Innings Close",
        "city": "Basilbridge",
    },
  },
  {
    "person_id": "7363626383",
    "firstname": "Carl",
    "lastname": "Simmons",
    "dateofbirth": ISODate("1998-12-26T13:13:55Z"),
    "vocation": "ENGINEER",
    "address": {
        "number": 187,
        "street": "Hillside Road",
        "city": "Kenningford",
    },
  },
]);
```

## Defining the aggregation pipeline

You will now define a pipeline that applies a number of stages to implement the aggregation:

```
var pipeline = [
  // Match engineers only
  {"$match": {
    "vocation": "ENGINEER",
  }},

  // Sort by youngest person first
  {"$sort": {
    "dateofbirth": -1,
  }},
```

```
// Only include the first 3 youngest people
{"$limit": 3},

// Exclude unrequired fields from each person record
{"$unset": [
  "_id",
  "vocation",
  "address",
]},
];
```

## Executing the aggregation pipeline

Next, run the following commands to do the following:

1. Execute the aggregation using the defined pipeline:

   ```
   db.persons.aggregate(pipeline);
   ```

2. Generate its explain plan:

   ```
   db.persons.explain("executionStats").aggregate(pipeline);
   ```

## Expected pipeline results

Once executed, the aggregation should return three documents representing the three youngest people who are engineers (ordered by youngest first), omitting the _id and address attributes of each person:

```
[
  {
    person_id: '7363626383',
    firstname: 'Carl',
    lastname: 'Simmons',
    dateofbirth: ISODate('1998-12-26T13:13:55.000Z')
  },
  {
    person_id: '1723338115',
    firstname: 'Olive',
    lastname: 'Ranieri',
    dateofbirth: ISODate('1985-05-12T23:14:30.000Z'),
    gender: 'FEMALE'
  },
```

```
  {
    person_id: '6392529400',
    firstname: 'Elise',
    lastname: 'Smith',
    dateofbirth: ISODate('1972-01-13T09:32:07.000Z')
  }
]
```

## Pipeline observations

- **Use index**: In this basic aggregation pipeline, because multiple records belong to the collection, a compound index for `vocation + dateofbirth` should exist to enable the database to fully optimize the execution of the pipeline, combining the filter of the `$match` stage with the sort from the `sort` stage and the limit of the `limit` stage.

- **Use unset**: An `$unset` stage is used rather than a `$project` stage. This enables the pipeline to avoid being verbose. More importantly, it means the pipeline does not have to be modified if a new field appears in documents added in the future (for example, see the `gender` field that appears in only *Olive's* record).

- **MongoDB Query Language similarity**: For reference, the MongoDB Query Language equivalent for you to achieve the same result is shown here (you can try this in the *MongoDB Shell*):

```
db.persons.find(
    {"vocation": "ENGINEER"},
    {"_id": 0, "vocation": 0, "address": 0},
).sort(
    {"dateofbirth": -1}
).limit(3);
```

# Group and total

This next section provides an example of the most commonly used pattern for grouping and summarizing data from a collection.

## Scenario

You need to generate a report to show what each shop customer purchased in 2020. You will group the individual order records by customer, capturing each customer's first purchase date, the number of orders they made, the total value of all their orders, and a list of their order items sorted by date.

## Populating the sample data

To start with, drop any old version of the database (if it exists) and then populate a new orders collection with nine order documents spanning 2019-2021, for three different unique customers. Each order record will contain a *customer ID*, the *date of the order*, and the dollar *total for the order*:

```
db = db.getSiblingDB("book-group-and-total");
db.dropDatabase();

// Create index for an orders collection
db.orders.createIndex({"orderdate": -1});

// Insert records into the orders collection
db.orders.insertMany([
  {
    "customer_id": "elise_smith@myemail.com",
    "orderdate": ISODate("2020-05-30T08:35:52Z"),
    "value": NumberDecimal("231.43"),
  },
  {
    "customer_id": "elise_smith@myemail.com",
    "orderdate": ISODate("2020-01-13T09:32:07Z"),
    "value": NumberDecimal("99.99"),
  },
  {
    "customer_id": "oranieri@warmmail.com",
    "orderdate": ISODate("2020-01-01T08:25:37Z"),
    "value": NumberDecimal("63.13"),
  },
```

```
    {
      "customer_id": "tj@wheresmyemail.com",
      "orderdate": ISODate("2019-05-28T19:13:32Z"),
      "value": NumberDecimal("2.01"),
    },
    {
      "customer_id": "tj@wheresmyemail.com",
      "orderdate": ISODate("2020-11-23T22:56:53Z"),
      "value": NumberDecimal("187.99"),
    },
    {
      "customer_id": "tj@wheresmyemail.com",
      "orderdate": ISODate("2020-08-18T23:04:48Z"),
      "value": NumberDecimal("4.59"),
    },
    {
      "customer_id": "elise_smith@myemail.com",
      "orderdate": ISODate("2020-12-26T08:55:46Z"),
      "value": NumberDecimal("48.50"),
    },
    {
      "customer_id": "tj@wheresmyemail.com",
      "orderdate": ISODate("2021-02-29T07:49:32Z"),
      "value": NumberDecimal("1024.89"),
    },
    {
      "customer_id": "elise_smith@myemail.com",
      "orderdate": ISODate("2020-10-03T13:49:44Z"),
      "value": NumberDecimal("102.24"),
    },
]);
```

# Defining the aggregation pipeline

You will now define a pipeline that applies a number of stages to implement the aggregation:

```
var pipeline = [
  // Match only orders made in 2020
  {"$match": {
    "orderdate": {
      "$gte": ISODate("2020-01-01T00:00:00Z"),
      "$lt": ISODate("2021-01-01T00:00:00Z"),
    },
  }},

  // Sort by order date ascending (to pick out 'first_purchase_date' below)
  {"$sort": {
    "orderdate": 1,
  }},

  // Group by customer
  {"$group": {
    "_id": "$customer_id",
    "first_purchase_date": {"$first": "$orderdate"},
    "total_value": {"$sum": "$value"},
    "total_orders": {"$sum": 1},
    "orders": {"$push": {"orderdate": "$orderdate", "value": "$value"}},
  }},

  // Sort by each customer's first purchase date
  {"$sort": {
    "first_purchase_date": 1,
  }},

  // Set customer's ID to be value of the field that was grouped on
  {"$set": {
    "customer_id": "$_id",
  }},

  // Omit unwanted fields
  {"$unset": [
    "_id",
  ]},
];
```

## Executing the aggregation pipeline

Next, run the following commands to do the following:

1.  Execute the aggregation using the defined pipeline:

    ```
    db.orders.aggregate(pipeline);
    ```

2.  Generate its explain plan:

    ```
    db.orders.explain("executionStats").aggregate(pipeline);
    ```

## Expected pipeline result

Once executed, the aggregation should return three documents representing the three customers, each showing the customer's first purchase date, the total value of all their orders, the number of orders they made, and a list of each order's detail, for 2020 only:

```
[
  {
    customer_id: 'oranieri@warmmail.com',
    first_purchase_date: ISODate('2020-01-01T08:25:37.000Z'),
    total_value: NumberDecimal('63.13'),
    total_orders: 1,
    orders: [
      {
        orderdate: ISODate('2020-01-01T08:25:37.000Z'),
        value:NumberDecimal('63.13')
      }
    ]
  },
  {
    customer_id: 'elise_smith@myemail.com',
    first_purchase_date: ISODate('2020-01-13T09:32:07.000Z'),
    total_value: NumberDecimal('482.16'),
    total_orders: 4,
    orders: [
      {
        orderdate: ISODate('2020-01-13T09:32:07.000Z'),
        value:NumberDecimal('99.99')
      },
```

```
      {
        orderdate: ISODate('2020-05-30T08:35:52.000Z'),
        value:NumberDecimal('231.43')
      },
      {
        orderdate: ISODate('2020-10-03T13:49:44.000Z'),
       value:NumberDecimal('102.24')
      },
      {
        orderdate: ISODate('2020-12-26T08:55:46.000Z'),
        value: NumberDecimal('48.50')
      }
    ]
  },
  {
    customer_id: 'tj@wheresmyemail.com',
    first_purchase_date: ISODate('2020-08-18T23:04:48.000Z'),
    total_value: NumberDecimal('192.58'),
    total_orders: 2,
    orders: [
      {
        orderdate: ISODate('2020-08-18T23:04:48.000Z'),
        value: NumberDecimal('4.59')
      },
      {
        orderdate: ISODate('2020-11-23T22:56:53.000Z'),
        value: NumberDecimal('187.99')
      }
    ]
  }
]
```

**Note**
The order of fields shown for each document may vary.

## Pipeline observations

- **Use of double sort**: It is necessary to perform $sort on the order date both before and after the $group stage. The $sort stage before the $group stage is required because the $group stage uses a $first group accumulator to capture just the first order's orderdate value for each grouped customer. The $sort after the $group stage is required because the act of having just grouped on customer ID will mean that the records are no longer sorted by purchase date for the records coming out of the $group stage.

- **Renaming the group**: Toward the end of the pipeline, you will see what a typical pattern for pipelines that use $group is, consisting of a combination of $set and $unset stages, to essentially take the group's key (which is always called _id) and substitute it with a more meaningful name (customer_id).

- **High-precision decimals**: You may notice that the pipeline uses a NumberDecimal() function to ensure the order amounts in the inserted records are using a high-precision decimal type, IEEE 754 decimal128. In this example, if you use a JSON float or double type instead, the order totals will significantly lose precision. For instance, for the customer elise_smith@myemail.com, if you use a double type, the total_value result will have the value shown in the second line of the following example, rather than the first line:

```
// Desired result achieved by using decimal128 types
total_value: NumberDecimal('482.16')

// Result that occurs if using float or double types instead
total_value: 482.15999999999997
```

# Unpack arrays and group differently

You applied filters and groups to whole documents in the previous two examples. In this example, you will work with an array field contained in each document, unraveling each array's contents to enable you to subsequently group the resulting raw data in a way that helps you produce a critical business summary report.

## Scenario

You want to generate a retail report to list the total value and quantity of expensive products sold (valued over 15 dollars). The source data is a list of shop orders, where each order contains the set of products purchased as part of the order.

## Populating the sample data

Drop any old version of the database (if it exists) and then populate a new orders collection where each document contains an array of products purchased. Each order document contains an *order ID* plus a *list of products* purchased as part of the order, including each *product's ID*, *name*, and *price*:

```
db = db.getSiblingDB("book-unpack-array-group-differently");
db.dropDatabase();

// Insert 4 records into the orders collection each with 1+ product items
db.orders.insertMany([
  {
    "order_id": 6363763262239,
    "products": [
      {
        "prod_id": "abc12345",
        "name": "Asus Laptop",
        "price": NumberDecimal("431.43"),
      },
      {
        "prod_id": "def45678",
        "name": "Karcher Hose Set",
        "price": NumberDecimal("22.13"),
      },
    ],
  },
  {
    "order_id": 1197372932325,
    "products": [
      {
```

```
          "prod_id": "abc12345",
          "name": "Asus Laptop",
          "price": NumberDecimal("429.99"),
        },
      ],
    },
    {
      "order_id": 9812343774839,
      "products": [
        {
          "prod_id": "pqr88223",
          "name": "Morphy Richards Food Mixer",
          "price": NumberDecimal("431.43"),
        },
        {
          "prod_id": "def45678",
          "name": "Karcher Hose Set",
          "price": NumberDecimal("21.78"),
        },
      ],
    },
    {
      "order_id": 4433997244387,
      "products": [
        {
          "prod_id": "def45678",
          "name": "Karcher Hose Set",
          "price": NumberDecimal("23.43"),
        },
        {
          "prod_id": "jkl77336",
          "name": "Picky Pencil Sharpener",
          "price": NumberDecimal("0.67"),
        },
        {
          "prod_id": "xyz11228",
          "name": "Russell Hobbs Chrome Kettle",
          "price": NumberDecimal("15.76"),
        },
      ],
    },
]);
```

## Defining the aggregation pipeline

You will now define a pipeline that applies a number of stages to implement the aggregation:

```
var pipeline = [
  // Unpack each product from each order's product as a new separate record
  {"$unwind": {
    "path": "$products",
  }},

  // Match only products valued greater than 15.00
  {"$match": {
    "products.price": {
      "$gt": NumberDecimal("15.00"),
    },
  }},

  // Group by product type, capturing each product's total value + quantity
  {"$group": {
    "_id": "$products.prod_id",
    "product": {"$first": "$products.name"},
    "total_value": {"$sum": "$products.price"},
    "quantity": {"$sum": 1},
  }},

  // Set product id to be the value of the field that was grouped on
  {"$set": {
    "product_id": "$_id",
  }},

  // Omit unwanted fields
  {"$unset": [
    "_id",
  ]},
];
```

## Executing the aggregation pipeline

Next, run the following commands to do the following:

1.  Execute the aggregation using the defined pipeline:

    ```
    db.orders.aggregate(pipeline);
    ```

2.  Generate its explain plan:

    ```
    db.orders.explain("executionStats").aggregate(pipeline);
    ```

## Expected pipeline results

Once executed, the aggregation should return four documents representing only the four expensive products that were referenced multiple times in the customer orders, each showing the product's total order value and amount sold:

```
[
  {
    product_id: 'pqr88223',
    product: 'Morphy Richards Food Mixer',
    total_value: NumberDecimal('431.43'),
    quantity: 1
  },
  {
    product_id: 'abc12345',
    product: 'Asus Laptop',
    total_value: NumberDecimal('861.42'),
    quantity: 2
  },
  {
    product_id: 'def45678',
    product: 'Karcher Hose Set',
    total_value: NumberDecimal('67.34'),
    quantity: 3
  },
  {
    product_id: 'xyz11228',
    product: 'Russell Hobbs Chrome Kettle',
    total_value: NumberDecimal('15.76'),
    quantity: 1
  }
]
```

> **Note**
> The order of fields shown for each document may vary.

## Pipeline observations

- **Unwinding arrays**: The $unwind stage is a powerful concept, although often unfamiliar to many developers initially. Distilled down, it does one simple thing: it generates a new record for each element in an array field of every input document. If a source collection has 3 documents and each document contains an array of 4 elements, then performing an $unwind stage on that array field for all the records produces 12 records (3 x 4).

- **Introducing a partial match**: The current example pipeline scans all documents in the collection and then filters out unpacked products where `price > 15.00`. If the pipeline executed this filter as the first stage, it would incorrectly produce some result product records with a value of 15 dollars or less. This would be the case for an order composed of both inexpensive and expensive products. However, you can still improve the pipeline by including an additional *partial match* filter at the start of the pipeline for products valued at over 15 dollars. The aggregation could leverage an index (on `products.price`), resulting in a partial rather than full collection scan. This extra filter stage is beneficial if the input dataset is large, and many customer orders are for inexpensive items only. This approach is described in *Chapter 3, Optimizing Pipelines for Performance*.

# Distinct list of values

A common requirement in the user interface of an application is to provide a *drop-down picklist* of possible values in an input field of a form ready for the application user to select one of the values. Here, you will learn how to populate a list of unique values ready for use in a drop-down widget.

## Scenario

You want to query a collection of people where each document contains data on one or more languages spoken by the person. The query result should be an alphabetically sorted list of unique languages that a developer can subsequently use to populate a list of values in a user interface's *drop-down* widget.

This example is the equivalent of a SELECT DISTINCT statement in SQL.

## Populating the sample data

Drop any old versions of the database (if they exist) and then populate a new *persons* collection. Each person document includes the person's *first name*, *last name*, *vocation*, and *spoken languages*:

```
db = db.getSiblingDB("book-distinct-values");
db.dropDatabase();

// Insert records into the persons collection
db.persons.insertMany([
  {
    "firstname": "Elise",
    "lastname": "Smith",
    "vocation": "ENGINEER",
    "language": "English",
  },
  {
    "firstname": "Olive",
    "lastname": "Ranieri",
    "vocation": "ENGINEER",
    "language": ["Italian", "English"],
  },
  {
    "firstname": "Toni",
    "lastname": "Jones",
    "vocation": "POLITICIAN",
    "language": ["English", "Welsh"],
  },
```

```
  {
    "firstname": "Bert",
    "lastname": "Gooding",
    "vocation": "FLORIST",
    "language": "English",
  },
  {
    "firstname": "Sophie",
    "lastname": "Celements",
    "vocation": "ENGINEER",
    "language": ["Gaelic", "English"],
  },
  {
    "firstname": "Carl",
    "lastname": "Simmons",
    "vocation": "ENGINEER",
    "language": "English",
  },
  {
    "firstname": "Diego",
    "lastname": "Lopez",
    "vocation": "CHEF",
    "language": "Spanish",
  },
  {
    "firstname": "Helmut",
    "lastname": "Schneider",
    "vocation": "NURSE",
    "language": "German",
  },
  {
    "firstname": "Valerie",
    "lastname": "Dubois",
    "vocation": "SCIENTIST",
    "language": "French",
  },
]);
```

## Defining the aggregation pipeline

You will now define a pipeline that applies a number of stages to implement the aggregation:

```
var pipeline = [
  // Unpack each language field which may be an array or a single value
  {"$unwind": {
    "path": "$language",
  }},

  // Group by language
  {"$group": {
    "_id": "$language",
  }},

  // Sort languages alphabetically
  {"$sort": {
    "_id": 1,
  }},

  // Change _id field's name to 'language'
  {"$set": {
    "language": "$_id",
    "_id": "$$REMOVE",
  }},
];
```

## Executing the aggregation pipeline

Next, perform the following steps:

1. Execute the aggregation using the defined pipeline:

```
db.persons.aggregate(pipeline);
```

2. Generate its explain plan:

```
db.persons.explain("executionStats").aggregate(pipeline);
```

## Expected pipeline result

Once executed, the aggregation should return seven unique language names sorted in alphabetical order:

```
[
  {language: 'English'},
  {language: 'French'},
  {language: 'Gaelic'},
  {language: 'German'},
  {language: 'Italian'},
  {language: 'Spanish'},
  {language: 'Welsh'}
]
```

## Pipeline observations

- **Unwinding non-arrays**: In some of the documents returned, the `language` field is an array, while in others, the field is a simple string value. The `$unwind` stage can seamlessly deal with both field types and does not throw an error if it encounters a non-array value. Instead, if the field is not an array, the stage outputs a single record using the field's string value in the same way it would if the field were an array containing just one element. If you are sure the field in every document will only ever be a simple field rather than an array, you can omit this first stage (`$unwind`) from the pipeline.

- **Group ID provides unique values**: By grouping on a single field and not accumulating other fields, such as total or count, the output of a `$group` stage is just every unique group's ID, which in this case is every unique language.

- **Unset alternative**: For the pipeline to be consistent with earlier examples in this book, it could have included an additional `$unset` stage to exclude the `_id` field. However, partly to show another way, the example pipeline used here marks the `_id` field for exclusion in the `$set` stage by being assigned the `$$REMOVE` variable.

# Summary

You started this chapter by looking at a simple example for extracting a sorted top subset of data from a collection. Then, you moved on to applying strategies for grouping and summarizing data, followed by how to unpack arrays of values to group differently. Finally, you finished with an aggregation to generate a list of unique values from a collection.

In the next chapter, you'll see how to use various approaches to join data from two different collections.

# 7

# Joining Data Examples

This chapter offers guidance on joining together data from two collections. Contrary to what you may have heard, MongoDB is quite capable of performing these joins. The method of data manipulation will differ depending on whether you're executing a one-to-one or one-to-many join. You will explore solutions for both scenarios.

This chapter will cover the following:

- Implementing one-to-one joins
- Implementing one-to-many joins
- Dealing with multiple fields on each side of the join

# One-to-one join

Sometimes, you need to join data between two collections, where one document in the first collection maps to one, and only one, document in the second collection. This section provides an example of performing this one-to-one join using the $lookup aggregation stage in MongoDB.

> **Note**
>
> For this example, you require MongoDB version 4.4 or above. This is because you will use the $first array operator introduced in version 4.4.

## Scenario

You want to generate a report to list all shop purchases for 2020, showing the product's name and category for each order, rather than the product's ID. To achieve this, you need to take the customer *orders* collection and join each order record to the corresponding product record in the *products* collection. There is a many-to-one relationship between both collections, resulting in a one-to-one join when matching an order to a product. The join will use a single field comparison between both sides, based on the product's ID.

Let's start by choosing the dataset and setting it up for the aggregation pipeline.

## Populating the sample data

Drop any old version of the database (if it exists) and then populate new *products* and *orders* collections with documents spanning 2019-2021. Each product will have an *ID*, *name*, *category*, and *description*. Each order will have a *customer ID*, *order date*, *product ID*, and *dollar value*:

```
db = db.getSiblingDB("book-one-to-one-join");
db.dropDatabase();

// Create index for a products collection
db.products.createIndex({"id": 1});

// Insert 4 records into the products collection
db.products.insertMany([
  {
    "id": "a1b2c3d4",
    "name": "Asus Laptop",
    "category": "ELECTRONICS",
    "description": "Good value laptop for students",
  },
  {
```

```
    "id": "z9y8x7w6",
    "name": "The Day Of The Triffids",
    "category": "BOOKS",
    "description": "Classic post-apocalyptic novel",
  },
  {
    "id": "ff11gg22hh33",
    "name": "Morphy Richards Food Mixer",
    "category": "KITCHENWARE",
    "description": "Luxury mixer turning good cakes into great",
  },
  {
    "id": "pqr678st",
    "name": "Karcher Hose Set",
    "category": "GARDEN",
    "description": "Hose + nosels + winder for tidy storage",
  },
]);

// Create index for a orders collection
db.orders.createIndex({"orderdate": -1});

// Insert 4 records into the orders collection
db.orders.insertMany([
  {
    "customer_id": "elise_smith@myemail.com",
    "orderdate": ISODate("2020-05-30T08:35:52Z"),
    "product_id": "a1b2c3d4",
    "value": NumberDecimal("431.43"),
  },
  {
    "customer_id": "tj@wheresmyemail.com",
    "orderdate": ISODate("2019-05-28T19:13:32Z"),
    "product_id": "z9y8x7w6",
    "value": NumberDecimal("5.01"),
  },
  {
    "customer_id": "oranieri@warmmail.com",
    "orderdate": ISODate("2020-01-01T08:25:37Z"),
    "product_id": "ff11gg22hh33",
    "value": NumberDecimal("63.13"),
  },
```

```
  {
    "customer_id": "jjones@tepidmail.com",
    "orderdate": ISODate("2020-12-26T08:55:46Z"),
    "product_id": "a1b2c3d4",
    "value": NumberDecimal("429.65"),
  },
]);
```

## Defining the aggregation pipeline

You will now define a pipeline that applies a number of stages to implement the aggregation:

```
var pipeline = [
  // Match only orders made in 2020
  {"$match": {
    "orderdate": {
      "$gte": ISODate("2020-01-01T00:00:00Z"),
      "$lt": ISODate("2021-01-01T00:00:00Z"),
    }
  }},

  // Join "product_id" in orders collection to "id" in products" collection
  {"$lookup": {
    "from": "products",
    "localField": "product_id",
    "foreignField": "id",
    "as": "product_mapping",
  }},

  // For this data model, will always be 1 record in right-side
  // of join, so take 1st joined array element
  {"$set": {
    "product_mapping": {"$first": "$product_mapping"},
  }},

  // Extract the joined embeded fields into top level fields
  {"$set": {
    "product_name": "$product_mapping.name",
    "product_category": "$product_mapping.category",
  }},
```

```
  // Omit unwanted fields
  {"$unset": [
    "_id",
    "product_id",
    "product_mapping",
  ]},
];
```

## Executing the aggregation pipeline

Next, run the following commands to do the following:

1.  Execute the aggregation using the defined pipeline:

    ```
    db.orders.aggregate(pipeline);
    ```

2.  Generate its explain plan:

    ```
    db.orders.explain("executionStats").aggregate(pipeline);
    ```

## Expected pipeline result

Once executed, the aggregation should return three documents, representing three customer orders that occurred in 2020, but with each order's product_id field replaced by two new looked-up fields, product_name and product_category, as shown in the following output:

```
[
  {
    customer_id: 'elise_smith@myemail.com',
    orderdate: ISODate('2020-05-30T08:35:52.000Z'),
    value: NumberDecimal('431.43'),
    product_name: 'Asus Laptop',
    product_category: 'ELECTRONICS'
  },
  {
    customer_id: 'oranieri@warmmail.com',
    orderdate: ISODate('2020-01-01T08:25:37.000Z'),
    value: NumberDecimal('63.13'),
    product_name: 'Morphy Richards Food Mixer',
    product_category: 'KITCHENWARE'
  },
```

```
    {
      customer_id: 'jjones@tepidmail.com',
      orderdate: ISODate('2020-12-26T08:55:46.000Z'),
      value: NumberDecimal('429.65'),
      product_name: 'Asus Laptop',
      product_category: 'ELECTRONICS'
    }
  ]
```

## Pipeline observations

- **Single field match**: This pipeline includes a $lookup join between a single field from each collection. To see how a join based on two or more matching fields is performed, see the next section, *Multi-field join and one-to-many*.

- **First element assumption**: In this particular data model example, the join between the two collections is one-to-one. Therefore, the returned array of joined elements coming out of the $lookup stage always contains precisely one array element. As a result, the pipeline extracts the data from this first array element only, using the $first operator. To see how a one-to-many join is performed, see the next section, *Multi-field join and one-to-many*.

- **First element for earlier MongoDB versions**: MongoDB only introduced the $first array operator expression in version 4.4. However, it is straightforward for you to replace its use in the pipeline with an equivalent solution, using the $arrayElemAt operator, to then allow the pipeline to work in MongoDB versions preceding version 4.4:

```
// $first equivalent
"product_mapping": {"$arrayElemAt": ["$product_mapping", 0]},
```

# Multi-field join and one-to-many

The previous example illustrated how to solve a one-to-one join. However, you may need to perform a one-to-many join, where a document in the first collection maps to potentially many records in the second collection. Here, you will learn how to achieve this in a pipeline.

## Scenario

You want to generate a report to list all the orders made for each product in 2020. To achieve this, you need to take a shop's *products* collection and join each product record to all its orders stored in an *orders* collection. There is a one-to-many relationship between both collections, based on a match of two fields on each side. Rather than joining on a single field such as `product_id` (which doesn't exist in this dataset), you need to use two common fields to join (`product_name` and `product_variation`).

> **Note**
> The requirement to perform a one-to-many join does not mandate the need to join the two collections by multiple fields on each side. However, in this example, there is a benefit to showing both aspects in one place.

## Populating the sample data

Like the previous example, you will first drop any old version of the database (if it exists) and then populate new *products* and *orders* collections with documents spanning 2019-2021. Each product will have a name, type variation, category, and description. Each order will have a *customer ID*, *order date*, *product name*, *product variation*, and *dollar value*:

```
db = db.getSiblingDB("book-multi-one-to-many");
db.dropDatabase();

// Insert 6 records into the products collection
db.products.insertMany([
  {
    "name": "Asus Laptop",
    "variation": "Ultra HD",
    "category": "ELECTRONICS",
    "description": "Great for watching movies",
  },
```

```
  {
    "name": "Asus Laptop",
    "variation": "Normal Display",
    "category": "ELECTRONICS",
    "description": "Good value laptop for students",
  },
  {
    "name": "The Day Of The Triffids",
    "variation": "1st Edition",
    "category": "BOOKS",
    "description": "Classic post-apocalyptic novel",
  },
  {
    "name": "The Day Of The Triffids",
    "variation": "2nd Edition",
    "category": "BOOKS",
    "description": "Classic post-apocalyptic novel",
  },
  {
    "name": "Morphy Richards Food Mixer",
    "variation": "Deluxe",
    "category": "KITCHENWARE",
    "description": "Luxury mixer turning good cakes into great",
  },
  {
    "name": "Karcher Hose Set",
    "variation": "Full Monty",
    "category": "GARDEN",
    "description": "Hose + nosels + winder for tidy storage",
  },
]);


// Create index for the orders collection
db.orders.createIndex({"product_name": 1, "product_variation": 1});

// Insert 4 records into the orders collection
db.orders.insertMany([
```

```
  {
    "customer_id": "elise_smith@myemail.com",
    "orderdate": ISODate("2020-05-30T08:35:52Z"),
    "product_name": "Asus Laptop",
    "product_variation": "Normal Display",
    "value": NumberDecimal("431.43"),
  },
  {
    "customer_id": "tj@wheresmyemail.com",
    "orderdate": ISODate("2019-05-28T19:13:32Z"),
    "product_name": "The Day Of The Triffids",
    "product_variation": "2nd Edition",
    "value": NumberDecimal("5.01"),
  },
  {
    "customer_id": "oranieri@warmmail.com",
    "orderdate": ISODate("2020-01-01T08:25:37Z"),
    "product_name": "Morphy Richards Food Mixer",
    "product_variation": "Deluxe",
    "value": NumberDecimal("63.13"),
  },
  {
    "customer_id": "jjones@tepidmail.com",
    "orderdate": ISODate("2020-12-26T08:55:46Z"),
    "product_name": "Asus Laptop",
    "product_variation": "Normal Display",
    "value": NumberDecimal("429.65"),
  },
]);
```

## Defining the aggregation pipeline

You will now define a pipeline that applies a number of stages to implement the aggregation:

```
var pipeline = [
  // Join by 2 fields in products collection to 2 fields in orders collection
  {"$lookup": {
    "from": "orders",
    "let": {
      "prdname": "$name",
      "prdvartn": "$variation",
    },
```

```
      // Embedded pipeline to control how the join is matched
      "pipeline": [
        // Join by two fields in each side
        {"$match":
          {"$expr":
            {"$and": [
              {"$eq": ["$product_name",  "$$prdname"]},
              {"$eq": ["$product_variation",  "$$prdvartn"]},
            ]},
          },
        },

        // Match only orders made in 2020
        {"$match": {
          "orderdate": {
            "$gte": ISODate("2020-01-01T00:00:00Z"),
            "$lt": ISODate("2021-01-01T00:00:00Z"),
          }
        }},

        // Exclude some unwanted fields from the right side of the join
        {"$unset": [
          "_id",
          "product_name",
          "product_variation",
        ]},
      ],
      as: "orders",
    }},

  // Only show products that have at least one order
  {"$match": {
    "orders": {"$ne": []},
  }},

  // Omit unwanted fields
  {"$unset": [
    "_id",
  ]},
];
```

## Executing the aggregation pipeline

Next, perform the following steps:

1. Execute the aggregation using the defined pipeline:

```
db.products.aggregate(pipeline);
```

2. Generate its explain plan:

```
db.products.explain("executionStats").aggregate(pipeline);
```

## Expected pipeline result

Once executed, the aggregation should return two documents representing the two products that had one or more orders in 2020, with the orders embedded in an array against each product:

```
[
  {
    name: 'Asus Laptop',
    variation: 'Normal Display',
    category: 'ELECTRONICS',
    description: 'Good value laptop for students',
    orders: [
      {
        customer_id: 'elise_smith@myemail.com',
        orderdate: ISODate('2020-05-30T08:35:52.000Z'),
        value: NumberDecimal('431.43')
      },
      {
        customer_id: 'jjones@tepidmail.com',
        orderdate: ISODate('2020-12-26T08:55:46.000Z'),
        value: NumberDecimal('429.65')
      }
    ]
  },
  {
    name: 'Morphy Richards Food Mixer',
    variation: 'Deluxe',
    category: 'KITCHENWARE',
    description: 'Luxury mixer turning good cakes into great',
    orders: [
      {
        customer_id: 'oranieri@warmmail.com',
```

```
        orderdate: ISODate('2020-01-01T08:25:37.000Z'),
        value: NumberDecimal('63.13')
      }
    ]
  }
]
```

## Pipeline observations

- **Multiple join fields**: To join two or more fields between the two collections, you must use a `let` parameter rather than specifying the `localField` and `foreignField` parameters used in a single field join. With a `let` parameter, you bind multiple fields from the first collection into variables ready to be used in the joining process. You use an embedded `pipeline` inside the `$lookup` stage to match the *bind* variables with fields in the second collection's records. In this instance, because the `$expr` operator performs an equality comparison specifically (as opposed to a range comparison), the aggregation runtime can employ an appropriate index for this match even if the underlying MongoDB version is older than 5.0.

- **Reducing array content**: The presence of an embedded pipeline in the `$lookup` stage provides an opportunity to filter out three unwanted fields brought in from the second collection. Instead, you could use an `$unset` stage later in the top-level pipeline to project out these unwanted array elements. Suppose you need to perform more complex array content filtering rules. In that case, you can use the approach described in *Chapter 3, Optimizing Pipelines for Performance*, specifically the *Avoid unwinding and regrouping documents just to process each array's elements* section.

## Summary

In this chapter, you learned techniques for solving the two common scenarios for joining data (one-to-one and one-to-many joins). You also looked at how to deal with multiple fields on each side of the join.

In the next chapter, you will explore how to address situations where the data quality in a collection is suboptimal, such as containing incorrect data types or incomplete fields, and provide solutions for rectifying these issues.

# 8

# Fixing and Generating Data Examples

This chapter provides you with tools and techniques to cleanse the data within your dataset. Sometimes, collections may store number and boolean fields as strings, or date fields as text without essential details such as the applicable time zone. Without proper typing, it can be almost impossible for users to execute range-based queries or ask for the results from querying the data to be sorted. You will also learn how to generate new sample data from scratch to help with your testing.

This chapter covers the following:

- Converting text fields to strongly typed fields
- Fixing incomplete date strings
- Generating new mock data

# Strongly typed conversion

It's not uncommon for someone to import data into a MongoDB collection and neglect to apply strong typing for the date, number, and boolean fields and store them as strings. This situation is likely to cause friction for subsequent users of the data. This example will show you how to restore these fields to their proper types.

## Scenario

A third party has imported a set of *retail orders* into a MongoDB collection but with all data typing lost (they have stored all field values as strings). You want to reestablish correct typing for all the documents and copy them into a new *cleaned* collection. You can incorporate such transformation logic in the aggregation pipeline because you know each field's type in the original record structure.

> **Note**
>
> Unlike most examples in this book, in this example, the aggregation pipeline writes its output to a collection rather than streaming the results back to the calling application.

## Populating the sample data

To begin with, drop any old version of the database (if it exists) and then populate a new `orders` collection with three order documents, where each order has text fields only, that is, for *order date*, *dollar value*, *item quantity*, and *issue reported*:

> **Note**
>
> The second document is intentionally missing the `reported` field for the `further_info` sub-document.

```
db = db.getSiblingDB("book-convert-to-strongly-typed");
db.dropDatabase();

// Insert orders documents
db.orders.insertMany([
  {
    "customer_id": "elise_smith@myemail.com",
    "order_date": "2020-05-30T08:35:52",
    "value": "231.43",
    "further_info": {
      "item_qty": "3",
      "reported": "false",
    },
  },
  {
    "customer_id": "oranieri@warmmail.com",
    "order_date": "2020-01-01T08:25:37",
    "value": "63.13",
    "further_info": {
      "item_qty": "2",
    },
  },
  {
    "customer_id": "tj@wheresmyemail.com",
    "order_date": "2019-05-28T19:13:32",
    "value": "2.01",
    "further_info": {
      "item_qty": "1",
      "reported": "true",
    },
  },
]);
```

## Defining the aggregation pipeline

You will now define a pipeline that applies a number of stages to implement the aggregation:

```
var pipeline = [
  // Convert strings to required types
  {"$set": {
    "order_date": {"$toDate": "$order_date"},
    "value": {"$toDecimal": "$value"},
    "further_info.item_qty": {"$toInt": "$further_info.item_qty"},
    "further_info.reported": {"$switch": {
      "branches": [
        {"case":
          {"$eq": [{"$toLower": "$further_info.reported"}, "true"]},
          "then": true
        },
        {"case":
          {"$eq": [{"$toLower": "$further_info.reported"}, "false"]},
          "then": false
        },
      ],
      "default":
        {"$ifNull": ["$further_info.reported", "$$REMOVE"]},
    }},
  }},

  // Output to an unsharded or sharded collection
  {"$merge": {
    "into": "orders_typed",
  }},
];
```

## Executing the aggregation pipeline

Next, execute the aggregation using the defined pipeline to generate and populate a new collection called `orders_typed`:

```
db.orders.aggregate(pipeline);
```

Then, check the contents of the new `orders_typed` collection to ensure the relevant fields are now appropriately typed:

```
db.orders_typed.find();
```

Now, view the explain plan for the aggregation pipeline:

```
db.orders.explain("executionStats").aggregate(pipeline);
```

## Expected pipeline result

Once executed, you'll see that the same number of documents appear in the new `orders_typed` collection as the source collection had, with the same field structure and fields names, but now using the strongly-typed boolean, date, integer, and decimal values where appropriate, as shown in the following result:

```
[
  {
    _id: ObjectId('6064381b7aa89666258201fd'),
    customer_id: 'elise_smith@myemail.com',
    further_info: {
      item_qty: 3,
      reported: false
    },
    order_date: ISODate('2020-05-30T08:35:52.000Z'),
    value: NumberDecimal('231.43')
  },
  {
    _id: ObjectId('6064381b7aa89666258201fe'),
    customer_id: 'oranieri@warmmail.com',
    further_info: {
      item_qty: 2
    },
    order_date: ISODate('2020-01-01T08:25:37.000Z'),
    value: NumberDecimal('63.13')
  },
  {
    _id: ObjectId('6064381b7aa89666258201ff'),
    customer_id: 'tj@wheresmyemail.com',\
    further_info: {
      item_qty: 1,
      reported: true
    },
    order_date: ISODate('2019-05-28T19:13:32.000Z'),
    value: NumberDecimal('2.01')
  }
]
```

## Pipeline observations

- **Boolean conversion**: The pipeline's conversion for integers, decimals, and dates are straightforward using the corresponding operator expressions, $toInt, $toDecimal, and $toDate. However, the $toBool operator expression is not used for the boolean conversion. This is because $toBool will convert any non-empty string to *true* regardless of its value. As a result, the pipeline uses a $switch operator to compare the lowercase version of strings with the text 'true' and 'false', returning the matching boolean.

- **Preserving non-existent fields**: The further_info.reported field is an optional field in this scenario. The field may not always appear in a document, as illustrated by one of the three documents in the example. If a field is absent from a document, this potentially significant fact should never be lost. The pipeline includes additional logic for the further_info.reported field to preserve this information. The pipeline ensures the field is not included in the output document if it didn't exist in the source document. An $ifNull conditional operator is used, which returns the $$REMOVE marker flag if the field is missing, instructing the aggregation engine to omit it.

- **Output to a collection**: The pipeline uses a $merge stage to instruct the aggregation engine to write the output to a collection rather than returning a stream of results. For this example, the default settings for $merge are sufficient. Each transformed record coming out of the aggregation pipeline becomes a new record in the target collection. The pipeline could have used an $out stage rather than a $merge stage. However, because $merge supports both unsharded and sharded collections, whereas $out only supports the former, $merge provides a more universally applicable solution. If your aggregation needs to create a brand new unsharded collection, $out may be a little faster because the aggregation will completely replace the existing collection if it exists. Using $merge, the system has to perform more checks for every record the aggregation inserts (even though, in this case, it will be to a new collection).

- **Trickier date conversions**: In this example, the date strings contain all the date parts required by the $toDate operator to perform a conversion correctly. In some situations, this may not be the case, and a date string may be missing some valuable information (e.g., which century a two-character year string is for, such as 19 or 21). To understand how to deal with these cases, see the next example.

# Converting incomplete date strings

Sometimes, you will encounter datasets with dates stored as strings and lacking critical details such as the century and time zone. As with the prior example, this poses challenges for database users. The next example will demonstrate how to amend these dates and add the missing information.

## Scenario

An application is ingesting payment documents into a MongoDB collection where each document's payment date field contains a string looking vaguely like a date-time, such as `"01-JAN-20 01.01.01.123000000"`. When aggregating the payments, you want to convert each payment date into a valid *BSON* (BSON is a binary encoding for JSON data types, making it easier and more performant for MongoDB to process and enabling support for more data types than the JSON standard) date type. However, the payment date fields contain only some of the information required to determine the exact date-time accurately. Therefore, you cannot use the *date operator expressions* (for example, `$dateFromString` and `$dateToParts`) in MongoDB directly to perform the text-to-date conversion. Each of these text fields is missing the following information:

- The specific century (1900s? 2000s?)

- The specific time zone (GMT? IST? PST?)

- The specific language the three-letter month abbreviation represents (is `"JAN"` in French? In English?)

You subsequently learn that all the payment records are for the 21st century only, the time zone used when ingesting the data is UTC, and the language used is English. Armed with this information, you build an aggregation pipeline to transform these text fields into date fields.

## Populating the sample data

Start by dropping any old version of the database (if it exists) and then populating a new payments collection with 12 sample payment documents. The inserted data provides coverage across all 12 months for 2020, with random *time*, *arbitrary account*, and *dollar amount* elements:

```
db = db.getSiblingDB("book-convert-incomplete-dates");
db.dropDatabase();

// Insert records into the payments collection
db.payments.insertMany([
  {
    "account": "010101",
    "paymentDate": "01-JAN-20 01.01.01.123000000",
    "amount": 1.01
  },
  {
    "account": "020202",
    "paymentDate": "02-FEB-20 02.02.02.456000000",
    "amount": 2.02
  },
  {
    "account": "030303",
    "paymentDate": "03-MAR-20 03.03.03.789000000",
    "amount": 3.03
  },
  {
    "account": "040404",
    "paymentDate": "04-APR-20 04.04.04.012000000",
    "amount": 4.04
  },
  {
    "account": "050505",
    "paymentDate": "05-MAY-20 05.05.05.345000000",
    "amount": 5.05
  },
```

```
    {
      "account": "060606",
      "paymentDate": "06-JUN-20 06.06.06.678000000",
      "amount": 6.06
    },
    {
      "account": "070707",
      "paymentDate": "07-JUL-20 07.07.07.901000000",
      "amount": 7.07
    },
    {
      "account": "080808",
      "paymentDate": "08-AUG-20 08.08.08.234000000",
      "amount": 8.08
    },
    {
      "account": "090909",
      "paymentDate": "09-SEP-20 09.09.09.567000000",
      "amount": 9.09
    },
    {
      "account": "101010",
      "paymentDate": "10-OCT-20 10.10.10.890000000",
      "amount": 10.10
    },
    {
      "account": "111111",
      "paymentDate": "11-NOV-20 11.11.11.111000000",
      "amount": 11.11
    },
    {
      "account": "121212",
      "paymentDate": "12-DEC-20 12.12.12.999000000",
      "amount": 12.12
    }
  ]);
```

## Defining the aggregation pipeline

You will now define a pipeline that applies a number of stages to implement the aggregation:

```
var pipeline = [
  // Change field from a string to a date, filling in the gaps
  {"$set": {
    "paymentDate": {
      "$let": {
        "vars": {
          "txt": "$paymentDate",  // Assign "paymentDate" field to variable
          "month": {"$substrCP": ["$paymentDate", 3, 3]},  // Extract month
        },
        "in": {
          "$dateFromString": {"format": "%d-%m-%Y %H.%M.%S.%L", "dateString":
            {"$concat": [
              {"$substrCP": ["$$txt", 0, 3]},  // Use 1st 3 chars in string
              {"$switch": {"branches": [  // Replace 3 chars with month num
                {"case": {"$eq": ["$$month", "JAN"]}, "then": "01"},
                {"case": {"$eq": ["$$month", "FEB"]}, "then": "02"},
                {"case": {"$eq": ["$$month", "MAR"]}, "then": "03"},
                {"case": {"$eq": ["$$month", "APR"]}, "then": "04"},
                {"case": {"$eq": ["$$month", "MAY"]}, "then": "05"},
                {"case": {"$eq": ["$$month", "JUN"]}, "then": "06"},
                {"case": {"$eq": ["$$month", "JUL"]}, "then": "07"},
                {"case": {"$eq": ["$$month", "AUG"]}, "then": "08"},
                {"case": {"$eq": ["$$month", "SEP"]}, "then": "09"},
                {"case": {"$eq": ["$$month", "OCT"]}, "then": "10"},
                {"case": {"$eq": ["$$month", "NOV"]}, "then": "11"},
                {"case": {"$eq": ["$$month", "DEC"]}, "then": "12"},
              ], "default": "ERROR"}},
              "-20",  // Add hyphen + hardcoded century 2 digits
              {"$substrCP": ["$$txt", 7, 15]}  // Ignore last 6 nanosecs
            ]
          }}
        }
      }
    },
  }},
```

```
    // Omit unwanted fields
    {"$unset": [
      "_id",
    ]},
  ];
];
```

## Executing the aggregation pipeline

Next, run the following commands to do the following:

1. Execute the aggregation using the defined pipeline:

```
db.payments.aggregate(pipeline);
```

2. Generate its explain plan:

```
db.payments.explain("executionStats").aggregate(pipeline);
```

## Expected pipeline result

Once executed, the aggregation will return 12 documents, corresponding to the original 12 source documents, but this time with the paymentDate field converted from *text* values to proper *date-typed* values:

```
[
  {
    account: '010101',
    paymentDate: ISODate('2020-01-01T01:01:01.123Z'),
    amount: 1.01
  },
  {
    account: '020202',
    paymentDate: ISODate('2020-02-02T02:02:02.456Z'),
    amount: 2.02
  },
  {
    account: '030303',
    paymentDate: ISODate('2020-03-03T03:03:03.789Z'),
    amount: 3.03
  },
  {
    account: '040404',
    paymentDate: ISODate('2020-04-04T04:04:04.012Z'),
    amount: 4.04
```

```
    },
    {
      account: '050505',
      paymentDate: ISODate('2020-05-05T05:05:05.345Z'),
      amount: 5.05
    },
    {
      account: '060606',
      paymentDate: ISODate('2020-06-06T06:06:06.678Z'),
      amount: 6.06
    },
    {
      account: '070707',
      paymentDate: ISODate('2020-07-07T07:07:07.901Z'),
      amount: 7.07
    },
    {
      account: '080808',
      paymentDate: ISODate('2020-08-08T08:08:08.234Z'),
      amount: 8.08
    },
    {
      account: '090909',
      paymentDate: ISODate('2020-09-09T09:09:09.567Z'),
      amount: 9.09
    },
    {
      account: '101010',
      paymentDate: ISODate('2020-10-10T10:10:10.890Z'),
      amount: 10.1
    },
    {
      account: '111111',
      paymentDate: ISODate('2020-11-11T11:11:11.111Z'),
      amount: 11.11
    },
    {
      account: '121212',
      paymentDate: ISODate('2020-12-12T12:12:12.999Z'),
      amount: 12.12
    }
  ]
```

## Pipeline observations

- **Concatenation explanation**: In this pipeline, the *text* fields (e.g., `'12-DEC-20 12.12.12.999000000'`) are each converted to *date* fields (e.g., `2020-12-12T12:12:12.999Z`). The pipeline achieves this by concatenating the following four example elements before passing them to the `$dateFromString` operator to convert to a *date* type:

  - `'12-'` (*day of the month from the input string plus the hyphen suffix already present in the text*)

  - `'12'` (*replacing "DEC"*)

  - `'-20'` (*hard-coded hyphen plus hard-coded century*)

  - `'20 12.12.12.999'` (*the rest of the input string apart from the last 6 nanosecond digits*)

- **Temporary reusable variables**: The pipeline includes a `$let` operator to define two variables ready to be reused in multiple places in the central part of the data conversion logic belonging to the `$dateFromString` operator. The `txt` variable provides a minor convenience to ensure the main part of the expression logic works regardless of whether the referenced field path is currently named `$paymentDate` or changes in a future version of the source collection (e.g., to `$transactionDate`). The `month` variable is more valuable, ensuring the pipeline does not have to repeat the same *substring* logic in multiple places.

# Generating mock test data

The ability to generate test data is necessary for most IT projects, but this can be quite a tedious and time-consuming process. The MongoDB aggregation framework provides operators that a pipeline can include to make generating mock test data easy for certain types of test scenarios.

> **Note**
>
> For this example, you require MongoDB version 6.0 or above. This is because you'll be using the $densify and $fill stages introduced in version 6.0.

## Scenario

You want to generate a load of sample data into a MongoDB collection so you can subsequently educate yourself by experimenting with MongoDB Query Language and defining indexes to determine how to improve the response time of your test queries. You don't have much time, so you want to use a low-effort way to quickly produce a collection of half a million documents using an aggregation pipeline. The specific fields you want each sample document to have include the following:

- A monotonically increasing datetime field
- A *key* with one of four values to logically relate a quarter of the documents together as part of the same *partition*
- A monotonically increasing progress numerical field
- A score field which that takes an entirely random float value between 0 and 1
- A preference field with one of three possible values (the primary colors) picked at random

## Populating the sample data

First, drop any old version of the sample database (if it exists) and then populate a new source collection with some sample documents to define boundaries for the dataset the pipeline will generate. These records include a key field for the different partitions of data, a datetime field with the earliest or latest timestamps required, and a progress field with the minimum or maximum values required:

```
db = db.getSiblingDB("book-generate-mock-data");
db.dropDatabase();

// Insert 6 records into the 'source' collection
db.source.insertMany([
```

```
  {
    "key": "A",
    "datetime": ISODate("2009-04-27T00:00:00.000Z"),
    "progress": 1
  },
  {
    "key": "B",
    "datetime": ISODate("2009-04-27T00:00:00.000Z"),
    "progress": 1
  },
  {
    "key": "C",
    "datetime": ISODate("2009-04-27T00:00:00.000Z"),
    "progress": 1
  },
  {
    "key": "D",
    "datetime": ISODate("2009-04-27T00:00:00.000Z"),
    "progress": 1
  },
  {
    "key": "A",
    "datetime": ISODate("2023-07-31T06:59:59.000Z"),
    "progress": 9
  },
  {
    "key": "B",
    "datetime": ISODate("2023-07-31T06:59:59.000Z"),
    "progress": 9
  },
  {
    "key": "C",
    "datetime": ISODate("2023-07-31T06:59:59.000Z"),
    "progress": 9
  },
  {
    "key": "D",
    "datetime": ISODate("2023-07-31T06:59:59.000Z"),
    "progress": 9
  },
]);
```

## Defining the aggregation pipeline

You will now define a pipeline that applies a number of stages to implement the aggregation:

```
var pipeline = [
  // Add new records every hour between the current first datetime
  // to current last datetime for each existing key value
  {"$densify": {
    "field": "datetime",
    "partitionByFields": ["key"],
    "range": {"bounds": "full", "step": 1, "unit": "hour"},
  }},

  // For the existing records, where 'progress' field is not set add a field
  // with a value that progressively increases for each existing key
  {"$fill": {
    "sortBy": {"datetime": 1},
    "partitionBy": {"key": "$key"},
    "output": {
      "progress": {"method": "linear"}
    },
  }},

  {"$set": {
    // Set score field to be a random number
    "score": {"$rand": {}},

    // Set preference field to one of 3 values randomly
    "preference": {
      "$let": {
        "vars": {
          "values": ["RED", "YELLOW", "BLUE"],
        },
        "in": {
          "$arrayElemAt": [
            "$$values",
            {"$floor": {"$multiply": [{"$size": "$$values"}, {"$rand": {}}]}},
          ]
        }
      }
    },
  }},
```

```
  {"$merge": {
    "into": "destination",
  }},
];
```

## Executing the aggregation pipeline

Next, run the following commands to do the following:

1. Execute the aggregation using the defined pipeline:

   ```
   db.source.aggregate(pipeline);
   ```

2. Generate its explain plan:

   ```
   db.source.explain("executionStats").aggregate(pipeline);
   ```

3. Then, run the commands to count the number of documents created in the new *destination* collection and then view its first few documents and last few documents:

   ```
   db.destination.countDocuments();

   db.destination.find().sort({"datetime": 1});

   db.destination.find().sort({"datetime": -1});
   ```

## Expected pipeline result

Running the *count* operation should indicate that the new collection contains half a million documents:

```
500000
```

Running the query for the first few records should include results similar to the following (the score field values will differ because they are random):

```
[
  {
    _id: ObjectId("64c931d08d90d71f25510365"),
    datetime: ISODate("2009-04-27T00:00:00.000Z"),
    key: 'A',
    preference: 'YELLOW',
    progress: 1,
    score: 0.6667974140557414
  },
  ....
```

```
  {
    _id: ObjectId("64c931db9840b32286c9236e"),
    datetime: ISODate("2009-04-27T01:00:00.000Z"),
    key: 'A',
    preference: 'BLUE',
    progress: 1.0000640005121464,
    score: 0.23781158031443062
  },
  ....
]
```

Running the query for the last few records should include results similar to the following (the score field values will differ because they are random):

```
[
  {
    _id: ObjectId("64c931d08d90d71f25510369"),
    datetime: ISODate("2023-07-31T06:59:59.000Z"),
    key: 'A',
    preference: 'RED',
    progress: 9,
    score: 0.5651984473548808
  }
  ....
  {
    _id: ObjectId("64c931df9840b32286cb0bb8"),
    datetime: ISODate("2023-07-31T06:00:00.000Z"),
    key: 'A',
    preference: 'RED',
    progress: 8.999936017265775,
    score: 0.6065233080691302
  },
  ....
]
```

## Pipeline observations

- **Densification of records**: You will have noticed that only eight records are included in the source collection to seed the subsequent generation of half a million records. Four of these inserted records act as the start boundary for subsequently generated records with the keys *A*, *B*, *C* and *D*. The other four records act as the end boundary for new records with those keys. The pipeline then uses the $densify operator to fill in missing documents between these two boundaries for each key, setting the datetime field for each new record with the next incremental hour between the datetime of the start and end boundary records. This first pipeline stage ($densify) essentially creates the missing 499,992 records in the gap.

- **Filling missing fields**: The pipeline's second stage ($fill) plays a different role. Rather than fill in missing records, it fills in some missing fields in the sequence of now-existing records. The stage defines that the thousands of records with the same key are given a linearly increasing floating value between the two boundary records with values 0 and 1 for the generated progress field.

- **Random value generation**: The pipeline uses the $rand operator to generate random numbers at two places by the pipeline. The pipeline uses $rand directly to assign a random value between 0 and 1 to a new field called score in each record (including the preexisting eight records). The pipeline also indirectly uses $rand to randomly choose one of three values, RED, YELLOW, and BLUE, to set the value of a new field called preference in each existing and newly generated record.

- **Output to a collection**: The pipeline uses a $merge stage to instruct the aggregation engine to write the output to a collection rather than returning a stream of results. The pipeline could have used an $out rather than a $merge stage. However, because $merge supports both unsharded and sharded collections, whereas $out only supports the former, $merge provides a more universally applicable example. If your aggregation needs to create a brand new unsharded collection, $out may be a little faster because the aggregation will completely replace the existing collection if it exists. Using $merge, the system has to perform more checks for every record the aggregation inserts (even though, in this case, it will be to a new collection).

- **Limit to the amount of documents generated by densify**: The $densify stage limits the number of documents a pipeline can generate to 500,000. There is a workaround, which involves inserting multiple $densify stages in the same pipeline. If you want to generate one million records, you need to include two stages. If employing this workaround, you must change the definition of the bounds field in each $densify stage. Rather than defining "bounds": "full", you define an explicit bounds range instead. For this example, you can use the following bounds field definitions:

```
// Defined in the FIRST $densify stage you employ in your pipeline
"bounds": [ISODate("1995-01-22T16:00:00.000Z"), ISODate("2009-04-
27T00:00:00.000Z")],
```

```
// Defined in the SECOND $densify stage you employ in your pipeline
"bounds": [ISODate("2009-04-27T00:00:00.000Z"), ISODate("2023-07-
31T06:59:59.000Z")],
```

For this to work correctly, you must change the initial script that inserts the eight seed records into the database to define the first four records with an earlier start date, as illustrated here:

```
{
  "key": "A",
  "datetime": ISODate("1995-01-22T16:00:00.000Z"),
  "progress": 1
},
{
  "key": "B",
  "datetime": ISODate("1995-01-22T16:00:00.000Z"),
  "progress": 1
},
{
  "key": "C",
  "datetime": ISODate("1995-01-22T16:00:00.000Z"),
  "progress": 1
  },
{
  "key": "D",
  "datetime": ISODate("1995-01-22T16:00:00.000Z"),
  "progress": 1
},
```

## Summary

In this chapter, you learned techniques for fixing existing data in your database, helping to fill in missing bits, and converting fields to be strongly typed.

In the next chapter, you will explore examples for analyzing datasets to pinpoint trends, categories, and relationships.

# 9

# Trend Analysis Examples

This chapter showcases the capabilities of the MongoDB aggregation framework in performing advanced data analytics. The framework empowers users to analyze rich datasets, discerning trends, classifications, and relationships.

This chapter will cover the following:

- Classifying data by different facets
- Traversing the graph of relationships between documents in the same collection
- Performing incremental analytics to generate reports

# Faceted classification

A typical scenario, often seen as a navigation bar on the left-hand side of an e-commerce product search website, is the need to characterize the same data across multiple dimensions or facets. This example will show you how to perform these faceting queries from a single aggregation pipeline.

## Scenario

You want to provide *faceted search* capability on your retail website to enable customers to refine their product search by selecting specific characteristics against the product results listed on the web page. It is beneficial to classify the products by different dimensions, where each dimension, or facet, corresponds to a particular field in a product record (e.g., *product rating* or *product price*).

Each facet should be broken down into a separate range so that a customer can select a specific sub-range (e.g., *4-5 stars*) for a particular facet (e.g., *rating*). The aggregation pipeline will analyze the *products* collection by each facet's field (*rating* and *price*) to determine each facet's spread of values.

## Populating the sample data

Start by dropping any old version of the database (if it exists) and then populate a new products collection with 16 documents. Each product record will contain the product's *name, category, description, price,* and *rating*:

```
db = db.getSiblingDB("book-faceted-classfctn");
db.dropDatabase();

// Insert first 8 records into the collection
db.products.insertMany([
  {
    "name": "Asus Laptop",
    "category": "ELECTRONICS",
    "description": "Good value laptop for students",
    "price": NumberDecimal("431.43"),
    "rating": NumberDecimal("4.2"),
  },
  {
    "name": "The Day Of The Triffids",
    "category": "BOOKS",
    "description": "Classic post-apocalyptic novel",
    "price": NumberDecimal("5.01"),
    "rating": NumberDecimal("4.8"),
  },
```

```
{
  "name": "Morphy Richards Food Mixer",
  "category": "KITCHENWARE",
  "description": "Luxury mixer turning good cakes into great",
  "price": NumberDecimal("63.13"),
  "rating": NumberDecimal("3.8"),
},
{
  "name": "Karcher Hose Set",
  "category": "GARDEN",
  "description": "Hose + nozzles + winder for tidy storage",
  "price": NumberDecimal("22.13"),
  "rating": NumberDecimal("4.3"),
},
{
  "name": "Oak Coffee Table",
  "category": "HOME",
  "description": "size is 2m x 0.5m x 0.4m",
  "price": NumberDecimal("22.13"),
  "rating": NumberDecimal("3.8"),
},
{
  "name": "Lenovo Laptop",
  "category": "ELECTRONICS",
  "description": "High spec good for gaming",
  "price": NumberDecimal("1299.99"),
  "rating": NumberDecimal("4.1"),
},
{
  "name": "One Day in the Life of Ivan Denisovich",
  "category": "BOOKS",
  "description": "Brutal life in a labour camp",
  "price": NumberDecimal("4.29"),
  "rating": NumberDecimal("4.9"),
},
{
  "name": "Russell Hobbs Chrome Kettle",
  "category": "KITCHENWARE",
  "description": "Nice looking budget kettle",
  "price": NumberDecimal("15.76"),
  "rating": NumberDecimal("3.9"),
},
```

```
{
  "name": "Tiffany Gold Chain",
  "category": "JEWELERY",
  "description": "Looks great for any age and gender",
  "price": NumberDecimal("582.22"),
  "rating": NumberDecimal("4.0"),
},
{
  "name": "Raleigh Racer 21st Century Classic",
  "category": "BICYCLES",
  "description": "Modern update to a classic 70s bike design",
  "price": NumberDecimal("523.00"),
  "rating": NumberDecimal("4.5"),
},
{
  "name": "Diesel Flare Jeans",
  "category": "CLOTHES",
  "description": "Top end casual look",
  "price": NumberDecimal("129.89"),
  "rating": NumberDecimal("4.3"),
},
{
  "name": "Jazz Silk Scarf",
  "category": "CLOTHES",
  "description": "Style for the winter months",
  "price": NumberDecimal("28.39"),
  "rating": NumberDecimal("3.7"),
},
{
  "name": "Dell XPS 13 Laptop",
  "category": "ELECTRONICS",
  "description": "Developer edition",
  "price": NumberDecimal("1399.89"),
  "rating": NumberDecimal("4.4"),
},
{
  "name": "NY Baseball Cap",
  "category": "CLOTHES",
  "description": "Blue & white",
  "price": NumberDecimal("18.99"),
  "rating": NumberDecimal("4.0"),
},
```

```
  {
    "name": "Tots Flower Pots",
    "category": "GARDEN",
    "description": "Set of three",
    "price": NumberDecimal("9.78"),
    "rating": NumberDecimal("4.1"),
  },
  {
    "name": "Picky Pencil Sharpener",
    "category": "Stationery",
    "description": "Ultra budget",
    "price": NumberDecimal("0.67"),
    "rating": NumberDecimal("1.2"),
  },
]);
```

## Defining the aggregation pipeline

Now define a pipeline that applies a number of stages to implement the aggregation:

```
var pipeline = [
  // Group products by 2 facets: 1) by price ranges, 2) by rating ranges
  {"$facet": {

    // Group by price ranges
    "by_price": [
      // Group into 3: inexpensive small range to expensive large range
      {"$bucketAuto": {
        "groupBy": "$price",
        "buckets": 3,
        "granularity": "1-2-5",
        "output": {
          "count": {"$sum": 1},
          "products": {"$push": "$name"},
        },
      }},

      // Tag range info as "price_range"
      {"$set": {
        "price_range": "$_id",
      }},
```

```
      // Omit unwanted fields
      {"$unset": [
        "_id",
      ]},
    ],

    // Group by rating ranges
    "by_rating": [
      // Group products evenly across 5 rating ranges from low to high
      {"$bucketAuto": {
        "groupBy": "$rating",
        "buckets": 5,
        "output": {
          "count": {"$sum": 1},
          "products": {"$push": "$name"},
        },
      }},

      // Tag range info as "rating_range"
      {"$set": {
        "rating_range": "$_id",
      }},

      // Omit unwanted fields
      {"$unset": [
        "_id",
      ]},
    ],
  }},
];
```

## Executing the aggregation pipeline

Next, perform the following steps:

1.  Execute the aggregation using the defined pipeline:

    ```
    db.products.aggregate(pipeline);
    ```

2.  Generate its explain plan:

    ```
    db.products.explain("executionStats").aggregate(pipeline);
    ```

## Expected pipeline result

Once executed, this aggregation will return a single document containing two facets (keyed off
by_price and by_rating, respectively), where each facet shows its sub-range of values and the
products belonging to each sub-range:

```
[
  {
    by_price: [
      {
        count: 6,
        products: [
          'Picky Pencil Sharpener',
          'One Day in the Life of Ivan Denisovich',
          'The Day Of The Triffids', 'Tots Flower Pots',
          'Russell Hobbs Chrome Kettle', 'NY Baseball Cap'
        ],
        price_range: {
          min: NumberDecimal('0.500000000000000'),
          max: NumberDecimal('20.0000000000000')
        }
      },
      {
        count: 5,
        products: [
          'Karcher Hose Set', 'Oak Coffee Table', 'Jazz Silk Scarf',
          'Morphy Richards Food Mixer', 'Diesel Flare Jeans'
        ],
        price_range: {
          min: NumberDecimal('20.0000000000000'),
          max: NumberDecimal('200.0000000000000')
        }
      },
      {
        count: 5,
        products: [
          'Asus Laptop', 'Raleigh Racer 21st Century Classic',
          'Tiffany Gold Chain', 'Lenovo Laptop', 'Dell XPS 13 Laptop'
        ],
        price_range: {
          min: NumberDecimal('200.0000000000000'),
          max: NumberDecimal('2000.0000000000000')
```

```
        }
      }
    ],
    by_rating: [
      {
        count: 4,
        products: [
          'Picky Pencil Sharpener', 'Jazz Silk Scarf',
          'Morphy Richards Food Mixer', 'Oak Coffee Table'
        ],
        rating_range: {
          min: NumberDecimal('1.2'),
          max: NumberDecimal('3.9')
        }
      },
      {
        count: 3,
        products: [
          'Russell Hobbs Chrome Kettle', 'Tiffany Gold Chain',
          'NY Baseball Cap'
        ],
        rating_range: {
          min: NumberDecimal('3.9'),
          max: NumberDecimal('4.1')
        }
      },
      {
        count: 3,
        products: [
          'Lenovo Laptop', 'Tots Flower Pots', 'Asus Laptop'
        ],
        rating_range: {
          min: NumberDecimal('4.1'),
          max: NumberDecimal('4.3')
        }
      },
      {
        count: 3,
        products: [
          'Karcher Hose Set', 'Diesel Flare Jeans', 'Dell XPS 13 Laptop'
```

```
      ],
      rating_range: {
        min: NumberDecimal('4.3'),
        max: NumberDecimal('4.5')
      }
    },
    {
      count: 3,
      products: [
        'Raleigh Racer 21st Century Classic', 'The Day Of The Triffids',
        'One Day in the Life of Ivan Denisovich'
      ],
      rating_range: {
        min: NumberDecimal('4.5'),
        max: NumberDecimal('4.9')
      }
    }
  ]
  }
]
```

## Pipeline observations

- **Multiple pipelines**: The $facet stage doesn't have to be employed for you to use the $bucketAuto stage. In most *faceted search* scenarios, you will want to understand a collection by multiple dimensions simultaneously (*price* and *rating*, in this case). The $facet stage is convenient because it allows you to define various $bucketAuto dimensions in one go in a single pipeline. Otherwise, a client application must invoke an aggregation multiple times, each using a new $bucketAuto stage to process a different field. In fact, each section of a $facet stage is just a regular aggregation (sub-) pipeline, able to contain any type of stage (with a few specific *documented exceptions*, see https://www.mongodb.com/docs/manual/reference/operator/aggregation/facet/#behavior), and may not even use $bucketAuto or $bucket stages at all.

- **Single document result**: Allowing the result of a $facet-based aggregation to be multiple documents will cause a problem. The results will contain a mix of records originating from different facets but with no way of ascertaining the facet to which each result record belongs. Consequently, when using $facet, a single document is always returned, containing top-level fields identifying each facet. Having only a single result record is not usually a problem. A typical requirement for faceted search is to return a small amount of grouped summary data about a collection rather than large amounts of raw data from the collection. Therefore, the 16 MB document size limit should not be an issue.

- **Spread of ranges**: In this example, each of the two employed bucketing facets uses a different granularity number scheme to spread out the sub-ranges of values. You choose a numbering scheme based on what you know about the nature of the facet. For instance, most of the *ratings* values in the sample collection have scores bunched between late 3s and early 4s. If a chosen numbering scheme reflects an even spread of ratings, most products will appear in the same sub-range bucket, and some sub-ranges will contain no products (e.g., ratings 2 to 3 in this example). This wouldn't provide website customers with much selectivity on product ratings.

- **Faster facet computation**: The aggregation in this example has no choice but to perform a *full collection scan* to construct the faceted results. For large collections, the amount of time the user has to wait on the website to see these results may be prohibitively long. However, you can employ an alternative mechanism to generate faceted results faster, using *Atlas Search*, as highlighted in *Chapter 13, Full-Text Search Examples*, specifically the *Facets and counts text search* section. Therefore, if you can adopt Atlas Search, you should use its faceted search capability rather than the general-purpose faceted search capability in MongoDB.

# Largest graph network

Sometimes your data may include graph relationships between records within a single collection. Take, for instance, a document management system database that houses whitepapers citing other whitepapers within the same collection. Visualizing the chain of dependencies becomes crucial in such situations. This example shows how you can traverse these sorts of relationships within a collection.

## Scenario

Your organization wants to know the best targets for a new marketing campaign based on a social network database such as *Twitter*.

You want to search the collection of social network users, each holding a user's name and the names of others who follow them. You want to *traverse* each user record's `followed_by` array to determine which user has the most extensive *network reach*.

> **Note**
>
> This example uses a simple data model for brevity. However, this is unlikely to be an optimum data model for using `$graphLookup` at scale for social network users with many followers or running in a sharded environment. For more guidance modeling large networks of relationships at scale, see this reference application: *Socialite* (see `https://github.com/mongodb-labs/socialite`).

## Populating the sample data

Start by dropping any old version of the database (if it exists) and then populate a new `users` collection with 10 social network user documents, plus an index to help optimize the *graph traversal*:

```
db = db.getSiblingDB("book-largest-graph-network");
db.dropDatabase();

// Create index on field which each graph traversal hop will connect to
db.users.createIndex({"name": 1});

// Insert records into the users collection
db.users.insertMany([
  {"name": "Paul", "followed_by": []},
  {"name": "Toni", "followed_by": ["Paul"]},
  {"name": "Janet", "followed_by": ["Paul", "Toni"]},
  {"name": "David", "followed_by": ["Janet", "Paul", "Toni"]},
  {"name": "Fiona", "followed_by": ["David", "Paul"]},
  {"name": "Bob", "followed_by": ["Janet"]},
```

```
    {"name": "Carl", "followed_by": ["Fiona"]},
    {"name": "Sarah", "followed_by": ["Carl", "Paul"]},
    {"name": "Carol", "followed_by": ["Helen", "Sarah"]},
    {"name": "Helen", "followed_by": ["Paul"]},
  ]);
```

## Defining the aggregation pipeline

You will now define a pipeline that applies a number of stages to implement the aggregation:

```
var pipeline = [
  // For each social network user, traverse their 'followed_by' people list
  {"$graphLookup": {
    "from": "users",
    "startWith": "$followed_by",
    "connectFromField": "followed_by",
    "connectToField": "name",
    "depthField": "depth",
    "as": "extended_network",
  }},

  // Add new accumulating fields
  {"$set": {
    // Count the extended connection reach
    "network_reach": {
      "$size": "$extended_network"
    },

    // Gather the list of the extended connections' names
    "extended_connections": {
      "$map": {
        "input": "$extended_network",
        "as": "connection",
        "in": "$$connection.name", // Get name field from each element
      }
    },
  }},

  // Omit unwanted fields
  {"$unset": [
    "_id",
    "followed_by",
```

```
    "extended_network",
  ]},

  // Sort by person with greatest network reach first, in descending order
  {"$sort": {
    "network_reach": -1,
  }},
];
```

## Executing the aggregation pipeline

Next, run the following commands to do as follows:

1. Execute the aggregation using the defined pipeline:

   ```
   db.users.aggregate(pipeline);
   ```

2. Generate its explain plan:

   ```
   db.users.explain("executionStats").aggregate(pipeline);
   ```

## Expected pipeline result

Once executed, the aggregation should return 10 documents corresponding to the original 10 social network users, with each document including a count of the user's *network reach* and the names of their *extended connections*, sorted by the user with the most extensive network reach first:

```
[
  {
    name: 'Carol',
    network_reach: 8,
    extended_connections: [ 'David', 'Toni', 'Fiona', 'Sarah', 'Helen',
                            'Carl', 'Paul',  'Janet' ]
  },
  {
    name: 'Sarah',
    network_reach: 6,
    extended_connections: [ 'David', 'Toni', 'Fiona', 'Carl', 'Paul',
                            'Janet']
  },
```

```
    {
      name: 'Carl',
      network_reach: 5,
      extended_connections: [ 'David', 'Toni', 'Fiona', 'Paul', 'Janet' ]
    },
    {
      name: 'Fiona',
      network_reach: 4,
      extended_connections: [ 'David', 'Toni', 'Paul', 'Janet' ]
    },
    {
      name: 'David',
      network_reach: 3,
      extended_connections: [ 'Toni', 'Paul', 'Janet' ]
    },
    {
      name: 'Bob',
      network_reach: 3,
      extended_connections: [ 'Toni', 'Paul', 'Janet' ]
    },
    {
      name: 'Janet',
      network_reach: 2,
      extended_connections: [ 'Toni', 'Paul' ]
    },
    {
      name: 'Toni',
      network_reach: 1,
      extended_connections: [ 'Paul']
    },
    {
      name: 'Helen',
      network_reach: 1,
      extended_connections: [ 'Paul' ]
    },
    { name: 'Paul',
      network_reach: 0,
      extended_connections: []
    }
  ]
```

## Pipeline observations

- **Following graphs**: The $graphLookup stage helps you traverse relationships between records, looking for patterns that aren't necessarily evident from looking at each record in isolation. In this example, by looking at *Paul's* record in isolation, it is evident that *Paul* has no *friends* and thus has the lowest network reach. However, it is not obvious that *Carol* has the greatest network reach just by looking at the number of people *Carol* is directly followed by, which is two. *David*, for example, is followed by three people (one more than *Carol*). However, the executed aggregation pipeline can deduce that *Carol* has the most extensive network reach.

- **Index use**: The $graphLookup stage can leverage the index on the name field for each of its connectToField hops. Without this, the aggregation would take an eternity to navigate an extensive network.

- **Extracting one field from each array element**: The pipeline uses the $map array operator to only take one field from each *user* element matched by the $graphLookup stage. The $map logic loops through each matched *user*, adding the value of the user's name field to the $map's array of results and ignoring the other field ( followed_by). For more information about using the $map operator, see *Chapter 4, Harnessing the Power of Expressions*.

# Incremental analytics

As a company matures, its volume of historical business data expands. This growth presents a significant challenge for the business intelligence department tasked with producing daily sales reports that must capture trends spanning years. The rising data volume increasingly delays the reporting process, impeding swift decision-making based on current financial data. The following example shows how you can avoid an increasing slowdown in reporting.

## Scenario

You have accumulated *shop orders* over many years, with the retail channel continuously adding new order records to the *orders* collection throughout each trading day. You want to frequently generate a summary report so management can understand the state of the business and react to changing business trends. Over the years, it has taken increasingly longer to generate the report of all daily sums and averages because there has been increasingly more data to process each day.

From now on, to address this problem, you will only generate each new day's summary analysis at the end of the day and store it in a different collection, which accumulates the daily summary records over time.

> **Note**
>
> Unlike most examples in this book, the aggregation pipeline writes its output to a collection rather than streaming the results back to the calling application. This approach is sometimes referred to as an **on-demand materialized view**.

## Populating the sample data

First, drop any old versions of the database (if any exist) and then add nine documents to the orders collection, representing five orders for 01-Feb-2021 and four orders for 02-Feb-2021. Each order will have an *order date* and a *value*:

```
db = db.getSiblingDB("book-incremental-analytics");
db.dropDatabase();

// Create index for a daily_orders_summary collection
db.daily_orders_summary.createIndex({"day": 1}, {"unique": true});

// Create index for a orders collection
db.orders.createIndex({"orderdate": 1});
```

```
// Insert records into the orders collection
// (5 orders for 1st Feb, 4 orders for 2nd Feb)
db.orders.insertMany([
  {
    "orderdate": ISODate("2021-02-01T08:35:52Z"),
    "value": NumberDecimal("231.43"),
  },
  {
    "orderdate": ISODate("2021-02-01T09:32:07Z"),
    "value": NumberDecimal("99.99"),
  },
  {
    "orderdate": ISODate("2021-02-01T08:25:37Z"),
    "value": NumberDecimal("63.13"),
  },
  {
    "orderdate": ISODate("2021-02-01T19:13:32Z"),
    "value": NumberDecimal("2.01"),
  },
  {
    "orderdate": ISODate("2021-02-01T22:56:53Z"),
    "value": NumberDecimal("187.99"),
  },
  {
    "orderdate": ISODate("2021-02-02T23:04:48Z"),
    "value": NumberDecimal("4.59"),
  },
  {
    "orderdate": ISODate("2021-02-02T08:55:46Z"),
    "value": NumberDecimal("48.50"),
  },
  {
    "orderdate": ISODate("2021-02-02T07:49:32Z"),
    "value": NumberDecimal("1024.89"),
  },
  {
    "orderdate": ISODate("2021-02-02T13:49:44Z"),
    "value": NumberDecimal("102.24"),
  },
]);
```

## Defining the aggregation pipeline

Now, you will do something that's a little different. Rather than defining a pipeline as a variable, you will define a function to create a pipeline, but with the *start* and *end* date parameterized, ready to be used to perform the aggregation multiple times for different days:

```
function getDayAggPipeline(startDay, endDay) {
  return [
    // Match orders for one day only
    {"$match": {
      "orderdate": {
        "$gte": ISODate(startDay),
        "$lt": ISODate(endDay),
      }
    }},

    // Group all orders together into one summary record for the day
    {"$group": {
      "_id": null,
      "date_parts": {"$first": {"$dateToParts": {"date": "$orderdate"}}},
      "total_value": {"$sum": "$value"},
      "total_orders": {"$sum": 1},
    }},

    // Get date parts from 1 order (need year+month+day, for UTC)
    {"$set": {
      "day": {
        "$dateFromParts": {
          "year": "$date_parts.year",
          "month": "$date_parts.month",
          "day":"$date_parts.day"
        }
      },
    }},

    // Omit unwanted field
    {"$unset": [
      "_id",
      "date_parts",
    ]},
```

```
    // Add day summary to summary collection (overwrite if already exists)
    {"$merge": {
      "into": "daily_orders_summary",
      "on": "day",
      "whenMatched": "replace",
      "whenNotMatched": "insert"
    }},
  ];
}
```

## Executing the aggregation pipeline

First, for 01-Feb-2021 orders only, build the pipeline and execute the aggregation:

```
// Get the pipeline for the 1st day
var pipeline = getDayAggPipeline("2021-02-01T00:00:00Z",
                                 "2021-02-02T00:00:00Z");

// Run aggregation for 01-Feb-2021 orders & put result in summary collection
db.orders.aggregate(pipeline);

// View the summary collection content (should be 1 record only)
db.daily_orders_summary.find();
```

From the results, you can see that only a single order summary was generated for 01- Feb-2021, containing the *total value* and *number of orders* for that day.

Now, for the next day only (for 02-Feb-2021 orders), build the pipeline and execute the aggregation:

```
// Get the pipeline for the 2nd day
var pipeline = getDayAggPipeline("2021-02-02T00:00:00Z",
                                 "2021-02-03T00:00:00Z");

// Run aggregation for 02-Feb-2021 orders & put result in summary collection
db.orders.aggregate(pipeline);

// View the summary collection content (should be 2 record now)
db.daily_orders_summary.find();
```

From the results, you can see that order summaries exist for both days. To simulate the organization's occasional need to correct an old order retrospectively, go back and add a new *high value* order for the first day. Then, rerun the aggregation for the first day only (01-Feb-2021) to show that you can safely and correctly recalculate the summary for just one day:

```
// Retrospectively add an order to an older day (01-Feb-2021)
db.orders.insertOne(
  {
    "orderdate": ISODate("2021-02-01T09:32:07Z"),
    "value": NumberDecimal("11111.11"),
  },
)


// Get the pipeline for the 1st day again
var pipeline = getDayAggPipeline("2021-02-01T00:00:00Z",
                                 "2021-02-02T00:00:00Z");


// Re-run agg for 01-Feb-2021 overwriting 1st record in summary collection
db.orders.aggregate(pipeline);


// View summary collection (should still be 2 records but 1st changed)
db.daily_orders_summary.find();
```

From the results, you can see that two order summaries still exist, one for each of the two trading days, but the total value and order count for the first day have changed.

For completeness, also view the explain plan for the aggregation pipeline:

```
db.products.explain("executionStats").aggregate(pipeline);
```

## Expected pipeline result

The content of the daily_orders_summary collection after running the aggregation for just the first day should be similar to the following:

```
[
  {
    _id: ObjectId('6062102e7eeb772e6ca96bc7'),
    total_value: NumberDecimal('584.55'),
    total_orders: 5,
    day: ISODate('2021-02-01T00:00:00.000Z')
  }
]
```

The content of the daily_orders_summary collection after running the aggregation for the second day should be similar to the following:

```
[
  {
```

```
    _id: ObjectId('6062102e7eeb772e6ca96bc7'),
    total_value: NumberDecimal('584.55'),
    total_orders: 5,
    day: ISODate('2021-02-01T00:00:00.000Z')
  },
  {
    _id: ObjectId('606210377eeb772e6ca96bcc'),
    total_value: NumberDecimal('1180.22'),
    total_orders: 4,
    day: ISODate('2021-02-02T00:00:00.000Z')
  }
]
```

After rerunning the aggregation for the first day following the addition of the missed order, the content of the `daily_orders_summary` collection should be similar to the following (notice the first record now shows a value of one greater than before for `total_orders`, and for `total_value`, the amount is now significantly higher):

```
[
  {
    _id: ObjectId('6062102e7eeb772e6ca96bc7'),
    total_value: NumberDecimal('11695.66'),
    total_orders: 6,
    day: ISODate('2021-02-01T00:00:00.000Z')
  },
  {
    _id: ObjectId('606210377eeb772e6ca96bcc'),
    total_value: NumberDecimal('1180.22'),
    total_orders: 4,
    day: ISODate('2021-02-02T00:00:00.000Z')
  }
]
```

## Pipeline observations

- **Merging results**: The pipeline uses a $merge stage to instruct the aggregation engine to write the output to a collection rather than returning a stream of results. In this example, with the options you provide to $merge, the aggregation inserts a new record in the destination collection if a matching one doesn't already exist. If a matching record already exists, it replaces the previous version.

- **Incremental updates**: The example illustrates just two days of shop orders, albeit with only a few orders, to keep the example simple. At the end of each new trading day, you run the aggregation pipeline to generate the current day's summary only. Even after the source collection has increased in size over many years, the time it takes you to bring the summary collection up to date again stays constant. In a real-world scenario, the business might expose a graphical chart showing the changing daily orders trend over the last rolling year. This charting dashboard is not burdened by the cost of periodically regenerating values for all days in the year. There could be hundreds of thousands of orders received per day for real-world retailers, especially large ones. A day's summary may take many seconds to generate in that situation. Without an *incremental analytics* approach, if you need to generate a year's worth of daily summaries every time, it would take hours to refresh the business dashboard.

- **Idempotency**: If a retailer is aggregating tens of thousands of orders per day, then during end-of-day processing, it may choose to generate 24 hourly summary records rather than a single daily record. This provides the business with finer granularity to understand trends better. As with any software process, when generating hourly results into the summary collection, there is the risk of not fully completing if a system failure occurs. If an in-flight aggregation terminates abnormally, it may not have written all 24 summary collection records. The failure leaves the summary collection in an indeterminate and incomplete state for one of its days. However, this isn't a problem because of the way the aggregation pipeline uses the $merge stage. When an aggregation fails to complete, it can just be rerun. When the aggregation is rerun, it will regenerate all the results for the day, replacing existing summary records and filling in the missing ones. The aggregation pipeline is idempotent, and you can run it repeatedly without damaging the summary collection. The overall solution is self-healing and naturally tolerant of inadvertently aborted aggregation jobs.

- **Retrospective changes**: Sometimes, an organization may need to go back and correct records from the past, as illustrated in this example. For instance, a bank may need to fix a past payment record due to a settlement issue that only comes to light weeks later. With the approach used in this example, it is straightforward to re-execute the aggregation pipeline for a prior date, using the updated historical data. This will correctly update the specific day's summary data only, to reflect the business's current state.

# Summary

In this chapter, you learned various methods for performing advanced analytics and reporting efficiently against data in a MongoDB database.

In the next chapter, you will explore examples of using aggregation pipelines to access and distribute data securely.

# 10

# Securing Data Examples

Data management systems often need to apply filtering and masking on data and apply strict access control rules to maintain data security, privacy, and regulatory compliance. Organizations need to protect sensitive information from unauthorized access. In this chapter, you will discover ways to use aggregation pipelines to help secure the data in a MongoDB database to reduce the risk of a data breach.

This chapter will cover the following:

- Providing views that filter out sensitive records and fields
- Masking and obfuscating the data of sensitive fields
- Applying programmatic access control rules over which users can access specific subsets of data

# Redacted view

A typical data security requirement is to expose views of data to users, omitting specific sensitive records and fields. For instance, a personnel database might hide salary details while showing employee names. Due to a confidentiality clause, the system may even need to omit some employees from query results entirely. In this example, you will discover how to build an aggregation pipeline to apply such filtering rules for a view.

## Scenario

You have a user management system containing data about various people in a database, and you need to ensure a particular client application cannot view the sensitive parts of the data relating to each person.

Consequently, you will provide a read-only view of each person's data. You will use the view, named *adults*, to redact personal data and expose this view to the client application as the only way it can access personal information. The view will apply the following two rules to restrict data access:

- Only show people aged 18 and above (by checking each person's `dateofbirth` field)
- Exclude each person's `social_security_num` field from the results

> **Note**
>
> In a real-world situation, you would combine this approach with applying the MongoDB **role-based access control** (**RBAC**) rules to limit the client application to only access the view and not have access to the original collection.

## Populating the sample data

First, drop any old version of the database (if it exists), create an index, and populate the new `persons` collection with five records. Each user will include the *person's ID, name, date of birth, email address, social security number*, and *address*:

```
db = db.getSiblingDB("book-redacted-view");
db.dropDatabase();

// Create index for a persons collection
db.persons.createIndex({"dateofbirth": -1});

// Create index for non-$expr part of filter in MongoDB version < 5.0
db.persons.createIndex({"gender": 1});
```

```
// Create index for combo of $expr & non-$expr filter in MDB version >= 5.0
db.persons.createIndex({"gender": 1, "dateofbirth": -1});

// Insert records into the persons collection
db.persons.insertMany([
  {
    "person_id": "6392529400",
    "firstname": "Elise",
    "lastname": "Smith",
    "dateofbirth": ISODate("1972-01-13T09:32:07Z"),
    "gender": "FEMALE",
    "email": "elise_smith@myemail.com",
    "social_security_num": "507-28-9805",
    "address": {
        "number": 5625,
        "street": "Tipa Circle",
        "city": "Wojzinmoj",
    },
  },
  {
    "person_id": "1723338115",
    "firstname": "Olive",
    "lastname": "Ranieri",
    "dateofbirth": ISODate("1985-05-12T23:14:30Z"),
    "gender": "FEMALE",
    "email": "oranieri@warmmail.com",
    "social_security_num": "618-71-2912",
    "address": {
        "number": 9303,
        "street": "Mele Circle",
        "city": "Tobihbo",
    },
  },
  {
    "person_id": "8732762874",
    "firstname": "Toni",
    "lastname": "Jones",
    "dateofbirth": ISODate("2014-11-23T16:53:56Z"),
    "gender": "FEMALE",
    "email": "tj@wheresmyemail.com",
    "social_security_num": "001-10-3488",
    "address": {
```

```
            "number": 1,
            "street": "High Street",
            "city": "Upper Abbeywoodington",
        },
    },
    {
        "person_id": "7363629563",
        "firstname": "Bert",
        "lastname": "Gooding",
        "dateofbirth": ISODate("1941-04-07T22:11:52Z"),
        "gender": "MALE",
        "email": "bgooding@tepidmail.com",
        "social_security_num": "230-43-7633",
        "address": {
            "number": 13,
            "street": "Upper Bold Road",
            "city": "Redringtonville",
        },
    },
    {
        "person_id": "1029648329",
        "firstname": "Sophie",
        "lastname": "Celements",
        "dateofbirth": ISODate("2013-07-06T17:35:45Z"),
        "gender": "FEMALE",
        "email": "sophe@celements.net",
        "social_security_num": "377-30-5364",
        "address": {
            "number": 5,
            "street": "Innings Close",
            "city": "Basilbridge",
        },
    },
]);
```

## Defining the aggregation pipeline

You will now define a pipeline that applies a number of stages to implement the aggregation:

```
var pipeline = [
  // Filter out any persons aged 18 ($expr required to reference '$$NOW')
  {"$match":
    {"$expr":{
      "$lt": [
        "$dateofbirth",
        {"$subtract": ["$$NOW", 18*365.25*24*60*60*1000]}
      ]
    }},
  },

  // Exclude fields to be filtered out by the view
  {"$unset": [
    "_id",
    "social_security_num",
  ]},
];
```

## Executing the aggregation pipeline

Firstly, to test the defined aggregation pipeline (before using it to create a view), run the following commands to do as follows:

1. Execute the aggregation using the defined pipeline:

   ```
   db.persons.aggregate(pipeline);
   ```

2. Generate its explain plan:

   ```
   db.persons.explain("executionStats").aggregate(pipeline);
   ```

3. Now create the new *adults* view, which will automatically apply the aggregation pipeline whenever anyone queries the view:

   ```
   db.createView("adults", "persons", pipeline);
   ```

4. Execute a regular query against the view, without any filter criteria, and also run the command to observe its explain plan:

```
db.adults.find();
```

```
db.adults.explain("executionStats").find();
```

5. Execute a MongoDB Query Language query against the view, but this time with a filter to return only adults who are female, and again run the command to observe its explain plan to see how the *gender* filter affects the plan:

```
db.adults.find({"gender": "FEMALE"});
```

```
db.adults.explain("executionStats").find({"gender": "FEMALE"});
```

## Expected pipeline result

Once executed, the result for both the aggregate() command and the find() command executed on the *view* should be the same, with three documents returned, representing the three persons who are over 18 and omitting each person's social security number:

```
[
  {
    person_id: '6392529400',
    firstname: 'Elise',
    lastname: 'Smith',
    dateofbirth: ISODate('1972-01-13T09:32:07.000Z'),
    gender: 'FEMALE',
    email: 'elise_smith@myemail.com',
    address: { number: 5625,
               street: 'Tipa Circle',
               city: 'Wojzinmoj' }
  },
  {
    person_id: '1723338115',
    firstname: 'Olive',
    lastname: 'Ranieri',
    dateofbirth: ISODate('1985-05-12T23:14:30.000Z'),
    gender: 'FEMALE',
    email: 'oranieri@warmmail.com',
    address: { number: 9303,
               street: 'Mele Circle',
               city: 'Tobihbo' }
  },
```

```
  {
    person_id: '7363629563',
    firstname: 'Bert',
    lastname: 'Gooding',
    dateofbirth: ISODate('1941-04-07T22:11:52.000Z'),
    gender: 'MALE',
    email: 'bgooding@tepidmail.com',
    address: { number: 13,
               street: 'Upper Bold Road',
               city: 'Redringtonville' }
  }
]
```

The result of running `find()` against the *view* with the `"gender"`: `"FEMALE"` filter should contain only two females records because the male record has been excluded:

```
[
  {
    person_id: '6392529400',
    firstname: 'Elise',
    lastname: 'Smith',
    dateofbirth: ISODate('1972-01-13T09:32:07.000Z'),
    gender: 'FEMALE',
    email: 'elise_smith@myemail.com',
    address: { number: 5625, street: 'Tipa Circle', city: 'Wojzinmoj' }
  },
  {
    person_id: '1723338115',
    firstname: 'Olive',
    lastname: 'Ranieri',
    dateofbirth: ISODate('1985-05-12T23:14:30.000Z'),
    gender: 'FEMALE',
    email: 'oranieri@warmmail.com',
    address: { number: 9303, street: 'Mele Circle', city: 'Tobihbo' }
  }
]
```

## Pipeline observations

- **$expr and indexes:** The `NOW` system variable used here returns the current system date-time. However, you can only access this system variable via an *aggregation expression* and not directly via the regular MongoDB query syntax used by MongoDB Query Language and `$match`. You must wrap an expression using `$$NOW` inside an `$expr` operator, as described in *Chapter 4, Harnessing the Power of Expressions*, specifically the *Restrictions when using expressions within $match* section. If you use an `$expr` query operator to perform a range comparison, you can't make use of an index in versions of MongoDB earlier than version 5.0. Therefore, in this example, unless you use MongoDB 5.0 or greater, the aggregation will not take advantage of an index on `dateofbirth`. For a view, because you specify the pipeline earlier than it is ever run, you cannot obtain the current date-time at runtime by other means.

- **View finds and indexes:** Even for earlier versions before MongoDB 5.0, the explain plan for the *gender query* run against the view shows an index has been used (the index defined for the *gender field*). At runtime, a view is essentially just an aggregation pipeline you define *ahead of time*. When `db.adults.find({"gender": "FEMALE"})` is executed, the database engine dynamically appends a new `$match` stage to the end of the pipeline for the gender match. It then optimizes the pipeline by moving the content of the new `$match` stage to the pipeline's start, where possible. Finally, it adds the filter extracted from the extended `$match` stage to the aggregation's initial query, and hence it can leverage an index containing the `gender` field. The following two excerpts, from an explain plan from a version earlier than MongoDB 5.0, illustrate how the filter on `gender` and the filter on `dateofbirth` combine at runtime and how the index for `gender` is used to avoid a full collection scan:

```
'$cursor': {
  queryPlanner: {
    plannerVersion: 1,
    namespace: 'book-redacted-view.persons',
    indexFilterSet: false,
    parsedQuery: {
      '$and': [
        { gender: { '$eq': 'FEMALE' } },
        {
          '$expr': {
            '$lt': [
              '$dateofbirth',
              {
                '$subtract': [ '$$NOW', { '$const': 568036800000 } ]
                ...

  inputStage: {
    stage: 'IXSCAN',
    keyPattern: { gender: 1 },
    indexName: 'gender_1',
    direction: 'forward',
    indexBounds: { gender: [ '["FEMALE", "FEMALE"]' ] }
}
```

In MongoDB 5.0 and greater, the explain plan will show the aggregation runtime executing the pipeline more optimally by entirely using the compound index based on both the fields (gender and dateofbirth).

---

**Note**

Just because the aggregation runtime moves the content of the $match stage from the base of the pipeline to the top of this pipeline, it doesn't imply this optimization can happen in all pipelines. For example, if the middle part of the pipeline includes a $group stage, then the runtime can't move the $match stage ahead of the $group stage because this would change the functional behavior and outcome of the pipeline. See the *Aggregation Pipeline Optimization* documentation (see https://www.mongodb.com/docs/manual/core/aggregation-pipeline-optimization/) for the runtime optimizations the MongoDB database engine can apply.

# Mask sensitive fields

Data masking, or data obfuscation, is a technique that allows an organization to alter sensitive data, maintaining its structure but removing the actual sensitive content. This ensures developers and testers can work with realistic datasets without risking data misuse and allowing the organization to protect sensitive information. In this example, we will discover how to use a pipeline to mask the fields of a document.

> **Note**
>
> This example requires MongoDB version 4.4 or above. This is because you'll be using the `$rand` operator introduced in version 4.4.

## Scenario

You want to perform irreversible masking on the sensitive fields in a collection of *credit card payments*, ready to provide the output dataset to a third party for analysis, without exposing sensitive information to that third party.

The specific changes that you need to make to the payment fields include the following:

- Partially obfuscate the cardholder's name

- Obfuscate the first 12 digits of the card's number, retaining only the final 4 digits

- Adjust the card's expiry *date-time* by adding or subtracting a random amount up to a maximum of 30 days (~1 month)

- Replace the card's three-digit security code with a random set of three digits

- Adjust transaction amounts by adding or subtracting a random amount, up to a maximum of 10% of the original amount

- Change the `reported` field's boolean value to the opposite value for roughly 20% of the records

- If the embedded `customer_info` sub-document's `category` field is set to `RESTRICTED`, exclude the whole `customer_info` sub-document

## Populating the sample data

First, drop any old version of the database (if it exists) and then populate a new `payments` collection with two credit card payment documents containing sensitive data. Each document includes typical data about both the credit card and the specific payment transaction the credit card was used for:

```
db = db.getSiblingDB("book-mask-sensitive-fields");
db.dropDatabase();

// Insert records into the payments collection
db.payments.insertMany([
  {
    "card_name": "Mrs. Jane A. Doe",
    "card_num": "1234567890123456",
    "card_expiry": ISODate("2023-08-31T23:59:59Z"),
    "card_sec_code": "123",
    "card_type": "CREDIT",
    "transaction_id": "eb1bd77836e8713656d9bf2debba8900",
    "transaction_date": ISODate("2021-01-13T09:32:07Z"),
    "transaction_amount": NumberDecimal("501.98"),
    "reported": false,
    "customer_info": {
      "category": "RESTRICTED",
      "rating": 89,
      "risk": 3,
    },
  },
  {
    "card_name": "Jim Smith",
    "card_num": "9876543210987654",
    "card_expiry": ISODate("2022-12-31T23:59:59Z"),
    "card_sec_code": "987",
    "card_type": "DEBIT",
    "transaction_id": "634c416a6fbcf060bb0ba90c4ad94f60",
    "transaction_date": ISODate("2020-11-24T19:25:57Z"),
    "transaction_amount": NumberDecimal("64.01"),
    "reported": true,
    "customer_info": {
      "category": "NORMAL",
      "rating": 78,
      "risk": 55,
    },
  },
]);
```

## Defining the aggregation pipeline

You will now define a pipeline that applies a number of stages to implement the aggregation:

```
var pipeline = [
  // Replace a subset of fields with new values
  {"$set": {
    // Extract last word from the name , eg: 'Doe' from 'Mrs. Jane A. Doe'
    "card_name": {"$regexFind": {"input": "$card_name", "regex": /(\S+)$/}},

    // Mask card num 1st part retaining last 4 chars,
    // eg: '1234567890123456' -> 'XXXXXXXXXXXX3456'
    "card_num": {"$concat": [
                  "XXXXXXXXXXXX",
                  {"$substrCP": ["$card_num", 12, 4]},
                ]},

    // Add/subtract random time amount of max 30 days (~1 month) each-way
    "card_expiry": {"$add": [
                    "$card_expiry",
                    {"$floor": {
                      "$multiply": [
                        {"$subtract": [{"$rand": {}}, 0.5]},
                        2*30*24*60*60*1000
                      ]
                    }},
                  ]},

    // Replace each digit with random digit, eg: '133' -> '472'
    "card_sec_code": {"$concat": [
                      {"$toString": {
                        "$floor": {"$multiply": [{"$rand": {}}, 10]}}
                      },
                      {"$toString": {
                        "$floor": {"$multiply": [{"$rand": {}}, 10]}}
                      },
                      {"$toString": {
                        "$floor": {"$multiply": [{"$rand": {}}, 10]}}
                      },
                    ]},
```

```
    // Add/subtract random percent of amount's value up to 10% max each-way
    "transaction_amount": {"$add": [
                        "$transaction_amount",
                        {"$multiply": [
                          {"$subtract": [{"$rand": {}}, 0.5]},
                          0.2,
                          "$transaction_amount"
                        ]},
                      ]},

    // Retain field's bool value 80% of time on average, setting to the
    // opposite value 20% of time
    "reported": {"$cond": {
                "if":   {"$lte": [{"$rand": {}}, 0.8]},
                "then": "$reported",
                "else": {"$not": ["$reported"]},
            }},

    // Exclude sub-doc if sub-doc's category field's value is 'RESTRICTED'
    "customer_info": {"$cond": {
                    "if": {
                      "$eq": ["$customer_info.category", "RESTRICTED"]
                    },
                    "then": "$$REMOVE",
                    "else": "$customer_info",
                }},

    // Mark _id field to excluded from results
    "_id": "$$REMOVE",
  }},

// Take regex matched last word from the card name
// and prefix it with hardcoded value
{"$set": {
  "card_name": {"$concat": [
    "Mx. Xxx ",
    {"$ifNull": ["$card_name.match", "Anonymous"]}
  ]},
 }},
];
```

## Executing the aggregation pipeline

Next, perform the following steps:

1. Execute the aggregation using the defined pipeline:

```
db.payments.aggregate(pipeline);
```

2. Generate its explain plan:

```
db.payments.explain("executionStats").aggregate(pipeline);
```

## Expected pipeline result

Once executed, the aggregation will return two documents corresponding to the original two source documents, but this time with many of their fields redacted and obfuscated, plus the customer_info embedded document omitted for one record due to it having been marked as RESTRICTED:

```
[
  {
    card_name: 'Mx. Xxx Doe',
    card_num: 'XXXXXXXXXXXX3456',
    card_expiry: ISODate('2023-08-31T23:29:46.460Z'),
    card_sec_code: '295',
    card_type: 'CREDIT',
    transaction_id: 'eb1bd77836e8713656d9bf2debba8900',
    transaction_date: ISODate('2021-01-13T09:32:07.000Z'),
    transaction_amount: NumberDecimal('492.4016988351474881660000000000000'),
    reported: false
  },
  {
    card_name: 'Mx. Xxx Smith',
    card_num: 'XXXXXXXXXXXX7654',
    card_expiry: ISODate('2023-01-01T00:34:49.330Z'),
    card_sec_code: '437',
    card_type: 'DEBIT',
    transaction_id: '634c416a6fbcf060bb0ba90c4ad94f60',
    transaction_date: ISODate('2020-11-24T19:25:57.000Z'),
    transaction_amount: NumberDecimal('58.36081337486762223600000000000000'),
    reported: false,
    customer_info: { category: 'NORMAL', rating: 78, risk: 55 }
  }
]
```

## Pipeline observations

- **Targeted redaction**: The pipeline uses a $cond operator to return the $$REMOVE marker variable if the category field equals RESTRICTED. This informs the aggregation engine to exclude the whole customer_info sub-document from the stage's output for the document. Alternatively, the pipeline could have used a $redact stage to achieve the same. However, $redact typically has to perform more processing work as it checks every field in the document. Hence, if a pipeline is only to redact one specific sub-document, use the approach outlined in this example.

- **Regular expression**: For masking the card_name field, a regular expression operator is used to extract the last word of the field's original value. $regexFind returns metadata into the stage's output records, indicating if the match succeeded and what the matched value is. Therefore, an additional $set stage is required later in the pipeline to extract the actual matched word from this metadata and prefix it with some hard-coded text. MongoDB version 5.0 introduced a new $getField operator, which you can instead use to directly extract the *regex* result field (match). Consequently, if you are using MongoDB 5.0 or greater, you can eliminate the second $set stage from the end of your pipeline and then replace the line of code that sets the masked value of the card_name field to the following:

```
// Prefix with a hard-coded value followed by the regex extracted last
word of the card name
"card_name": {"$concat": ["Mx. Xxx ", {"$ifNull": [{"$getField":
{"field": "match", "input": {"$regexFind": {"input": "$card_name",
"regex": /(\S+)$/}}}}, "Anonymous"]}]},
```

- **Meaningful insights**: Even though the pipeline is irreversibly obfuscating fields, it doesn't mean that the masked data is useless for performing analytics to gain insights. The pipeline masks some fields by fluctuating the original values by a small but limited random percentage (e.g., card_expiry, transaction_amount), rather than replacing them with completely random values (e.g., card_sec_code). In such cases, if the input dataset is sufficiently large, then minor variances will be equaled out. For the fields that are only varied slightly, users can derive similar trends and patterns from analyzing the masked data as they would the original data.

# Role programmatic restricted view

MongoDB provides robust RBAC solutions, allowing administrators to specify user access to resources declaratively. However, there are instances when you need to programmatically apply detailed logic to limit data access based on roles. In this example, you will explore how to regulate data access using programmatic RBAC within an aggregation pipeline.

> **Note**
>
> This example requires MongoDB version 7.0 or above. This is because you'll be using the `USER_ROLES` system variable introduced in version 7.0.

## Scenario

At a medical establishment, the central IT system holds patient data that you need to share with different applications (and their users) according to the application's user role: *receptionist, nurse,* or *doctor*. Consequently, you will provide a read-only view of patient data, but the view will filter out specific sensitive fields depending on the application user's role. For example, the *receptionist's* application should not be able to access the patient's current *weight* and *medication*. However, the *doctor's* application needs this information to enable them to perform their job.

> **Note**
>
> Essentially, this example illustrates how you can apply both *record-level* (a.k.a. *row-level*) and *field-level* (a.k.a. *column-level*) access control in MongoDB. The pipeline will apply programmatic RBAC rules rather than declarative ones to enforce what data users can access within a view. In a real-world situation, you would additionally use a declarative role to limit the client application with access only to the view and not the underlying collection.

## Populating the sample data

Assuming you are using a self-installed MongoDB deployment, run the commands shown in the following code block to create the necessary roles and users to help with implementing programmatic access control:

> **Note**
>
> If you're using a *MongoDB Atlas database cluster*, then instead, use the *Atlas console* to define the roles and users for your Atlas project and its database cluster.

```
var dbName = "book-role-programmatic-restricted-view";
db = db.getSiblingDB(dbName);
db.dropDatabase();
db.dropAllRoles();
db.dropAllUsers();

// Create 3 roles to use for programmatic access control
db.createRole({"role": "Receptionist", "roles": [], "privileges": []});
db.createRole({"role": "Nurse", "roles": [], "privileges": []});
db.createRole({"role": "Doctor", "roles": [], "privileges": []});

// Create 3 users where each user will have a different role
db.createUser({
  "user": "front-desk",
  "pwd": "abc123",
  "roles": [
     {"role": "Receptionist", "db": dbName},
  ]
});
db.createUser({
  "user": "nurse-station",
  "pwd": "xyz789",
  "roles": [
    {"role": "Nurse", "db": dbName},
  ]
});
db.createUser({
  "user": "exam-room",
  "pwd": "mno456",
  "roles": [
    {"role": "Doctor", "db": dbName},
  ]
});
```

Then, you need to populate a new patients collection with four records. Each patient record includes the *patient's ID*, *name*, *date of birth*, *weight*, and *current medication*:

```
db = db.getSiblingDB("book-role-programmatic-restricted-view");

// Insert 4 records into the patients collection
db.patients.insertMany([
  {
    "id": "D40230",
    "first_name": "Chelsea",
    "last_Name": "Chow",
    "birth_date": ISODate("1984-11-07T10:12:00Z"),
    "weight": 145,
    "medication": ["Insulin", "Methotrexate"],
  },
  {
    "id": "R83165",
    "first_name": "Pharrell",
    "last_Name": "Phillips",
    "birth_date": ISODate("1993-05-30T19:44:00Z"),
    "weight": 137,
    "medication": ["Fluoxetine"],
  },
  {
    "id": "X24046",
    "first_name": "Billy",
    "last_Name": "Boaty",
    "birth_date": ISODate("1976-02-07T23:58:00Z"),
    "weight": 223,
    "medication": [],
  },
  {
    "id": "P53212",
    "first_name": "Yazz",
    "last_Name": "Yodeler",
    "birth_date": ISODate("1999-12-25T12:51:00Z"),
    "weight": 156,
    "medication": ["Tylenol", "Naproxen"],
  },
]);
```

# Defining the aggregation pipeline

You will now define a pipeline that applies a number of stages to implement the aggregation:

```
var pipeline = [
  {"$set": {
    // Exclude weight if user does not have right role
    "weight": {
      "$cond": {
        "if": {
          "$eq": [
            {"$setIntersection": [
              "$$USER_ROLES.role",
              ["Doctor", "Nurse"]
            ]},
            []
          ]
        },
        "then": "$$REMOVE",
        "else": "$weight"
      }
    },

    // Exclude weight if user does not have right role
    "medication": {
      "$cond": {
        "if": {
          "$eq": [
            {"$setIntersection":
              ["$$USER_ROLES.role",
              ["Doctor"]
            ]},
            []
          ]
        },
        "then": "$$REMOVE",
        "else": "$medication"
      }
    },

    // Always exclude _id
    "_id": "$$REMOVE",
  }},
]
```

Then, create a new view called `patients_view`, which will automatically apply the aggregation pipeline whenever anyone queries the view:

```
db.createView("patients_view", "patients", pipeline);
```

## Executing the aggregation pipeline

Now, authenticate as `front-desk`, which has the `Receptionist` role, and execute a query against the view to observe which fields of each record the application can see:

```
db.auth("front-desk", "abc123");

db.patients_view.find();
```

Then, authenticate as `nurse-station`, which has the `Nurse` role, and execute a query against the view to observe which fields of each record the application can see:

```
db.auth("nurse-station", "xyz789");

db.patients_view.find();
```

Then, authenticate as `exam-room`, which has the `Doctor` role, and execute a query against the view to observe which fields of each record the application can see:

```
db.auth("exam-room", "mno456");

db.patients_view.find();
```

Finally, also view the explain plan for the aggregation pipeline:

```
db.patients_view.explain("executionStats").find();
```

## Expected pipeline result

Running a query on the view for `front-desk` (*receptionist*) includes patient data in the results but omits each patient's weight and medication fields because the user's role does not have sufficient privileges to access those fields:

```
[
  {
    id: 'D40230',
    first_name: 'Chelsea',
    last_Name: 'Chow',
    birth_date: ISODate("1984-11-07T10:12:00.000Z")
  },
```

```
  {
    id: 'R83165',
    first_name: 'Pharrell',
    last_Name: 'Phillips',
    birth_date: ISODate("1993-05-30T19:44:00.000Z")
  },
  {
    id: 'X24046',
    first_name: 'Billy',
    last_Name: 'Boaty',
    birth_date: ISODate("1976-02-07T23:58:00.000Z")
  },
  {
    id: 'P53212',
    first_name: 'Yazz',
    last_Name: 'Yodeler',
    birth_date: ISODate("1999-12-25T12:51:00.000Z")
  }
]
```

Running a query on the view for nurse-station (*nurse*) includes patient data in the results similar to the previous user, but with the weight field also shown for each record:

```
[
  {
    id: 'D40230',
    first_name: 'Chelsea',
    last_Name: 'Chow',
    birth_date: ISODate("1984-11-07T10:12:00.000Z"),
    weight: 145
  },
  {
    id: 'R83165',
    first_name: 'Pharrell',
    last_Name: 'Phillips',
    birth_date: ISODate("1993-05-30T19:44:00.000Z"),
    weight: 137
  },
```

```
  {
    id: 'X24046',
    first_name: 'Billy',
    last_Name: 'Boaty',
    birth_date: ISODate("1976-02-07T23:58:00.000Z"),
    weight: 223
  },
  {
    id: 'P53212',
    first_name: 'Yazz',
    last_Name: 'Yodeler',
    birth_date: ISODate("1999-12-25T12:51:00.000Z"),
    weight: 156
  }
]
```

Running a query on the view for exam-room (*doctor*) includes each patient's entire data in the results, including the weight and medication fields, due to the user having sufficient privileges to access those fields:

```
[
  {
    id: 'D40230',
    first_name: 'Chelsea',
    last_Name: 'Chow',
    birth_date: ISODate("1984-11-07T10:12:00.000Z"),
    weight: 145,
    medication: [ 'Insulin', 'Methotrexate' ]
  },
  {
    id: 'R83165',
    first_name: 'Pharrell',
    last_Name: 'Phillips',
    birth_date: ISODate("1993-05-30T19:44:00.000Z"),
    weight: 137,
    medication: [ 'Fluoxetine' ]
  },
```

```
  {
    id: 'X24046',
    first_name: 'Billy',
    last_Name: 'Boaty',
    birth_date: ISODate("1976-02-07T23:58:00.000Z"),
    weight: 223,
    medication: []
  },
  {
    id: 'P53212',
    first_name: 'Yazz',
    last_Name: 'Yodeler',
    birth_date: ISODate("1999-12-25T12:51:00.000Z"),
    weight: 156,
    medication: [ 'Tylenol', 'Naproxen' ]
  }
].
```

## Pipeline observations

- **Programmatic versus declarative RBAC**: MongoDB provides RBAC to enable an administrator to govern access to database resources. The administrator achieves this by *declaratively* granting system users to one or more roles (e.g., `readWrite`, `find`) against one or more resources (e.g., `collectionABC`, `viewXYZ`). However, this chapter's example goes further by allowing you to include business logic to enforce *programmatic* access rules based on the connecting system user's role. In the example, these *rules* are captured in aggregation expressions, which use the `$$USER_ROLES` system variable to look up the roles associated with the current requesting system user. The pipeline's logic for both `weight` and `medication` uses a condition expression (`$cond`) to see whether the connected user is a member of a named role, and if not, it removes the field. Given the entire set of MongoDB aggregation operators at your disposal, you can implement whatever custom access control logic you want.

- **Avoid proliferation of views**: An alternative solution for this example is enabling a purely declarative RBAC approach by defining three different *hard-coded* views rather than mandating that you code programmatic rules in one view. You would specify one view per role (e.g., `receptionist_patients_view`, `nurse_patients_view`, `doctor_patients_view`). Each view would contain an almost identical aggregation pipeline, varying only in the specific fields it omits. However, such an approach introduces duplication; whenever developers change the view's core aggregation pipeline, they must apply the changes in three places. This proliferation of views will be exasperated when there are hundreds of roles involved in a non-trivial application. Thus, adding a programmatic RBAC approach to *fine-tune* access rules reduces maintenance costs and friction to increase agility.

- **Filtering on a view with index pushdowns**: As you saw in the *Redacted view* example in this chapter, the view's aggregation pipeline can leverage an index. In some situations, the aggregation runtime can move the view's filter to the start of the pipeline, pushing the filter down to leverage an index more optimally.

- **Field-level versus record-level access control**: The example view's pipeline applies field-level access control rules (e.g., the nurse role cannot access a document's medication field). However, adding logic to the pipeline to filter out specific documents is also straightforward, using the approach highlighted in the *Redacted view* example in this chapter to enforce record-level access control. You achieve this by optionally applying a $match operator in the pipeline if the user has a specific role (e.g., receptionist) rather than just filtering based on the value of some fields in each document (e.g., if a document's date field is less than a specific point in time).

- **Factor out logic to dynamic metadata**: The examples in this chapter use hard-coded logic to enforce access control rules. Every time the business needs to change a rule (e.g., adjust what fields Nurse can see), a developer must modify and retest the code. When such business rules frequently change in dynamic applications, it may be undesirable to mandate a code change and application rerelease for each change. Instead, you could factor out metadata into a new collection, capturing the mappings of the names of fields each role can access. A business administrator could dynamically modify the mappings in this *special* collection via an administrative user interface. At runtime, the view's pipeline would use a $lookup stage to map the current user's role (using USER_ROLES) to the fields the role can access. The pipeline would then use this list to conditionally show or omit values of each field in its result.

## Summary

In this chapter, you have learned techniques to apply filtering and masking on data and apply strict access control rules to maintain data security.

In the next chapter, you will explore how aggregations can be used to extract summarized information from time-series data.

# 11

# Time-Series Examples

Time-series data, characterized by its chronological sequence and high generation frequency, differs from conventional data. This time-series data is crucial for forecasting and trend analysis in many financial services and **Internet of Things (IoT)** applications. MongoDB provides specialized features tailored for processing vast amounts of data and distinct query patterns, such as windowing, associated with time-series use cases. In this chapter, you will look at examples of how you can use aggregation pipelines to extract insight from time-series data.

In this chapter, you will learn about the following:

- Analyzing rolling windows of data
- Computing the power consumption of devices
- Tracking behavior changes of devices

# IoT power consumption

In industrial IT, organizations must accurately compute the power consumption of devices to optimize energy use, reduce costs, and ensure sustainable operations. They need specialized database features to manage the vast and dynamic data generated by these devices and then offer real-time analytics for predictive modeling to maintain efficient energy management and operational continuity. In this example, you will explore how to build an aggregation pipeline to calculate the power consumption of devices.

> **Note**
>
> For this example, you require MongoDB version 5.0 or above. This is because you'll be using *time-series collections*, the $setWindowFields stage, and the $integral operator introduced in version 5.0.

## Scenario

You are monitoring various air-conditioning units running in two buildings on an industrial campus. Every 30 minutes, a device in each unit sends the unit's current power consumption reading back to base, which is persisted in a central database. You want to analyze this data to see how much energy in **kilowatt-hours (kWh)** each air-conditioning unit has consumed over the last hour for each reading received. Further, you want to compute the total energy consumed by all the air-conditioning units combined in each building for every hour.

## Populating the sample data

First, drop any old versions of the database (if they exist) and then populate a new device_readings collection with device readings spanning three hours of a day for air-conditioning units in two different buildings:

```
db = db.getSiblingDB("book-iot-power-consumption");
db.dropDatabase();

// Use a time-series collection for optimal processing
// NOTE: This command can be commented out & this example will still work
db.createCollection("device_readings", {
  "timeseries": {
    "timeField": "timestamp",
    "metaField": "deviceID",
    "granularity": "minutes"
  }
});
```

```
// Create cmpnd idx for performance of partitionBy/sortBy of setWindowFields
db.device_readings.createIndex({"deviceID": 1, "timestamp": 1});

// Insert 18 records into the device readings collection
db.device_readings.insertMany([
  // 11:29am device readings
  {
    "buildingID": "Building-ABC",
    "deviceID": "UltraAirCon-111",
    "timestamp": ISODate("2021-07-03T11:29:59Z"),
    "powerKilowatts": 8,
  },
  {
    "buildingID": "Building-ABC",
    "deviceID": "UltraAirCon-222",
    "timestamp": ISODate("2021-07-03T11:29:59Z"),
    "powerKilowatts": 7,
  },
  {
    "buildingID": "Building-XYZ",
    "deviceID": "UltraAirCon-666",
    "timestamp": ISODate("2021-07-03T11:29:59Z"),
    "powerKilowatts": 10,
  },

  // 11:59am device readings
  {
    "buildingID": "Building-ABC",
    "deviceID": "UltraAirCon-222",
    "timestamp": ISODate("2021-07-03T11:59:59Z"),
    "powerKilowatts": 9,
  },
  {
    "buildingID": "Building-ABC",
    "deviceID": "UltraAirCon-111",
    "timestamp": ISODate("2021-07-03T11:59:59Z"),
    "powerKilowatts": 8,
  },
  {
    "buildingID": "Building-XYZ",
    "deviceID": "UltraAirCon-666",
    "timestamp": ISODate("2021-07-03T11:59:59Z"),
    "powerKilowatts": 11,
```

```
  },

  // 12:29pm device readings
  {
    "buildingID": "Building-ABC",
    "deviceID": "UltraAirCon-222",
    "timestamp": ISODate("2021-07-03T12:29:59Z"),
    "powerKilowatts": 9,
  },
  {
    "buildingID": "Building-ABC",
    "deviceID": "UltraAirCon-111",
    "timestamp": ISODate("2021-07-03T12:29:59Z"),
    "powerKilowatts": 9,
  },
  {
    "buildingID": "Building-XYZ",
    "deviceID": "UltraAirCon-666",
    "timestamp": ISODate("2021-07-03T12:29:59Z"),
    "powerKilowatts": 10,
  },

  // 12:59pm device readings
  {
    "buildingID": "Building-ABC",
    "deviceID": "UltraAirCon-222",
    "timestamp": ISODate("2021-07-03T12:59:59Z"),
    "powerKilowatts": 8,
  },
  {
    "buildingID": "Building-ABC",
    "deviceID": "UltraAirCon-111",
    "timestamp": ISODate("2021-07-03T12:59:59Z"),
    "powerKilowatts": 8,
  },
  {
    "buildingID": "Building-XYZ",
    "deviceID": "UltraAirCon-666",
    "timestamp": ISODate("2021-07-03T12:59:59Z"),
    "powerKilowatts": 11,
  },
```

```
// 13:29pm device readings
{
  "buildingID": "Building-ABC",
  "deviceID": "UltraAirCon-222",
  "timestamp": ISODate("2021-07-03T13:29:59Z"),
  "powerKilowatts": 9,
},
{
  "buildingID": "Building-ABC",
  "deviceID": "UltraAirCon-111",
  "timestamp": ISODate("2021-07-03T13:29:59Z"),
  "powerKilowatts": 9,
},
{
  "buildingID": "Building-XYZ",
  "deviceID": "UltraAirCon-666",
  "timestamp": ISODate("2021-07-03T13:29:59Z"),
  "powerKilowatts": 10,
},

// 13:59pm device readings
{
  "buildingID": "Building-ABC",
  "deviceID": "UltraAirCon-222",
  "timestamp": ISODate("2021-07-03T13:59:59Z"),
  "powerKilowatts": 8,
},
{
  "buildingID": "Building-ABC",
  "deviceID": "UltraAirCon-111",
  "timestamp": ISODate("2021-07-03T13:59:59Z"),
  "powerKilowatts": 8,
},
{
  "buildingID": "Building-XYZ",
  "deviceID": "UltraAirCon-666",
  "timestamp": ISODate("2021-07-03T13:59:59Z"),
  "powerKilowatts": 11,
},
]);
```

## Defining the aggregation pipeline

You will be building two pipelines:

1.  Define a pipeline ready to perform an aggregation to calculate the energy an air-conditioning unit has consumed over the last hour for each reading received:

    ```
    var pipelineRawReadings = [
      // Calc each unit energy consumed in last hour for each reading
      {"$setWindowFields": {
        "partitionBy": "$deviceID",
        "sortBy": {"timestamp": 1},
        "output": {
          "consumedKilowattHours": {
            "$integral": {
              "input": "$powerKilowatts",
              "unit": "hour",
            },
            "window": {
              "range": [-1, "current"],
              "unit": "hour",
            },
          },
        },
      }},
    ];
    ```

2.  Define a pipeline ready to compute the total energy consumed by all the air-conditioning units combined in each building for every hour:

    ```
    var pipelineBuildingsSummary = [
      // Calc each unit energy consumed in last hour for each reading
      {"$setWindowFields": {
        "partitionBy": "$deviceID",
        "sortBy": {"timestamp": 1},
        "output": {
          "consumedKilowattHours": {
            "$integral": {
              "input": "$powerKilowatts",
              "unit": "hour",
            },
            "window": {
              "range": [-1, "current"],
              "unit": "hour",
            },
    ```

```
      },
    },
  }},

  // Sort each reading by unit/device and then by timestamp
  {"$sort": {
    "deviceID": 1,
    "timestamp": 1,
  }},

  // Group readings together for each hour for each device using
  // the last calculated energy consumption field for each hour
  {"$group": {
    "_id": {
      "deviceID": "$deviceID",
      "date": {
          "$dateTrunc": {
            "date": "$timestamp",
            "unit": "hour",
          }
      },
    },
    "buildingID": {"$last": "$buildingID"},
    "consumedKilowattHours": {"$last": "$consumedKilowattHours"},
  }},

  // Sum together the energy consumption for the whole building
  // for each hour across all the units in the building
  {"$group": {
    "_id": {
      "buildingID": "$buildingID",
      "dayHour": {
        "$dateToString": {
          "format": "%Y-%m-%d   %H",
          "date": "$_id.date"
        }
      },
    },
    "consumedKilowattHours": {"$sum": "$consumedKilowattHours"},
  }},

  // Sort the results by each building and then by each hourly summary
  {"$sort": {
```

```
        "_id.buildingID": 1,
        "_id.dayHour": 1,
      }},

      // Make the results more presentable with meaningful field names
      {"$set": {
        "buildingID": "$_id.buildingID",
        "dayHour": "$_id.dayHour",
        "_id": "$$REMOVE",
      }},
    ];
```

## Executing the aggregation pipeline

Execute an aggregation using the first pipeline to calculate the energy an air-conditioning unit has consumed over the last hour for each reading received, and also run the command to see its explain plan:

```
db.device_readings.aggregate(pipelineRawReadings);

db.device_readings.explain("executionStats").aggregate(pipelineRawReadings);
```

Execute an aggregation using the second pipeline to compute the total energy consumed by all the air-conditioning units combined in each building, for every hour, and also run the command to see its explain plan:

```
db.device_readings.aggregate(pipelineBuildingsSummary);

db.device_readings.explain("executionStats").
  aggregate(pipelineBuildingsSummary);
```

## Expected pipeline result

For the first executed pipeline to calculate the energy an air-conditioning unit has consumed over the last hour for each reading received, results like the following should be returned:

> **Note**
> The following code has been redacted for brevity and only shows the first few records.

```
[
  {
```

    _id: ObjectId("60ed5e679ea1f9f74814ca2b"),
    buildingID: 'Building-ABC',
    deviceID: 'UltraAirCon-111',
    timestamp: ISODate("2021-07-03T11:29:59.000Z"),
    powerKilowatts: 8,
    consumedKilowattHours: 0
  },
  {
    _id: ObjectId("60ed5e679ea1f9f74814ca2f"),
    buildingID: 'Building-ABC',
    deviceID: 'UltraAirCon-111',
    timestamp: ISODate("2021-07-03T11:59:59.000Z"),
    powerKilowatts: 8,
    consumedKilowattHours: 4
  },
  {
    _id: ObjectId("60ed5e679ea1f9f74814ca32"),
    buildingID: 'Building-ABC',
    deviceID: 'UltraAirCon-111',
    timestamp: ISODate("2021-07-03T12:29:59.000Z"),
    powerKilowatts: 9,
    consumedKilowattHours: 8.25
  },
  {
    _id: ObjectId("60ed5e679ea1f9f74814ca35"),
    buildingID: 'Building-ABC',
    deviceID: 'UltraAirCon-111',
    timestamp: ISODate("2021-07-03T12:59:59.000Z"),
    powerKilowatts: 8,
    consumedKilowattHours: 8.5
  },
  {
    _id: ObjectId("60ed5e679ea1f9f74814ca38"),
    buildingID: 'Building-ABC',
    deviceID: 'UltraAirCon-111',
    timestamp: ISODate("2021-07-03T13:29:59.000Z"),
    powerKilowatts: 9,
    consumedKilowattHours: 8.5
  },
  ...
  ...
]

For the second executed pipeline to compute the total energy consumed by all the air-conditioning units combined in each building for every hour, the following results should be returned:

```
[
  {
    buildingID: 'Building-ABC',
    dayHour: '2021-07-03  11',
    consumedKilowattHours: 8
  },
  {
    buildingID: 'Building-ABC',
    dayHour: '2021-07-03  12',
    consumedKilowattHours: 17.25
  },
  {
    buildingID: 'Building-ABC',
    dayHour: '2021-07-03  13',
    consumedKilowattHours: 17
  },
  {
    buildingID: 'Building-XYZ',
    dayHour: '2021-07-03  11',
    consumedKilowattHours: 5.25
  },
  {
    buildingID: 'Building-XYZ',
    dayHour: '2021-07-03  12',
    consumedKilowattHours: 10.5
  },
  {
    buildingID: 'Building-XYZ',
    dayHour: '2021-07-03  13',
    consumedKilowattHours: 10.5
  }
]
```

## Pipeline observations

- **Integral trapezoidal rule**: As documented in the *MongoDB Manual* (see `https://www.mongodb.com/docs/manual/reference/operator/aggregation/integral/`), the `$integral` operator *returns an approximation for the mathematical integral value, which is calculated using the trapezoidal rule.* For non-mathematicians, this explanation may be hard to understand. You may find it easier to comprehend the behavior of the `$integral` operator by studying *Figure 11.1* and the explanation that follows:

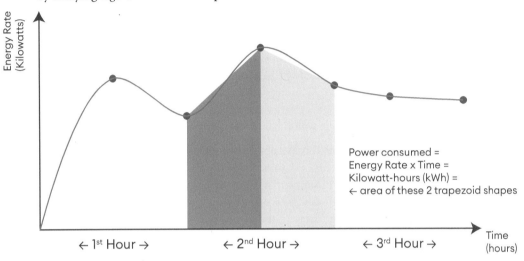

Figure 11.1: Integral trapezoidal rule

Essentially, the *trapezoidal rule* determines the area of a region between two points under a graph by matching the region with a trapezoid shape that approximately fits this region and then calculates the area of this trapezoid. You can see a set of points in *Figure 11.1* with the matched trapezoid shape underneath each pair of points. For this *IoT power consumption* example, the points on the graph represent an air-conditioning unit's power readings captured every 30 minutes. The *y* axis is the *energy rate (i.e., power rate)* in kilowatts, and the *x* axis is the *time* in hours to indicate when the device captured each reading. Consequently, for this example, the energy consumed by the air-conditioning unit for a given hour's span is the area of the hour's specific section under the graph. This section's area is approximately the area of the two trapezoids shown. Using the `$integral` operator for the window of time you define in the `$setWindowFields` stage, you are asking for this approximate area to be calculated, which is the kWh consumed by the air-conditioning unit in one hour.

- **Window range definition**: For every captured document representing a device reading, this example's pipeline identifies a window of *one hour* of previous documents relative to this *current* document. The pipeline uses this set of documents as the input for the $integral operator. It defines this window range in the range: [-1, "current"], unit: "hour" setting. The pipeline assigns the output of the $integral calculation to a new field called consumedKilowattHours.

- **One-hour range versus hours output**: The fact that the $setWindowFields stage in the pipeline defines unit: "hour" in two places may appear redundant at face value. However, this is not the case, and each serves a different purpose. As described in the previous observation, unit: "hour" for the "window" option helps dictate the window size of the previous number of documents to analyze. However, unit: "hour" for the $integral operator defines that the output should be in hours (*kWh* in this example), yielding the result consumedKilowattHours: 8.5 for one of the processed device readings. However, if the pipeline defined this $integral parameter to be "unit": "minute" instead, which is perfectly valid, the output value would be 510 kilowatt-minutes (i.e., 8.5 x 60 minutes).

- **Optional time-series collection**: This example uses a time-series collection to efficiently store sequences of device measurements over time. Employing a time-series collection is optional, as shown in the NOTE JavaScript comment in the example code. The aggregation pipeline does not need to be changed and achieves the same output if you use a regular collection instead. However, when dealing with large datasets, the aggregation will complete quicker by employing a time-series collection.

- **Index for partition by and sort by**: In this example, you define the index {deviceID: 1, timestamp: 1} to optimize the use of the combination of the partitionBy and sortBy parameters in the $setWindowFields stage. This means that the aggregation runtime does not have to perform a slow in-memory sort based on these two fields, and it also avoids the pipeline stage memory limit of 100 MB. It is beneficial to use this index regardless of whether you employ a regular collection or adopt a time-series collection.

# State change boundaries

Continuing on the industrial IT theme, an organization managing a large estate of devices needs to identify operating trends and rhythms across its devices to control costs and enable proactive measures, such as predictive maintenance. In this example, you will discover how to build an aggregation pipeline to identify patterns for when devices are in use or idle.

> **Note**
>
> For this example, you require MongoDB version 5.0 or above. This is because you will use time-series collections, the $setWindowFields stage, and the $shift operator introduced in version 5.0.

## Scenario

You are monitoring various industrial devices (e.g., heaters and fans) contained in the business locations of your clients. You want to understand the typical patterns of when these devices are on and off to help you optimize for sustainability by reducing energy costs and their carbon footprint. The source database contains periodic readings for every device, capturing whether each is currently on or off. You need a less verbose view that condenses this data, highlighting each device's timespan in a particular on or off state.

## Populating the sample data

First, drop any old versions of the database (if they exist) and then populate the device status collection. Each reading includes the *device's ID*, the *timestamp* when the measurement was taken, and the *state* of the device at the time (on or off):

```
db = db.getSiblingDB("book-state-change-boundaries");
db.dropDatabase();

// Use a time-series collection for optimal processing
// NOTE: This command can be commented out & the full example will still work
db.createCollection("device_status", {
  "timeseries": {
    "timeField": "timestamp",
    "metaField": "deviceID",
    "granularity": "minutes"
  }
});
```

```
// Create cmpnd idx for performance of partitionBy/sortBy of setWindowFields
db.device_status.createIndex({"deviceID": 1, "timestamp": 1});

// Insert 9 records into the deployments collection
db.device_status.insertMany([
  {
    "deviceID": "HEATER-111",
    "timestamp": ISODate("2021-07-03T11:09:00Z"),
    "state": "on",
  },
  {
    "deviceID": "FAN-999",
    "timestamp": ISODate("2021-07-03T11:09:00Z"),
    "state": "on",
  },
  {
    "deviceID": "HEATER-111",
    "timestamp": ISODate("2021-07-03T11:19:00Z"),
    "state": "on",
  },
  {
    "deviceID": "HEATER-111",
    "timestamp": ISODate("2021-07-03T11:29:00Z"),
    "state": "on",
  },
  {
    "deviceID": "FAN-999",
    "timestamp": ISODate("2021-07-03T11:39:00Z"),
    "state": "off",
  },
  {
    "deviceID": "HEATER-111",
    "timestamp": ISODate("2021-07-03T11:39:00Z"),
    "state": "off",
  },
  {
    "deviceID": "HEATER-111",
    "timestamp": ISODate("2021-07-03T11:49:00Z"),
    "state": "off",
  },
```

```
  {
    "deviceID": "HEATER-111",
    "timestamp": ISODate("2021-07-03T11:59:00Z"),
    "state": "on",
  },
  {
    "deviceID": "DEHUMIDIFIER-555",
    "timestamp": ISODate("2021-07-03T11:29:00Z"),
    "state": "on",
  },
]);
```

## Defining the aggregation pipeline

You will now define a pipeline that applies a number of stages to implement the aggregation:

```
var pipeline = [
  // Capture previous+next records' state into new fields in current record
  {"$setWindowFields": {
    "partitionBy": "$deviceID",
    "sortBy": {"timestamp": 1},
    "output": {
      "previousState": {
        "$shift": {
          "output": "$state",
          "by": -1,
        }
      },
      "nextState": {
        "$shift": {
          "output": "$state",
          "by": 1,
        }
      },
    }
  }},

  // Use current record's timestamp as "startTimestamp" only if state
  // changed from previous record in series, and only set "endMarkerDate"
  // to current record's timestamp if the state changes between current
  // and next records in the series
  {"$set": {
```

```
      "startTimestamp" : {
        "$cond": [
          {"$eq": ["$state", "$previousState"]},
          "$$REMOVE",
          "$timestamp",
        ]
      },
      "endMarkerDate" : {
        "$cond": [
          {"$eq": ["$state", "$nextState"]},
          "$$REMOVE",
          "$timestamp",
        ]
      },
    }},

    // Only keep records where the state has just changed or is just about
    // to change - therefore, this will be mostly start/end pairs, but not
    // always, if the state change only lasted one record
    {"$match": {
      "$expr": {
        "$or": [
          {"$ne": ["$state", "$previousState"]},
          {"$ne": ["$state", "$nextState"]},
        ]
      }
    }},

    // Set "nextMarkerDate" to the timestamp of the next record in the
    // series - this will be set to 'null', if there is no no next record,
    // to indicate 'unbounded'
    {"$setWindowFields": {
      "partitionBy": "$deviceID",
      "sortBy": {"timestamp": 1},
      "output": {
        "nextMarkerDate": {
          "$shift": {
            "output": "$timestamp",
            "by": 1,
          }
        },
      }
    }},
```

```
// Only keep records at the start of the state change boundaries (throw
// away matching pair end records, if any)
{"$match": {
  "$expr": {
    "$ne": ["$state", "$previousState"],
  }
}},


// If no boundary after this record (it's the last matching record in
// the series), set "endTimestamp" as unbounded (null).
//
// Otherwise, if this start boundary record was also an end boundary
// record (not paired - with only 1 record before state changed), set
// "endTimestamp" to end timestamp.
//
// Otherwise, set "endTimestamp" to what was the captured timestamp
// from the original matching pair in the series (where the end paired
// record has since been removed).
{"$set": {
  "endTimestamp" : {
    "$switch": {
      "branches": [
        // Unbounded, so no final timestamp in series
        {"case":
          {"$eq": [{"$type": "$nextMarkerDate"}, "null"]},
          "then": null
        },
        // Use end timestamp from what was same end record as start record
        {"case":
          {"$ne": [{"$type": "$endMarkerDate"}, "missing"]},
          "then": "$endMarkerDate"
        },
      ],
      // Use timestamp from what was an end record paired with
      // separate start record
      "default": "$nextMarkerDate",
    }
  },
}},
```

```
// Remove unwanted fields from the final result
{"$unset": [
  "_id",
  "timestamp",
  "previousState",
  "nextState",
  "endMarkerDate",
  "nextMarkerDate",
]}
];
```

## Executing the aggregation pipeline

Next, perform the following steps:

1.  Execute the aggregation using the defined pipeline:

    ```
    db.device_status.aggregate(pipeline);
    ```

2.  Generate its explain plan:

    ```
    db.device_status.explain("executionStats").aggregate(pipeline);
    ```

## Expected pipeline result

Once executed, the aggregation will return six documents, each of which captures the duration between two state change boundaries (on→off or off→on) for a device, as shown:

```
[
  {
    deviceID: 'DEHUMIDIFIER-555',
    state: 'on',
    startTimestamp: ISODate("2021-07-03T11:29:00.000Z"),
    endTimestamp: null
  },
  {
    deviceID: 'FAN-999',
    state: 'on',
    startTimestamp: ISODate("2021-07-03T11:09:00.000Z"),
    endTimestamp: ISODate("2021-07-03T11:39:00.000Z")
  },
```

```
  {
    deviceID: 'FAN-999',
    state: 'off',
    startTimestamp: ISODate("2021-07-03T11:39:00.000Z"),
    endTimestamp: null
  },
  {
    deviceID: 'HEATER-111',
    state: 'on',
    startTimestamp: ISODate("2021-07-03T11:09:00.000Z"),
    endTimestamp: ISODate("2021-07-03T11:29:00.000Z")
  },
  {
    deviceID: 'HEATER-111',
    state: 'off',
    startTimestamp: ISODate("2021-07-03T11:39:00.000Z"),
    endTimestamp: ISODate("2021-07-03T11:49:00.000Z")
  },
  {
    deviceID: 'HEATER-111',
    state: 'on',
    startTimestamp: ISODate("2021-07-03T11:59:00.000Z"),
    endTimestamp: null
  }
]
```

## Pipeline observations

- **Null end timestamps**: The last record for each specific device has the value of its `endTimestamp` field set to `null`. The `null` value indicates that this record contains the final known state of the device.

- **Peeking at one document from another**: You can apply aggregation operations spanning multiple documents using the windowing stage (`$setWindowFields`). Combined with its shift operator (`$shift`), you can peek at the content of preceding or following documents and bring some of that other document's content into the current document. In this example, you copy the device's state from the previous document (`-1` offset) and the following document (`+1` offset) into the current document. Capturing these adjacent values enables subsequent stages in your pipeline to determine whether the current device has changed state. Using `$shift` relies on the documents already being partitioned (e.g., by *device ID*) and sorted (e.g., by *timestamp*), which the containing `$setWindowFields` stage is enforcing.

- **Double use of a windowing stage**: The pipeline's first windowing stage and the subsequent matching stage capture device documents where the device's state has changed from `on` to `off` or vice versa. In many cases, this results in adjacent pairs of documents where the first document in the pair captures the first time the device has a new state, and the second document captures the last time it was in that same state before changing again. The example pipeline requires another windowing stage to condense each pair of *boundary* documents into one document. This second windowing stage again uses a shift operator to bring the timestamp of the pair's second document into a new field in the pair's first document. Consequently, single documents now exist containing both the start and end timestamps of a particular device's state. Finally, the pipeline employs further logic to clean things up because, in some situations, there won't be a pair of related documents. For example, if a device's recorded state changes and immediately changes again, or it's the last recorded state of the device, there will be no paired document marking the end state.

- **Time-series collection and indexes**: As with the previous example, the aggregation can optionally use a time-series collection to store sequences of device measurements over time for efficient storage and fast querying. Additionally, as with the previous example, the aggregation can leverage an index for `{deviceID: 1, timestamp: 1}` to avoid the `$setWindowFields` stage having to perform a slow in-memory sort operation.

# Summary

In this chapter, you explored examples of using time-series windowing aggregations to compute summaries and trends for industrial IoT devices.

In the next chapter, you will learn how to process and manipulate array fields contained in documents without having to unwind and regroup the content of each array.

# 12

# Array Manipulation Examples

Storing and processing documents with fields that contain arrays of sub-documents is an essential aspect of MongoDB. The aggregation framework offers rich operators to process array contents, which is important to avoid performance penalties from needlessly unwinding and regrouping arrays. The aggregation pipeline's ability to handle nested operations makes even the most challenging array manipulation tasks feasible. However, these solutions can sometimes appear complicated. In this chapter, you will learn how to break down array manipulation problems into manageable pieces, streamlining your assembly of solutions.

This chapter will cover the following topics:

- Generating summaries of array contents, such as highs and lows
- Sorting and changing the orientation of the contents of arrays
- Calculating averages and percentiles for arrays
- Grouping elements of arrays by common keys
- Joining elements from different array fields together
- Comparing the contents of two different array fields

# Summarizing arrays for first, last, minimum, maximum, and average values

Financial time-series data, such as the values of currency pairs (e.g., euro-to-US dollar), fluctuates due to changing market factors. Financial institutions need rapid analytics to identify highs, lows, and averages. Even basic immediate insight such as these enable institutions to make fast, informed trading decisions, capitalizing on opportunities and avoiding potential risks. In this example, you will discover how to generate summary data for fluctuating currency-pair values.

> **Note**
>
> This example requires MongoDB version 4.4 or above. This is because you'll be using the `$first` and `$last` array operators, which were first introduced in version 4.4.

## Scenario

You want to generate daily summaries for the exchange rates of foreign currency pairs. You need to analyze an array of persisted hourly rates for each currency pair for each day. You will output a daily summary of the *open* (first), *close* (last), *low* (minimum), *high* (maximum), and *average* exchange rate values for each currency pair.

## Populating the sample data

First, drop any old versions of the database (if they exist) and then populate the new *currency-pair daily* collection with a summary record for the values of a currency-pair on a given day. Each document includes the *name* of a currency pair, the *day* the document applies to, and an array of the *hourly values* of the currency pair for that day:

```
db = db.getSiblingDB("book-array-high-low-avg");
db.dropDatabase();

// Inserts records into the currency_pair_values collection
db.currency_pair_values.insertMany([
```

```
  {
    "currencyPair": "USD/GBP",
    "day": ISODate("2021-07-05T00:00:00.000Z"),
    "hour_values": [
      NumberDecimal("0.71903411"), NumberDecimal("0.72741832"),
      NumberDecimal("0.71997271"), NumberDecimal("0.73837282"),
      NumberDecimal("0.75262621"), NumberDecimal("0.74739202"),
      NumberDecimal("0.72972612"), NumberDecimal("0.73837292"),
      NumberDecimal("0.72393721"), NumberDecimal("0.72746837"),
      NumberDecimal("0.73787372"), NumberDecimal("0.73746483"),
      NumberDecimal("0.73373632"), NumberDecimal("0.75737372"),
      NumberDecimal("0.76783263"), NumberDecimal("0.75632828"),
      NumberDecimal("0.75362823"), NumberDecimal("0.74682282"),
      NumberDecimal("0.74628263"), NumberDecimal("0.74726262"),
      NumberDecimal("0.75376722"), NumberDecimal("0.75799222"),
      NumberDecimal("0.75545352"), NumberDecimal("0.74998835"),
    ],
  },
  {
    "currencyPair": "EUR/GBP",
    "day": ISODate("2021-07-05T00:00:00.000Z"),
    "hour_values": [
      NumberDecimal("0.86739394"), NumberDecimal("0.86763782"),
      NumberDecimal("0.87362937"), NumberDecimal("0.87373652"),
      NumberDecimal("0.88002736"), NumberDecimal("0.87866372"),
      NumberDecimal("0.87862628"), NumberDecimal("0.87374621"),
      NumberDecimal("0.87182626"), NumberDecimal("0.86892723"),
      NumberDecimal("0.86373732"), NumberDecimal("0.86017236"),
      NumberDecimal("0.85873636"), NumberDecimal("0.85762283"),
      NumberDecimal("0.85362373"), NumberDecimal("0.85306218"),
      NumberDecimal("0.85346632"), NumberDecimal("0.84647462"),
      NumberDecimal("0.84694720"), NumberDecimal("0.84723232"),
      NumberDecimal("0.85002222"), NumberDecimal("0.85468322"),
      NumberDecimal("0.85675656"), NumberDecimal("0.84811122"),
    ],
  },
]);
```

## Defining the aggregation pipeline

You will now define a pipeline that applies a number of stages to implement the aggregation:

```
var pipeline = [
  // Generate day summaries from the hourly array values
  {"$set": {
    "summary.open": {"$first": "$hour_values"},
    "summary.low": {"$min": "$hour_values"},
    "summary.high": {"$max": "$hour_values"},
    "summary.close": {"$last": "$hour_values"},
    "summary.average": {"$avg": "$hour_values"},
  }},

  // Exclude unrequired fields from each daily currency pair record
  {"$unset": [
    "_id",
    "hour_values",
  ]},
];
```

## Executing the aggregation pipeline

Next, run the following commands to do the following:

1.  Execute the aggregation using the defined pipeline:

    ```
    db.currency_pair_values.aggregate(pipeline);
    ```

2.  Generate its explain plan:

    ```
    db.currency_pair_values.explain("executionStats").aggregate(pipeline);
    ```

## Expected pipeline result

Once executed, the aggregation will return two documents now showing the daily summary *open*, *low*, *high*, *close*, and *average* prices for each currency pair:

```
[
  {
    currencyPair: 'USD/GBP',
    day: ISODate("2021-07-05T00:00:00.000Z"),
    summary: {
      open: NumberDecimal("0.71903411"),
      low: NumberDecimal("0.71903411"),
      high: NumberDecimal("0.76783263"),
      close: NumberDecimal("0.74998835"),
      average: NumberDecimal("0.74275533")
    }
  },
  {
    currencyPair: 'EUR/GBP',
    day: ISODate("2021-07-05T00:00:00.000Z"),
    summary: {
      open: NumberDecimal("0.86739394"),
      low: NumberDecimal("0.84647462"),
      high: NumberDecimal("0.88002736"),
      close: NumberDecimal("0.84811122"),
      average: NumberDecimal("0.86186929875")
    }
  }
]
```

## Pipeline observations

- **$first and $last for earlier MongoDB versions**: MongoDB only introduced the $first and $last array operator expressions in version 4.4. However, replacing these operators in the pipeline with an equivalent solution using the $arrayElemAt operator is straightforward. The following are alternatives you can use instead of $first and $last to operate correctly in versions earlier than MongoDB 4.4:

  ```
  // $first equivalent
  "summary.open": {"$arrayElemAt": ["$hour_values", 0]},

  // $last equivalent
  "summary.close": {"$arrayElemAt": ["$hour_values", -1]},
  ```

# Pivoting array items by a key

In some scenarios, an array field within documents contains a sequence of elements where some of the array's elements logically relate to each other. In this example, you will explore how to construct a pipeline that restructures arrays to represent these inherent groupings.

## Scenario

You have a set of geographically dispersed weather station zones where each zone has multiple sensor devices collecting readings such as temperature, humidity, and pressure. Each weather station assembles readings from its devices and once per hour transmits this set of measurements to a central database to store. The set of persisted readings is randomly ordered measurements for different devices in the zone. You need to take the mix of readings and group them by device, so the weather data is easier to consume by downstream dashboards and applications.

> **Note**
>
> This example's pipeline relies on some of the more difficult-to-understand array operator expressions, such as $map, $mergeObjects, and $filter. Make sure you have read *Chapter 4, Harnessing the Power of Expressions*, first, which explains how to use these operators. The pipeline also uses the $setUnion operator to find unique values in an array, which is explained in more detail in the *Pipeline observations* section at the end of this example.

## Populating the sample data

First, drop any old versions of the database (if they exist) and then populate the new hourly weather station measurements collection. Each weather measurement document contains the weather station's location and timestamps of its readings, along with the array of measurements from the various devices at the station's site:

```
db = db.getSiblingDB("book-pivot-array-by-key");
db.dropDatabase();

// Inserts records into the weather_measurements collection
db.weather_measurements.insertMany([
  {
    "weatherStationsZone": "FieldZone-ABCD",
    "dayHour": ISODate("2021-07-05T15:00:00.000Z"),
    "readings": [
      {"device": "ABCD-Device-123", "tempCelsius": 18},
      {"device": "ABCD-Device-789", "pressureMBar": 1004},
      {"device": "ABCD-Device-123", "humidityPercent": 31},
      {"device": "ABCD-Device-123", "tempCelsius": 19},
      {"device": "ABCD-Device-123", "pressureMBar": 1005},
      {"device": "ABCD-Device-789", "humidityPercent": 31},
      {"device": "ABCD-Device-123", "humidityPercent": 30},
      {"device": "ABCD-Device-789", "tempCelsius": 20},
      {"device": "ABCD-Device-789", "pressureMBar": 1003},
    ],
  },
  {
    "weatherStationsZone": "FieldZone-ABCD",
    "dayHour": ISODate("2021-07-05T16:00:00.000Z"),
    "readings": [
      {"device": "ABCD-Device-789", "humidityPercent": 33},
      {"device": "ABCD-Device-123", "humidityPercent": 32},
      {"device": "ABCD-Device-123", "tempCelsius": 22},
      {"device": "ABCD-Device-123", "pressureMBar": 1007},
      {"device": "ABCD-Device-789", "pressureMBar": 1008},
      {"device": "ABCD-Device-789", "tempCelsius": 22},
      {"device": "ABCD-Device-789", "humidityPercent": 34},
    ],
  },
]);
```

## Defining the aggregation pipeline

You will now define a pipeline that applies a number of stages to implement the aggregation:

```
var pipeline = [
  // Loop each unique device to accumulate array of devices & their readings
  {"$set": {
    "readings_device_summary": {
      "$map": {
        "input": {
          "$setUnion": "$readings.device"  // Get only unique device ids
        },
        "as": "device",
        "in": {
          "$mergeObjects": {  // Merge array of key:values into single object
            "$filter": {
              "input": "$readings",  // Iterate the "readings" array field
              "as": "reading",  // Name the current array element "reading"
              "cond": {  // Only include device props matching current device
                "$eq": ["$$reading.device", "$$device"]
              }
            }
          }
        }
      }
    },
  }},

  // Exclude unrequired fields from each record
  {"$unset": [
    "_id",
    "readings",
  ]},
];
```

## Executing the aggregation pipeline

Next, perform the following steps:

1.  Execute the aggregation using the defined pipeline:

    ```
    db.weather_measurements.aggregate(pipeline);
    ```

2.  Generate its explain plan:

    ```
    db.weather_measurements.explain("executionStats").aggregate(pipeline);
    ```

## Expected pipeline result

Once executed, the aggregation will return two documents, with the weather station hourly records containing a new array field of elements representing each device and its measurements:

```
[
  {
    weatherStationsZone: 'FieldZone-ABCD',
    dayHour: ISODate("2021-07-05T15:00:00.000Z"),
    readings_device_summary: [
      {
        device: 'ABCD-Device-123',
        tempCelsius: 19,
        humidityPercent: 30,
        pressureMBar: 1005
      },
      {
        device: 'ABCD-Device-789',
        pressureMBar: 1003,
        humidityPercent: 31,
        tempCelsius: 20
      }
    ]
  },
  {
    weatherStationsZone: 'FieldZone-ABCD',
    dayHour: ISODate("2021-07-05T16:00:00.000Z"),
    readings_device_summary: [
      {
        device: 'ABCD-Device-123',
        humidityPercent: 32,
        tempCelsius: 22,
```

```
          pressureMBar: 1007
      },
      {
        device: 'ABCD-Device-789',
        humidityPercent: 34,
        pressureMBar: 1008,
        tempCelsius: 22
      }
    ]
  }
]
```

## Pipeline observations

- **Pivoting items by a key**: The pipeline does not use the source array field directly to provide the initial list of items for the $map operator to loop through. Instead, it uses the $setUnion operator to capture each unique device name from the array of readings. This approach essentially allows you to group subsets of array items by a key. The array processing and grouping work is self-contained within each document for optimum aggregation performance.

- **Merging subset of array elements into one item**: For each $map iteration, a $filter operator collects the subset of readings from the original array, which match the unique device's name. The $mergeObjects operator then turns this subset of readings into an object, with the measurement type (e.g., temperature) as the key and the measurement (e.g., 21) as the value. Suppose more than one reading of the same type exists for a device (e.g., temperature=22 and temperature=23). In that case, the $mergeObject operator retains the last value only (e.g., 23), which is the desired behavior for this example scenario.

- **Adopting a better data model**: In this example, the weather station's hourly data is persisted directly into the database in the exact structure that the system receives it. However, if you can take control of exactly what structure you persist the data in initially, you should take this opportunity. You want to land the data in the database using the optimal model for consuming applications to access it. Adopting the **Bucket Pattern** (see https://www.mongodb.com/blog/post/building-with-patterns-the-bucket-pattern) for an IoT-type use case would be best, where time-series data is collected and analyzed downstream. However, if you use MongoDB version 5.0 or greater, you can use the *time-series* collection feature in MongoDB instead. This particular type of collection efficiently stores sequences of measurements over time to improve subsequent query efficiency. It automatically adopts a *Bucket Pattern* internally, meaning you don't have to explicitly design your data model for this.

# Array sorting and percentiles

The need to sort arrays and calculate summary data, such as the 99th percentile, is common. Recent versions of the MongoDB aggregation framework offer enhanced capabilities in this area. This example will guide you through implementing this using both an earlier and a more recent version of MongoDB.

## Scenario

You've conducted performance testing of an application with the results of each *test run* captured in a database. Each record contains a set of response times for the test run. You want to analyze the data from multiple runs to identify the slowest ones. You calculate the median (50th percentile) and 90th percentile response times for each test run and only keep results where the 90th percentile response time is greater than 100 milliseconds.

> **Note**
>
> For MongoDB version 5.0 and earlier, the example will use a macro function for inline sorting of arrays. Adopting this approach avoids the need for you to use the combination of the $unwind, $sort, and $group stages. Instead, you process each document's array in isolation for optimum performance, as explained in *Chapter 3, Optimizing Pipelines for Performance*. You can reuse this chapter's custom sortArray() function as is when you need to sort an array field's contents. For MongoDB version 6.0 and greater, you can use MongoDB's new $sortArray operator instead.
>
> MongoDB version 7.0 introduced the $percentile and $median operators. Combining these with the $sortArray operator can significantly simplify the solution. The final observation, as seen in the *Pipeline observations* section of this example, provides a far simpler pipeline for this example.

## Populating the sample data

First, drop any old versions of the database (if they exist) and then populate the test run results collection. Each document contains the test run number, the date of the run, and an array of response times for the tests performed in the run:

```
db = db.getSiblingDB("book-array-sort-percentiles");
db.dropDatabase();

// Insert 7 records into the performance_test_results collection
db.performance_test_results.insertMany([
```

```
{
  "testRun": 1,
  "datetime": ISODate("2021-08-01T22:51:27.638Z"),
  "responseTimesMillis": [
    62, 97, 59, 104, 97, 71, 62, 115, 82, 87,
  ],
},
{
  "testRun": 2,
  "datetime": ISODate("2021-08-01T22:56:32.272Z"),
  "responseTimesMillis": [
    34, 63, 51, 104, 87, 63, 64, 86, 105, 51, 73,
    78, 59, 108, 65, 58, 69, 106, 87, 93, 65,
  ],
},
{
  "testRun": 3,
  "datetime": ISODate("2021-08-01T23:01:08.908Z"),
  "responseTimesMillis": [
    56, 72, 83, 95, 107, 83, 85,
  ],
},
{
  "testRun": 4,
  "datetime": ISODate("2021-08-01T23:17:33.526Z"),
  "responseTimesMillis": [
    78, 67, 107, 110,
  ],
},
{
  "testRun": 5,
  "datetime": ISODate("2021-08-01T23:24:39.998Z"),
  "responseTimesMillis": [
    75, 91, 75, 87, 99, 88, 55, 72, 99, 102,
  ],
},
{
  "testRun": 6,
  "datetime": ISODate("2021-08-01T23:27:52.272Z"),
  "responseTimesMillis": [
    88, 89,
  ],
},
```

```
    },
    {
      "testRun": 7,
      "datetime": ISODate("2021-08-01T23:31:59.917Z"),
      "responseTimesMillis": [
        101,
      ],
    },
  ]);
```

## Defining the aggregation pipeline

If you are using version 5.0 or earlier of MongoDB, define the following custom sortArray()
function for inline sorting of the contents of an array field, ready for you to use in a pipeline:

```
// Macro function to generate a complex aggregation expression for sorting
// an array - this function isn't required for MongoDB version 5.2+ due to
// the new $sortArray operator
function sortArray(sourceArrayField) {
  return {
    // GENERATE NEW ARRAY TO CONTAIN ELEMENTS FROM SOURCE ARRAY BUT SORTED
    "$reduce": {
      "input": sourceArrayField,
      "initialValue": [],  // 1st VERSION OF TEMP SORTED ARRAY WILL BE EMPTY
      "in": {
        "$let": {
          "vars": {  // CAPTURE $$this & $$value FROM OUTER $reduce
            "resultArray": "$$value",
            "currentSourceArrayElement": "$$this"
          },
          "in": {
            "$let": {
              "vars": {
                // FIND EACH SOURCE ARRAY'S CURRENT ELEM POS IN SORTED ARRAY
                "targetArrayPosition": {
                  "$reduce": {
                    "input": {"$range": [0, {"$size": "$$resultArray"}]},
                    "initialValue": {  // INIT SORTED POS TO BE LAST ELEMNT
                      "$size": "$$resultArray"
                    },
```

```
                        "in": {   // LOOP THRU "0,1,2..."
                          "$cond": [
                            {"$lt": [
                              "$$currentSourceArrayElement",
                              {"$arrayElemAt": ["$$resultArray", "$$this"]}
                            ]},
                            {"$min": ["$$value", "$$this"]}, // IF NOT YET FOUND
                            "$$value"  // RETAIN INIT VAL AS NOT YET FOUND POSTN
                          ]
                        }
                      }
                    }
                  },
                  "in": {
                    // BUILD NEW ARRAY BY SLICING OLDER 1 INSERT NEW ELM BETWEEN
                    "$concatArrays": [
                      {"$cond": [  // RETAIN THE EXISTING 1st PART OF NEW ARRAY
                        {"$eq": [0, "$$targetArrayPosition"]},
                        [],
                        {"$slice": ["$$resultArray", 0, "$$targetArrayPosition"]},
                      ]},
                      ["$$currentSourceArrayElement"],  // PULL IN NEW ELEMENT
                      {"$cond": [  // RETAIN EXISTING LAST PART OF NEW ARRAY
                        {"$gt": [{"$size": "$$resultArray"}, 0]},
                        {"$slice": [
                          "$$resultArray",
                          "$$targetArrayPosition",
                          {"$size": "$$resultArray"}
                        ]},
                        [],
                      ]},
                    ]
                  }
                }
              }
            }
          }
        }
      }
    };
  }
```

Next, define the new `arrayElemAtPercentile()` function for capturing the element of a sorted array at the *n*th percentile position:

```
// Macro function to find nth percentile element of sorted version of array
function arrayElemAtPercentile(sourceArrayField, percentile) {
  return {
    "$let": {
      "vars": {
        "sortedArray": sortArray(sourceArrayField),
        // Comment out the line above & uncomment lines below if MDB 5.2+
        //"sortedArray": {
        //  "$sortArray": {"input": sourceArrayField, "sortBy": 1}
        //},
      },
      "in": {
        "$arrayElemAt": [   // FIND ELEMENT OF ARRAY AT NTH PERCENTILE POS
          "$$sortedArray",
          {"$subtract": [   // ARRAY IS 0-INDEX BASED: SUBTRACT 1 TO GET POS
            {"$ceil":   // FIND NTH ELEME IN ARRAY ROUNDED UP TO NEAREST INT
              {"$multiply": [
                {"$divide": [percentile, 100]},
                {"$size": "$$sortedArray"}
              ]}
            },
            1
          ]}
        ]
      }
    }
  };
}
```

> **Note**
> If you're running MongoDB version 6.0 or greater, you can comment or uncomment the specific lines indicated in the preceding code to leverage the new MongoDB $sortArray operator.

Now, define the pipeline ready to perform the aggregation:

```
var pipeline = [
  // Capture new fields for the ordered array + various percentiles
  {"$set": {
    "sortedResponseTimesMillis": sortArray("$responseTimesMillis"),
    // Comment out the line above & uncomment lines below if MDB 5.2+
    //"sortedResponseTimesMillis": {
    //  "$sortArray": {"input": "$responseTimesMillis", "sortBy": 1}
    //},
    "medianTimeMillis":
      arrayElemAtPercentile("$responseTimesMillis", 50),
    "ninetiethPercentileTimeMillis":
      arrayElemAtPercentile("$responseTimesMillis", 90),
  }},

  // Only show results for tests with slow latencies
  // (i.e. 90th%-ile responses >100ms)
  {"$match": {
    "ninetiethPercentileTimeMillis": {"$gt": 100},
  }},

  // Exclude unrequired fields from each record
  {"$unset": [
    "_id",
    "datetime",
    "responseTimesMillis",
  ]},
];
```

> **Note**
>
> If you're running MongoDB version 6.0 or greater, you can comment or uncomment the specific lines indicated in the preceding code to leverage the new MongoDB $sortArray operator.

## Executing the aggregation pipeline

Next, perform the following steps:

1.  Execute the aggregation using the defined pipeline:

    ```
    db.performance_test_results.aggregate(pipeline);
    ```

2. Generate its explain plan:

```
db.performance_test_results.explain("executionStats").
aggregate(pipeline);
```

## Expected pipeline result

Once executed, the aggregation will return 5 documents, representing the subset of documents with a 90th percentile response time greater than 100 milliseconds:

```
[
  {
    testRun: 1,
    sortedResponseTimesMillis: [
      59, 62, 62,  71,  82,
      87, 97, 97, 104, 115
    ],
    medianTimeMillis: 82,
    ninetiethPercentileTimeMillis: 104
  },
  {
    testRun: 2,
    sortedResponseTimesMillis: [
      34, 51, 51,  58,  59,  63,  63,
      64, 65, 65,  69,  73,  78,  86,
      87, 87, 93, 104, 105, 106, 108
    ],
    medianTimeMillis: 69,
    ninetiethPercentileTimeMillis: 105
  },
  {
    testRun: 3,
    sortedResponseTimesMillis: [
      56, 72,  83, 83,
      85, 95, 107
    ],
    medianTimeMillis: 83,
    ninetiethPercentileTimeMillis: 107
  },
```

```
  {
    testRun: 4,
    sortedResponseTimesMillis: [ 67, 78, 107, 110 ],
    medianTimeMillis: 78,
    ninetiethPercentileTimeMillis: 110
  },
  {
    testRun: 7,
    sortedResponseTimesMillis: [ 101 ],
    medianTimeMillis: 101,
    ninetiethPercentileTimeMillis: 101
  }
]
```

## Pipeline observations

- **Macro functions**: In this example, you employed two functions, `sortArray()` and `arrayElemAtPercentile()`, to generate portions of aggregation boilerplate code. These functions are essentially macros. You invoke these functions from within the pipeline you create in MongoDB Shell. Each function you invoke embeds the returned boilerplate code into the pipeline's code. You can see this in action by typing the text `pipeline` into the Shell and pressing *Enter*.

  > **Note**
  >
  > You may first have to increase the depth displayed in *mongosh* by issuing the *mongosh* `config.set("inspectDepth", 100)` command. This action will display a single large piece of code representing the whole pipeline, including the macro-generated code.

  The aggregation runtime never sees or runs custom functions such as `sortArray()` and `arrayElemAtPercentile()` directly. Of course, you won't use JavaScript functions to generate composite expressions if you use a different programming language and a `MongoDB driver`. You will use the relevant features of your specific programming language to assemble composite expression objects.

- **Sorting on primitives only**: The custom `sortArray()` function used for MongoDB versions 5.0 and earlier will sort arrays containing just primitive values, such as integers, floats, date-times, and strings. However, if an array's members are objects (i.e., each has its own fields and values), the code will not sort the array correctly. Enhancing the function to enable sorting an array of objects is possible, but this enhancement is not covered here. For MongoDB versions 6.0 and greater, the new `$sortArray` operator provides options to sort an array of objects easily.

- **Comparison with classic sorting algorithms**: Despite being more optimal than unwinding and regrouping arrays to bring them back into the same documents, the custom sorting code will be slower than commonly recognized computer science sorting algorithms. This situation is due to the limitations of the aggregation domain language compared with a general-purpose programming language. The performance difference will be negligible for arrays with few elements (probably up to a few tens of members). For larger arrays containing hundreds of members or more, the degradation in performance will be more profound. For MongoDB versions 6.0 and greater, the new $sortArray operator leverages a fully optimized sorting algorithm under the covers to avoid this issue.

- **Simplified pipeline in MongoDB 7.0**: Combining the $sortArray operator introduced in MongoDB version 6.0 and the $percentile and $median operators introduced in MongoDB version 7.0, you can employ a significantly simpler pipeline for the solution without requiring any macros, as shown:

```
var pipeline = [
  {"$set": {
    "sortedResponseTimesMillis": {
      "$sortArray": {
        "input": "$responseTimesMillis",
        "sortBy": 1
      }
    },

    "medianTimeMillis": {
      "$median": {
        "input": "$responseTimesMillis",
        "method": "approximate",
      }
    },

    "ninetiethPercentileTimeMillis": {
      "$first": {
        "$percentile": {
          "input": "$responseTimesMillis",
          "p": [0.90],
          "method": "approximate",
        }
      }
    }
  }},

  {"$match": {
    "ninetiethPercentileTimeMillis": {"$gt": 100},
  }},
];
```

# Array element grouping

Grouping data from documents in MongoDB is one of the most common tasks you will use the aggregation framework for. However, sometimes, you only need to group elements in an array field within each document in isolation rather than grouping data from different documents. Let's find out how we can do this efficiently in this example.

## Scenario

You want to provide a report for your online game showing the total *coin* rewards each gaming user has accumulated. The challenge is that the source collection captures each time the game awards a user with a type of coin in a growing array field containing many elements. However, for each gamer, you want to show the total for each coin type in an array instead. An extra complication exists in that you cannot know ahead of time what all the possible coin types can be when developing the solution. For example, the game could introduce different coin types in the future (e.g., *tungsten coins*).

## Populating the sample data

First, drop any old versions of the database (if they exist) and then populate the user rewards collection. Each document contains the user's *ID* and an array of the user's current coin *rewards* of different types and amounts:

```
db = db.getSiblingDB("book-array-element-grouping");
db.dropDatabase();

// Insert 3 records into the user_rewards collection
db.user_rewards.insertMany([
  {
    "userId": 123456789,
    "rewards": [
      {"coin": "gold", "amount": 25,
       "date": ISODate("2022-11-01T09:25:23Z")},
      {"coin": "bronze", "amount": 100,
       "date": ISODate("2022-11-02T11:32:56Z")},
      {"coin": "silver", "amount": 50,
       "date": ISODate("2022-11-09T12:11:58Z")},
      {"coin": "gold", "amount": 10,
       "date": ISODate("2022-11-15T12:46:40Z")},
      {"coin": "bronze", "amount": 75,
       "date": ISODate("2022-11-22T12:57:01Z")},
      {"coin": "gold", "amount": 50,
       "date": ISODate("2022-11-28T19:32:33Z")},
    ],
```

```
    },
    {
      "userId": 987654321,
      "rewards": [
        {"coin": "bronze", "amount": 200,
         "date": ISODate("2022-11-21T14:35:56Z")},
        {"coin": "silver", "amount": 50,
         "date": ISODate("2022-11-21T15:02:48Z")},
        {"coin": "silver", "amount": 50,
         "date": ISODate("2022-11-27T23:04:32Z")},
        {"coin": "silver", "amount": 50,
         "date": ISODate("2022-11-27T23:29:47Z")},
        {"coin": "bronze", "amount": 500,
         "date": ISODate("2022-11-27T23:56:14Z")},
      ],
    },
    {
      "userId": 888888888,
      "rewards": [
        {"coin": "gold", "amount": 500,
         "date": ISODate("2022-11-13T13:42:18Z")},
        {"coin": "platinum", "amount": 5,
         "date": ISODate("2022-11-19T15:02:53Z")},
      ],
    },
]);
```

## Defining the aggregation pipeline

First, you need to define the following two array element grouping functions ready for you to use in a pipeline (one to perform group *counting* and the other to perform group *summing*):

```
// Macro function to generate a complex expression to group an array field's
// content by the value of a field occurring in each array element, counting
// the number of times it occurs
function arrayGroupByCount(arraySubdocField, groupByKeyField) {
  return {
    "$map": {
      "input": {
        "$setUnion": {
          "$map": {
            "input": '$${arraySubdocField}',
```

```
                    "in": '$$this.${groupByKeyField}'
                }
            }
        },
        "as": "key",
        "in": {
          "id": "$$key",
          "count": {
            "$size": {
              "$filter": {
                "input": '$${arraySubdocField}',
                "cond": {
                  "$eq": ['$$this.${groupByKeyField}', "$$key"]
                }
              }
            }
          }
        }
      }
    };
}


// Macro function to generate a complex expression to group an array field's
// content by the value of a field occurring in each array element, summing
// the values from a corresponding amount field in each array element
function arrayGroupBySum(arraySubdocField, groupByKeyField, groupByValueField)
{
  return {
    "$map": {
      "input": {
        "$setUnion": {
          "$map": {
            "input": '$${arraySubdocField}',
            "in": '$$this.${groupByKeyField}'
          }
        }
      },
      "as": "key",
      "in": {
```

```
      "id": "$$key",
      "total": {
        "$reduce": {
          "input": '$${arraySubdocField}',
          "initialValue": 0,
          "in": {
            "$cond": {
              "if": {"$eq": ['$$this.${groupByKeyField}', "$$key"]},
              "then": {"$add": ['$$this.${groupByValueField}', "$$value"]},
              "else": "$$value"
            }
          }
        }
      }
    }
  };
}
```

Then, define the pipeline ready to perform the aggregation:

```
var pipeline = [
  // Capture new fields grouping elems of each array & remove unwanted fields
  {"$set": {
    "coinTypeAwardedCounts": arrayGroupByCount("rewards", "coin"),
    "coinTypeTotals": arrayGroupBySum("rewards", "coin", "amount"),
    "_id": "$$REMOVE",
    "rewards": "$$REMOVE",
  }},
];
```

## Executing the aggregation pipeline

Next, run the following commands to do the following:

1. Execute the aggregation using the defined pipeline:

   ```
   db.user_rewards.aggregate(pipeline);
   ```

2. Generate its explain plan:

   ```
   db.user_rewards.explain("executionStats").aggregate(pipeline);
   ```

## Expected pipeline result

Once executed, the aggregation will return three documents, representing the three gamers and showing the number of times they received each coin type with totals:

```
[
  {
    userId: 123456789,
    coinTypeAwardedCounts: [
      { id: 'bronze', count: 2 },
      { id: 'silver', count: 1 },
      { id: 'gold', count: 3 }
    ],
    coinTypeTotals: [
      { id: 'bronze', total: 175 },
      { id: 'silver', total: 50 },
      { id: 'gold', total: 85 }
    ]
  },
  {
    userId: 987654321,
    coinTypeAwardedCounts: [
      { id: 'bronze', count: 2 },
      { id: 'silver', count: 3 }
    ],
    coinTypeTotals: [
      { id: 'bronze', total: 700 },
      { id: 'silver', total: 150 }
    ]
  },
  {
    userId: 888888888,
    coinTypeAwardedCounts: [
      { id: 'gold', count: 1 },
      { id: 'platinum', count: 1 }
    ],
    coinTypeTotals: [
      { id: 'gold', total: 500 },
      { id: 'platinum', total: 5 }
    ]
  }
]
```

## Pipeline observations

- **Reusable macro functions**: As with the previous example, the aggregation uses macro functions to generate boilerplate code, which it inlines into the pipeline before the aggregation runtime executes it. In this example, both the `arrayGroupByCount()` and `arrayGroupBySum()` macro functions are general purpose and reusable, which you can employ as is for any other scenario where array elements need to be grouped and totaled.

- **Grouping array elements without unwinding first**: The `$group` stage is the standard tool for grouping elements and producing counts and totals for these groups. However, as discussed in *Chapter 4, Harnessing the Power of Expressions*, this is inefficient if you only need to manipulate each document's array field in isolation from other documents. You must unwind a document's array, process the unpacked data, and then regroup each array back into the same parent document. By regrouping, you are introducing a blocking and resource-limited step. This example's two macro functions enable you to avoid this overhead and achieve the array grouping you require, even when the keys you are grouping by are unknown to you ahead of time. The `$setUnion` operator used in both functions produces the set of unique keys to group by.

- **Variable reference and $$ potential confusion:**. In *Chapter 4, Harnessing the Power of Expressions*, you may recall that field paths begin with $ (e.g., `$rewards`) and variables begin with $$ (e.g., `$$currentItem`) for aggregation expressions. Therefore, you may be confused by the syntax `'$${arraySubdocField}'` used in both functions. This confusion is understandable. Employing ' backticks is part of the `template literals` feature of JavaScript. Therefore, before the pipeline executes, the JavaScript interpreter replaces `${arraySubdocField}` with the string `rewards`, which is the value of the `arraySubdocField` parameter passed to the function. So, `'$${arraySubdocField}'` becomes the field path `"$rewards"` before the macro function embeds it into the larger complex expression it is constructing.

# Array fields joining

Joining documents between two collections is an aggregation topic you explored extensively in *Chapter 7, Joining Data Examples*. However, sometimes, you only need to efficiently join two fields within the same document where at least one of the fields is an array. Let's look at how you can achieve this.

## Scenario

You are developing a new dating website using a database to hold the profiles of all registered users. For each user profile, you will persist a set of the user's specified hobbies, each with a description of how the user says they conduct their pursuit. Each user's profile also captures what they prefer to do depending on their mood (e.g., *happy*, *sad*, *chilling*, etc.). When you show the user profiles on the website to a person searching for a date, you want to describe how each candidate user conducts their hobbies for each mood to help the person spot their ideal match.

## Populating the sample data

First, drop any old versions of the database (if they exist) and then populate a new user profiles collection. Each profile contains several attributes about the user, a field with a set of their named hobbies and an array field of their favorite things to do depending on their mood:

```
db = db.getSiblingDB("book-array-fields-joining");
db.dropDatabase();

// Insert 2 records into the users collection
db.users.insertMany([
  {
    "firstName": "Alice",
    "lastName": "Jones",
    "dateOfBirth": ISODate("1985-07-21T00:00:00Z"),
    "hobbies": {
      "music": "Playing the guitar",
      "reading": "Science Fiction books",
      "gaming": "Video games, especially RPGs",
      "sports": "Long-distance running",
      "traveling": "Visiting exotic places",
      "cooking": "Trying out new recipes",
    },
```

```
        "moodFavourites": {
          "sad": ["music"],
          "happy": ["sports"],
          "chilling": ["music", "cooking"],
        },
    },
    {
        "firstName": "Sam",
        "lastName": "Brown",
        "dateOfBirth": ISODate("1993-12-01T00:00:00Z"),
        "hobbies": {
          "cycling": "Mountain biking",
          "writing": "Poetry and short stories",
          "knitting": "Knitting scarves and hats",
          "hiking": "Hiking in the mountains",
          "volunteering": "Helping at the local animal shelter",
          "music": "Listening to Jazz",
          "photography": "Nature photography",
          "gardening": "Growing herbs and vegetables",
          "yoga": "Practicing Hatha Yoga",
          "cinema": "Watching classic movies",
        },
        "moodFavourites": {
          "happy": ["gardening", "cycling"],
          "sad": ["knitting"],
        },
    },
]);
```

## Defining the aggregation pipeline

First, you need to define the following function to get the array values of named fields in a sub-document where each field's name is only known at runtime:

```
// Macro function to generate a complex expression to get array values of
// named fields in a sub-doc where each field's name is only known at runtime
function getValuesOfNamedFieldsAsArray(obj, fieldnames) {
  return {
    "$map": {
      "input": {
        "$filter": {
          "input": {"$objectToArray": obj},
          "as": "currElem",
          "cond": {"$in": ["$$currElem.k", fieldnames]},
        }
      },
      "in": "$$this.v"
    },
  };
}
```

Then, define the pipeline ready to perform the aggregation:

```
var pipeline = [
  // Set a field with activities each user likes doing according to their mood
  {"$set": {
    "moodActivities": {
      "$arrayToObject": {
        "$map": {
          "input": {"$objectToArray": "$moodFavourites"},
          "in": {
            "k": "$$this.k",
            "v": getValuesOfNamedFieldsAsArray("$hobbies", "$$this.v"),
          }
        },
      }
    }
  }},
```

```
    // Remove unwanted fields
    {"$unset": [
      "_id",
      "hobbies",
      "moodFavourites",
    ]},
  ]
```

## Executing the aggregation pipeline

Next, perform the following steps:

1. Execute the aggregation using the defined pipeline:

   ```
   db.users.aggregate(pipeline);
   ```

2. Generate its explain plan:

   ```
   db.users.explain().aggregate(pipeline);
   ```

## Expected pipeline result

Once executed, the aggregation will return two documents, each showing a new `moodActivities` array field containing descriptions of how a user conducts their preferred hobby for each mood:

```
[
  {
    firstName: 'Alice',
    lastName: 'Jones',
    dateOfBirth: ISODate("1985-07-21T00:00:00.000Z"),
    moodActivities: {
      sad: [ 'Playing the guitar' ],
      happy: [ 'Long-distance running' ],
      chilling: [ 'Playing the guitar', 'Trying out new recipes' ]
    }
  },
```

```
  {
    firstName: 'Sam',
    lastName: 'Brown',
    dateOfBirth: ISODate("1993-12-01T00:00:00.000Z"),
    moodActivities: {
      happy: [ 'Mountain biking', 'Growing herbs and vegetables' ],
      sad: [ 'Knitting scarves and hats' ]
    }
  }
]
```

## Pipeline observations

- **Joining between two fields in each record**: Each user document contains two sub-document fields the pipeline must join: hobbies and moodFavourites. The moodFavourites sub-document field holds arrays with values mapped to properties of the hobbies sub-document, and consequently, there is a many-to-many relationship between the two fields. A user's given hobby can appear as a favorite for more than one of their moods, and each user's mood can have multiple preferred hobbies. The getValuesOfNamedFieldsAsArray() function lets the pipeline look up multiple hobbies in one go for each *mood* that it iterates through.

- **Reusable macro functions**: As with many of the other *array manipulation examples*, the aggregation uses a macro function to generate boilerplate code for use in the pipeline. This is a general-purpose function and reusable as is in other solutions.

- **Grouping array elements without unwinding first**: As with the previous example, the aggregation avoids unnecessarily unwinding of each document's two arrays to group back together again, just to manipulate each document's array fields in isolation from other documents. It avoids introducing a blocking and resource-limited grouping step in the pipeline.

# Comparison of two arrays

Frequently, when analyzing data and computing summary values for different time periods, you also want to compare what has changed in the data between those periods. Such *last-mile* comparisons can be left to the client application to perform using the programming language available there. However, as you will discover in this example, an aggregation can invariably perform this action for you.

> **Note**
>
> For this example, you require MongoDB version 4.4 or above. This is because you'll be using the $first array operator introduced in MongoDB version 4.4.

## Scenario

You are an IT administrator managing virtual machine deployments in a data center to host a critical business application in a few environments (e.g., *production* and *QA*). A database collection captured the configuration state of each virtual machine across two days. You want to generate a report showing what configuration changes people made to the virtual machines (if any) between these two days.

## Populating the sample data

First, drop any old version of the database (if it exists) and then populate the deployments collection. Each deployment document contains the deployment name (e.g., `ProdServer`), a field containing an array of its old configuration settings, an array of its new configuration settings, and timestamps for when each of these two sets of settings was captured:

```
db = db.getSiblingDB("book-comparison-of-two-arrays");
db.dropDatabase();

// Insert 5 records into the deployments collection
db.deployments.insertMany([
  {
    "name": "ProdServer",
    "beforeTimestamp": ISODate("2022-01-01T00:00:00Z"),
    "afterTimestamp": ISODate("2022-01-02T00:00:00Z"),
    "beforeConfig": {
      "vcpus": 8,
      "ram": 128,
      "storage": 512,
      "state": "running",
    },
```

```
      "afterConfig": {
        "vcpus": 16,
        "ram": 256,
        "storage": 512,
        "state": "running",
      },
    },
    {
      "name": "QAServer",
      "beforeTimestamp": ISODate("2022-01-01T00:00:00Z"),
      "afterTimestamp": ISODate("2022-01-02T00:00:00Z"),
      "beforeConfig": {
        "vcpus": 4,
        "ram": 64,
        "storage": 512,
        "state": "paused",
      },
      "afterConfig": {
        "vcpus": 4,
        "ram": 64,
        "storage": 256,
        "state": "running",
        "extraParams": "disableTLS;disableCerts;"
      },
    },
    {
      "name": "LoadTestServer",
      "beforeTimestamp": ISODate("2022-01-01T00:00:00Z"),
      "beforeConfig": {
        "vcpus": 8,
        "ram": 128,
        "storage": 256,
        "state": "running",
      },
    },
```

```
{
    "name": "IntegrationServer",
    "beforeTimestamp": ISODate("2022-01-01T00:00:00Z"),
    "afterTimestamp": ISODate("2022-01-02T00:00:00Z"),
    "beforeConfig": {
      "vcpus": 4,
      "ram": 32,
      "storage": 64,
      "state": "running",
    },
    "afterConfig": {
      "vcpus": 4,
      "ram": 32,
      "storage": 64,
      "state": "running",
    },
  },
  {
    "name": "DevServer",
    "afterTimestamp": ISODate("2022-01-02T00:00:00Z"),
    "afterConfig": {
      "vcpus": 2,
      "ram": 16,
      "storage": 64,
      "state": "running",
    },
  },
]);
```

## Defining the aggregation pipeline

You first need to define the following two functions, one to get all the unique keys from two different arrays and the other to get the value of a field only known at runtime, ready for you to use in a pipeline:

```
// Macro function to generate a complex expression to get all the unique
// keys from two sub-documents returned as an array of the unique keys
function getArrayOfTwoSubdocsKeysNoDups(firstArrayRef, secondArrayRef) {
  return {
    "$setUnion": {
      "$concatArrays": [
        {"$map": {
          "input": {"$objectToArray": firstArrayRef},
          "in": "$$this.k",
        }},
        {"$map": {
          "input": {"$objectToArray": secondArrayRef},
          "in": "$$this.k",
        }},
      ]
    }
  };
}


// Macro function to generate a complex expression to get the value of a
// field in a document where the field's name is only known at runtime
function getDynamicField(obj, fieldname) {
  return {
    "$first": [
      {"$map": {
        "input": {
          "$filter": {
            "input": {"$objectToArray": obj},
            "as": "currObj",
            "cond": {"$eq": ["$$currObj.k", fieldname]},
            "limit": 1
          }
        },
        "in": "$$this.v"
      }},
    ]
  };
}
```

Then, define the pipeline ready to perform the aggregation:

```
var pipeline = [
  // Compare two different arrays in the same document & get the differences
  {"$set": {
    "differences": {
      "$reduce": {
        "input": getArrayOfTwoSubdocsKeysNoDups("$beforeConfig",
                                                "$afterConfig"),
        "initialValue": [],
        "in": {
          "$concatArrays": [
            "$$value",
            {"$cond": {
              "if": {
                "$ne": [
                  getDynamicField("$beforeConfig", "$$this"),
                  getDynamicField("$afterConfig", "$$this"),
                ]
              },
              "then": [{
                "field": "$$this",
                "change": {
                  "$concat": [
                    {"$ifNull": [
                      {"$toString":
                        getDynamicField("$beforeConfig", "$$this")},
                      "<not-set>"
                    ]},
                    " --> ",
                    {"$ifNull": [
                      {"$toString":
                        getDynamicField("$afterConfig", "$$this")},
                      "<not-set>"
                    ]},
                  ]
                },
              }],
              "else": [],
            }}
          ]
        }
      }
    }
  }
```

```
        }
      },
   }},


   // Add 'status' field & only show 'differences' field if differences exist
   {"$set": {
      // Set 'status' to ADDED, REMOVED, MODIFIED or UNCHANGED accordingly
      "status": {
        "$switch": {
          "branches": [
            {
              "case": {
                "$and": [
                  {"$in": [{"$type": "$differences"}, ["missing", "null"]]},
                  {"$in": [{"$type": "$beforeConfig"}, ["missing", "null"]]},
                ]
              },
              "then": "ADDED"
            },
            {
              "case": {
                "$and": [
                  {"$in": [{"$type": "$differences"}, ["missing", "null"]]},
                  {"$in": [{"$type": "$afterConfig"}, ["missing", "null"]]},
                ]
              },
              "then": "REMOVED"
            },
            {"case":
              {"$lte": [{"$size": "$differences"}, 0]},
              "then": "UNCHANGED"
            },
            {"case":
              {"$gt":  [{"$size": "$differences"}, 0]},
              "then": "MODIFIED"
            },
          ],
          "default": "UNKNOWN",
        }
      },
```

```
    // If there are diffs, keep the differences field, otherwise remove it
    "differences": {
      "$cond": [
        {"$or": [
          {"$in": [{"$type": "$differences"}, ["missing", "null"]]},
          {"$lte": [{"$size": "$differences"}, 0]},
        ]},
        "$$REMOVE",
        "$differences"
      ]
    },
  }},

  // Remove unwanted fields
  {"$unset": [
    "_id",
    "beforeTimestamp",
    "afterTimestamp",
    "beforeConfig",
    "afterConfig",
  ]},
];
```

## Executing the aggregation pipeline

Next, perform the following steps:

1.  Execute the aggregation using the defined pipeline:

    ```
    db.deployments.aggregate(pipeline);
    ```

2.  Generate its explain plan:

    ```
    db.deployments.explain("executionStats").aggregate(pipeline);
    ```

## Expected pipeline result

Once executed, the aggregation will return five documents, showing whether anyone *added*, *removed*, or *modified* a deployment or left it *unchanged*, with the deployment's changes listed if modified, as shown:

```
[
  {
    "name": "ProdServer",
    "status": "MODIFIED",
    "differences": [
      {
        "field": "vcpus",
        "change": "8 --> 16"
      },
      {
        "field": "ram",
        "change": "128 --> 256"
      }
    ]
  },
  {
    "name": "QAServer",
    "status": "MODIFIED",
    "differences": [
      {
        "field": "storage",
        "change": "512 --> 256"
      },
      {
        "field": "state",
        "change": "paused --> running"
      },
      {
        "field": "extraParams",
        "change": "<not-set> --> disableTLS;disableCerts;"
      }
    ]
```

```
  },
  {
    "name": "LoadTestServer",
    "status": "REMOVED"
  },
  {
    "name": "IntegrationServer",
    "status": "UNCHANGED"
  },
  {
    "name": "DevServer",
    "status": "ADDED"
  }
]
```

## Pipeline observations

- **Reusable macro functions**: As with many of the other *array manipulation examples*, the aggregation uses macro functions to generate boilerplate code for use in the pipeline. These functions are general purpose and reusable as is in other solutions.

- **Sub-document comparison**: The pipeline provides a generic way to compare the topmost fields hanging off two sub-document fields. The comparison will only work for sub-document fields with primitive values (e.g., *string, double, null, date, boolean*, etc.). The comparison will not work if a sub-document's field is an array or object. The pipeline finds all the field names (*keys*) appearing in either sub-document. For each field name, the pipeline then compares whether it exists in both sub-documents and if the values don't match, it incorporates the two different values in the output.

- **Potential need for earlier stages**: The example source documents already embed two fields to compare, each corresponding to the deployment's configuration captured at a different point in time (beforeTimestamp and afterTimestamp). In real-world data models, these two configuration snapshots would be more likely to correspond to two different records in a collection, not one combined record. However, it doesn't mean that this example is redundant. In such cases, you would include the following additional stages at the start of the example's pipeline:

  - $sort: To sort all records by timestamp regardless of which deployment each corresponds to.

  - $group: To group on the name of the deployment. Inside this group stage, you would use a $first operator to capture the first document's config into a new beforeConfig field, and a $last operator to capture the last document's config into a new afterConfig field.

The rest of the pipeline from the example would then be used unchanged.

# Jagged array condensing

Some data is best represented as an array of arrays, where each sub-array has an uneven length. These are called *jagged arrays*. Sometimes, you will need to condense the array of arrays into a single array of averages instead.

## Scenario

You are developing a healthcare IT system to track the results of clinical trials for different types of emerging medical drugs, where each clinical trial will involve multiple patients. In most cases, doctors will administer the medication to each patient over several sessions, measuring its effectiveness soon after each administered session to understand each patient's response. You want to capture the results of each clinical trial as a record in a database, including an array of participating patients. Each patient array element will contain an array of their administered drug sessions, showing the resulting effectiveness of each session. Essentially, you need to store a jagged array because some patients in the clinical trial will have the drug administered on more occasions than others.

Once the clinical trial finishes, you want to be able to run a report showing when the drug was most effective on average across the set of participating patients (e.g., after just a few administered sessions or after many sessions).

## Populating the sample data

First, drop any old versions of the database (if they exist) and then populate a new `drugTrialResults` collection with two documents. Each document contains the trial's *ID* and *name*, the name of the medical drug tested, and an array of patients, where each patient element is an array of test results:

```
db = db.getSiblingDB("book-jagged-array-condense");
db.dropDatabase();


// Insert 2 records into the drug trials results collection
db.drugTrialResults.insertMany([
  {
    "trial_id": 111111111,
    "trial_name": "Clinical Trial for Drug A",
    "drug_name": "Drug A",
    "patientsWithAdministeredSessions": [
      [30.3, 40.4, 50.3], // Patient 1 sessions (effectiveness scores)
      [55.5, 65.2, 75.4, 85.3], // Patient 2 sessions (effectiveness scores)
      [50.3, 66.4, 65.5, 87.6, 86.7], // Patient 3 sessions (scores)
      [40.1, 50.2, 60.1, 70.3], // Patient 4 sessions (effectiveness scores)
      [45.6, 55.7, 55.6, 75.5, 85.3, 91.8], // Patient 5 sessions (scores)
      [41.5, 40.2, 55.5, 65.3], // Patient 6 sessions (effectiveness scores)
```

```
          [38.4, 39.2, 47.9, 55.2], // Patient 7 sessions (effectiveness scores)
      ]
    },
    {
      "trial_id": 222222222,
      "trial_name": "Clinical Trial for Drug B",
      "drug_name": "Drug B",
      "patientsWithAdministeredSessions": [
          [87.7, 80.6, 70.5, 60.4], // Patient 1 sessions (effectiveness scores)
          [81.3, 83.4, 75.2], // Patient 2 sessions (effectiveness scores)
          [70.3, 60.1], // Patient 3 sessions (effectiveness scores)
          [75.5, 65.8, 55.7], // Patient 4 sessions (effectiveness scores)
          [60.4, 60.6, 40.4, 30.3], // Patient 5 sessions (effectiveness scores)
      ]
    },
]);
```

## Defining the aggregation pipeline

You first need to define the following two functions:

1.  To get the size of the largest sub-array within the outer array

2.  To condense the sub-arrays into a single array of sums and counts, ready for you to use in
    a pipeline:

```
// Macro function to generate a compound expression to get
// the size of the largest sub-array within an array
function getLargestSubArraySize(arrayOfSubArraysRef) {
  return {
    "$reduce": {
      "input": arrayOfSubArraysRef,
      "initialValue": 0,
      "in": {
        "$cond": [
          {"$gt": [{"$size": "$$this"}, "$$value"]},
          {"$size": "$$this"},
          "$$value"
        ]
      },
    },
  };
}
```

```
// Macro function to generate a compound expression to condense
// the sub-arrays in an array into a single array of sums and counts
function condenseSubArraysToSumsAndCounts(arrayOfSubArraysRef) {
  return {
    "$map": {  // Loop with counter "index" up to largest sub-array's length
      "input": {"$range": [0, getLargestSubArraySize(arrayOfSubArraysRef)]},
      "as": "index",
      "in": {
        "$reduce": {  // Loop with ref "this" thru each outer array member
          "input": {
            "$range": [0, {"$size": arrayOfSubArraysRef}]
          },
          "initialValue": {
            "sum": 0,
            "count": "",
          },
          "in": {
            // Total up the Nth sessions across all the patients
            "sum": {
              "$sum": [
                "$$value.sum",
                {"$arrayElemAt": [
                  {"$arrayElemAt": [arrayOfSubArraysRef, "$$this"]},
                  "$$index"
                ]}
              ]
            },
            // Count number of patients who conducted in the Nth session
            "count": {
              "$sum": [
                "$$value.count",
                {"$cond": [
                  {"$isNumber": {
                    "$arrayElemAt": [
                      {"$arrayElemAt": [arrayOfSubArraysRef, "$$this"]},
                      "$$index"
                    ]
                  }},
                  1,
```

```
                    0,
                  ]},
                ]
            },
          },
        },
      },
    },
  };
}
```

Then, define the pipeline ready to perform the aggregation:

```
var pipeline = [
  {"$set": {
    "sessionsAverageEffectiveness": {
      "$let": {
        "vars": {
          // Condense the sub-arrays into a single array of sums and counts
          "sessionsWithSumCountOfEffectiveness":
            condenseSubArraysToSumsAndCounts(
              "$patientsWithAdministeredSessions"),
        },
        "in": {
          // Create avg score for Nth session for all participating patients
          "$map": {
            "input": "$$sessionsWithSumCountOfEffectiveness",
            "in": {"$divide": ["$$this.sum", "$$this.count"]}
          }
        }
      },
    },
  }},

  {"$unset": [
    "_id",
    "patientsWithAdministeredSessions",
  ]},
];
```

## Executing the aggregation pipeline

Next, perform the following steps:

1.  Execute the aggregation using the defined pipeline:

    ```
    db.drugTrialResults.aggregate(pipeline);
    ```

2.  Generate its explain plan:

    ```
    db.drugTrialResults.explain("executionStats").aggregate(pipeline);
    ```

## Expected pipeline result

Once executed, the aggregation will return two documents, each showing the same drug trial records as before but with the patientsWithAdministeredSessions jagged array (array of arrays) field replaced with a sessionsAverageEffectiveness array of average session effectiveness results across all patients for that trial:

```
[
  {
    "trial_id": 111111111,
    "trial_name": "Clinical Trial for Drug A",
    "drug_name": "Drug A",
    "sessionsAverageEffectiveness": [
      43.1, 51.04285714285714, 58.61428571428571, 73.2, 86, 91.8
    ]
  },
  {
    "trial_id": 222222222,
    "trial_name": "Clinical Trial for Drug B",
    "drug_name": "Drug B",
    "sessionsAverageEffectiveness": [
      75.04, 70.1, 60.45, 45.35
    ]
  }
]
```

## Pipeline observations

- **Reusable macro functions**: As with many of the other *array manipulation examples*, the aggregation uses macro functions to generate boilerplate code for use in the pipeline. These functions are general purpose, and reusable as is in other solutions.

- **Dealing with uneven sub-array lengths**: Processing elements in the same position in each sub-array requires looping through each array position, but given that each sub-array is a different length, this is not straightforward. You could iterate each element in the first sub-array and then grab the corresponding position element of the other sub-arrays. However, if the first sub-array is not the longest, you will miss some elements from the longer array. Therefore, the example employs a macro function, `getLargestSubArraySize()`, to compare the sizes of every sub-array and return the largest size.

- **Calculating sums and counts across elements in different sub-arrays**: The new `condenseSubArraysToSumsAndCounts()` macro function performs the main logic on behalf of the pipeline to generate a new array of result averages from the original array of arrays of patient results. This function uses a `$map` operator to iterate through session result sub-arrays first rather than the outer patient's array. This approach checks position 0 of every patient's session result first, then position 1, then position 2, and so on. Inside this `$map` operator, a `$reduce` operator is used to sum and count drug session effectiveness for the current element position of each patient of the outer array. The `$arrayElemAt` and `$sum` operators used during the summing or counting process gracefully tolerate missing elements for the shorter sub-arrays. The looping process calculates both the sum and count values for each test session for a trial. If we were to print the values generated by this function for one of the records, they would look similar to the following:

```
[
    {"sum": 301.7, "count": 7},
    {"sum": 357.3, "count": 7},
    {"sum": 410.3, "count": 7},
    {"sum": 439.2, "count": 6},
    {"sum": 172, "count": 2},
    {"sum": 91.8, "count": 1}
]
```

The macro function is invoked via a `$let` variable in the main pipeline's body. As you can see with the count fields previously, the macro function has correctly identified that not all patients (seven patients maximum) were administered drugs for all the sessions (six sessions maximum) in this particular clinical trial.

- **Calculating averages across elements in different sub-arrays**: The final part of the main pipeline uses $map to iterate through the condensed sum and count for each session built by the macro function and held in the $let variable. For each session's sum and count pair, the pipeline simply divides the sum by the count to yield the average effectiveness of the drug for each session. The pipeline cannot use the MongoDB built-in $avg operator because $avg expects to calculate the average for a single array's elements. However, the pipeline calculates an average across elements of different sub-arrays in this scenario.

- **Inability to use the $zip operator**: There was potential for the whole pipeline to be simpler by using the $zip operator to merge the elements of each sub-array that occupy the same sub-array position. However, the $zip operator expects to be given an array of expressions and rejects any attempt to give it a single field path expression referencing a jagged array.

## Summary

In this chapter, you explored examples of dealing with complex array manipulation challenges by breaking down array processing into manageable pieces for various use cases.

In the next chapter, you will learn how to build aggregation pipelines to perform full-text searches on the text fields of documents.

# 13

# Full-Text Search Examples

Applications often require full-text search capabilities to enable partial and weighted matches over textual content beyond exact field matches. This feature could be necessary for a content management system to search for keywords, an e-commerce platform to search for product descriptions, or a customer support application to scan user feedback. In this chapter, you will explore how to build aggregation pipelines that leverage full-text search capabilities in MongoDB Atlas.

In this chapter, we will cover the following topics:

- An overview of Atlas Search
- Performing a text search on mandatory and optional keywords
- Using text search to generate facets and counts efficiently

# What is Atlas Search?

Atlas Search makes adding fast relevance-based full-text search to your applications easy. Atlas Search deploys an Apache Lucene index alongside your database, automatically handling data and schema synchronization between the source collection and this new search index. Atlas Search provides the following features, all backed by support for multiple language analyzers:

- Fuzzy matching

- Autocomplete

- Fast facets and counts

- Highlighting

- Relevance scoring

- Geospatial queries

- Synonyms

You reduce your cognitive load by invoking searches via the regular MongoDB drivers and aggregations API rather than a third-party Lucene API.

With the Atlas platform's integration of a database, search engine, and synchronization pipeline into a single, unified, and fully managed service, you can quickly build search features into your applications. Consequently these ease of use and functionality advantages mean you should use Atlas Search over the `$text` and `$regex` query operators of MongoDB when running your database in Atlas specifically.

# Compound text search criteria

Full-text search and regular database querying exhibit distinct usage patterns. Full-text search solutions primarily scan and retrieve unstructured data, such as paragraphs of text, by analyzing the semantics and frequency of terms, using elaborate algorithms to rank relevance and handle synonyms or related phrases. On the other hand, regular database querying usually targets highly structured data, leveraging precise field-based value matching to identify and retrieve records. In this example, you will develop an aggregation pipeline to execute an Atlas-based full-text search on a collection of documents.

## Scenario

You want to search a collection of e-commerce products for specific movie DVDs. Based on each DVD's full-text plot description, you want movies with a *post-apocalyptic* theme, especially those related to a *nuclear* disaster where some people *survive*. However, you aren't interested in seeing movies involving *zombies*.

> **Note**
>
> To execute this example, you need to use an Atlas cluster rather than a self-managed MongoDB deployment. Therefore, before you begin, you'll need to provision a free-tier Atlas cluster (see `https://www.mongodb.com/cloud/atlas`).

## Populating the sample data

First, drop any old version of the database (if it exists) and then populate a new *products* collection with some *DVD* and *book* records. Each record includes the product's *name, category* (book or DVD), and a textual *description*:

```
db = db.getSiblingDB("book-compound-text-search");
db.products.remove({});

// Insert 7 records into the products collection
db.products.insertMany([
  {
    "name": "The Road",
    "category": "DVD",
    "description": "In a dangerous post-apocalyptic world, a dying father
protects his surviving son as they try to reach the coast",
  },
```

```
    {
      "name": "The Day Of The Triffids",
      "category": "BOOK",
      "description": "Post-apocalyptic disaster where most people are blinded by
  a meteor shower and then die at the hands of a new type of plant",
    },
    {
      "name": "The Road",
      "category": "BOOK",
      "description": "In a dangerous post-apocalyptic world, a dying father
  protects his surviving son as they try to reach the coast",
    },
    {
      "name": "The Day the Earth Caught Fire",
      "category": "DVD",
      "description": "A series of nuclear explosions cause fires and earthquakes
  to ravage cities, with some of those that survive trying to rescue the post-
  apocalyptic world",
    },
    {
      "name": "28 Days Later",
      "category": "DVD",
      "description": "A caged chimp infected with a virus is freed from a lab,
  and the infection spreads to people who become zombie-like with just a few
  surviving in a post-apocalyptic country",
    },
    {
      "name": "Don't Look Up",
      "category": "DVD",
      "description": "Pre-apocalyptic situation where some astronomers warn
  humankind of an approaching comet that will destroy planet Earth",
    },
    {
      "name": "Thirteen Days",
      "category": "DVD",
      "description": "Based on the true story of the Cuban nuclear misile
  threat, crisis is averted at the last minute and the workd survives",
    },
  ]);
```

Now, using the simple procedure described in the *Appendix*, define an Atlas Search index. Select the new `book-compound-text search.products` database collection and enter the following JSON search index definition:

```
{
  "searchAnalyzer": "lucene.english",
  "mappings": {
    "dynamic": true
  }
}
```

This definition indicates that the index should use the `lucene.english` analyzer and include all document fields to be searchable with their inferred data types.

## Defining the aggregation pipeline

Once you have inserted the index and defined the search index, define a pipeline ready to perform the aggregation:

```
var pipeline = [
  // Search DVDs where desc must contain "apocalyptic" but not "zombie"
  {"$search": {
    "index": "default",
    "compound": {
      "must": [
        {"text": {
          "path": "description",
          "query": "apocalyptic",
        }},
      ],
      "should": [
        {"text": {
          "path": "description",
          "query": "nuclear survives",
        }},
      ],
      "mustNot": [
        {"text": {
          "path": "description",
          "query": "zombie",
        }},
      ],
```

```
        "filter": [
          {"text": {
            "path": "category",
            "query": "DVD",
          }},
        ],
      }
    }},

    // Capture the search relevancy score in the output and omit the _id field
    {"$set": {
      "score": {"$meta": "searchScore"},
      "_id": "$$REMOVE",
    }},
  ];
```

## Executing the aggregation pipeline

Next, perform the following steps:

1. Execute the aggregation using the defined pipeline:

   ```
   db.products.aggregate(pipeline);
   ```

2. Generate its explain plan:

   ```
   db.products.explain("executionStats").aggregate(pipeline);
   ```

## Expected pipeline result

Once executed, the aggregation will return three documents, showing products that are post-apocalyptic-themed DVDs:

```
[
  {
    name: 'The Day the Earth Caught Fire',
    category: 'DVD',
    description: 'A series of nuclear explosions cause fires and earthquakes
to ravage cities, with some of those that survive trying to rescue the post-
apocalyptic world',
    score: 0.8468831181526184
  },
  {
```

```
    name: 'The Road',
    category: 'DVD',
    description: 'In a dangerous post-apocalyptic world, a dying father
protects his surviving son as they try to reach the coast',
    score: 0.3709350824356079
  },
  {
    name: "Don't Look Up",
    category: 'DVD',
    description: 'Pre-apocalyptic situation where some astronomers warn
humankind of an approaching comet that will destroy planet Earth',
    score: 0.09836573898792267
  }
]
```

If you don't see any results, double-check that the system has finished generating your new full-text search index.

## Pipeline observations

- **Search stage**: The $search stage is only available in aggregation pipelines run against an Atlas-based MongoDB database, which leverages Atlas Search. A $search stage must be the first stage of an aggregation pipeline. Under the covers (see https://www.mongodb.com/docs/atlas/atlas-search/atlas-search-overview/#fts-architecture), it instructs the system to execute a text search operation against an internally synchronized Lucene full-text index. Inside the $search stage, you can only use one of the small sets of text-search-specific pipeline operators. In this example, the pipeline uses a $compound operator to define a combination of multiple $text text search operators.

- **Results and relevancy explanation**: The executed pipeline ignores four of the seven input documents and sorts the remaining three documents by highest relevancy first. It achieves this by applying the following actions:

  - It excludes two book-related records because the filter option executes a $text match on just DVD in the category field.

  - It ignores the 28 Days Later DVD record because the mustNot option's $text matches zombie in the description field.

  - It excludes the movie Thirteen Days because even though its description contains two of the optional terms (nuclear and survives), it doesn't include the mandatory term apocalyptic.

- It deduces the score of the remaining records based on the ratio of the number of matching terms (`apocalyptic`, `nuclear`, and `survives`) in each document's `description` field versus how infrequently those terms appear in other documents in the same collection.

- **English language analyzer**: Atlas Search provides multiple analyzer options for breaking down generated text indexes and executing text queries into searchable tokens. The default analyzer, `standard`, is not used here because the pipeline needs to match variations of the same English words. For example, `survives` and `surviving` need to refer to the same term. Hence, the text index uses the `lucene.english` analyzer.

- **Meta operator**: The `$meta` operator provides supplementary metadata about the results of a text search performed earlier in a pipeline. When leveraging an Atlas Search-based text search, the pipeline can look up a `searchScore` field in the metadata to access the relevancy score attributed to each text search result. This example uses `searchScore` to help you understand why the results are in a particular order, with some records having higher relevancy than others. In this example, it serves no other purpose, and you can omit it. However, in a different situation, you could use the search score to filter out low-relevancy results in a later `$match` stage of a pipeline.

# Facets and counts text search

In *Chapter 9, Trend Analysis Examples*, you learned about using a core MongoDB aggregation framework stage (`$facet`) to classify the data in a collection by different dimensions. However, as that chapter highlighted, the aggregation has no choice but to perform a *full-collection scan* to identify and assemble the faceted results. With Atlas, you can employ an alternative mechanism to generate faceted results faster, which you should prefer whenever Atlas is an option. This example will walk you through how to use Atlas Search to create facets for a collection.

> **Note**
>
> For this example, you require MongoDB version 4.4 or above. This is because you'll be using the `facet` option in the `$searchMeta` stage introduced in version 4.4.

## Scenario

You help run a bank's call center and want to analyze the summary descriptions of customer telephone inquiries recorded by call center staff. You want to look for customer calls that mention *fraud* and understand what periods of a specific day these fraud-related calls occur. This insight will help the bank plan its future staffing rotas for the fraud department.

> **Note**
>
> To execute this example, you need to use an Atlas cluster rather than a self-managed MongoDB deployment. Therefore, before you begin, you'll need to provision a free-tier Atlas cluster (see `https://www.mongodb.com/cloud/atlas`).

## Populating the sample data

First, drop any old versions of the database (if they exist) and then populate a new *enquiries* collection with new records. Each enquiry document has fields for the customer *account ID*, the *date* and *time* of the call, and a textual *summary* of what was discussed in the call:

```
db = db.getSiblingDB("book-facets-text-search");
db.enquiries.remove({});


// Insert records into the enquiries collection
db.enquiries.insertMany([
  {
    "accountId": "9913183",
    "datetime": ISODate("2022-01-30T08:35:52Z"),
    "summary": "They just made a balance enquiry only - no other issues",
  },
  {
    "accountId": "9913183",
    "datetime": ISODate("2022-01-30T09:32:07Z"),
    "summary": "Reported suspected fraud - froze cards, initiated chargeback
on the transaction",
  },
  {
    "accountId": "6830859",
    "datetime": ISODate("2022-01-30T10:25:37Z"),
    "summary": "Customer said they didn't make one of the transactions which
could be fraud - passed on to the investigations team",
  },
  {
    "accountId": "9899216",
    "datetime": ISODate("2022-01-30T11:13:32Z"),
    "summary": "Struggling financially this month hence requiring extended
overdraft - increased limit to 500 for 2 monts",
  },
  {
    "accountId": "1766583",
    "datetime": ISODate("2022-01-30T10:56:53Z"),
    "summary": "Fraud reported - fradulent direct debit established 3 months
ago - removed instruction and reported to crime team",
  },
```

```
  {
     "accountId": "9310399",
     "datetime": ISODate("2022-01-30T14:04:48Z"),
     "summary": "Customer rang on mobile whilst fraud call in progress on home
phone to check if it was valid - advised to hang up",
  },
  {
     "accountId": "4542001",
     "datetime": ISODate("2022-01-30T16:55:46Z"),
     "summary": "Enquiring for loan - approved standard loan for 6000 over 4
years",
  },
  {
     "accountId": "7387756",
     "datetime": ISODate("2022-01-30T17:49:32Z"),
     "summary": "Froze customer account when they called in as multiple fraud
transactions appearing even whilst call was active",
  },
  {
     "accountId": "3987992",
     "datetime": ISODate("2022-01-30T22:49:44Z"),
     "summary": "Customer called claiming fraud for a transaction which
confirmed looks suspicious and so issued chargeback",
  },
  {
     "accountId": "7362872",
     "datetime": ISODate("2022-01-31T07:07:14Z"),
     "summary": "Worst case of fraud I've ever seen - customer lost millions -
escalated to our high value team",
  },
]);
```

Now, using the simple procedure described in the *Appendix*, define a search index. Select the new `book-facets-text search.enquiries` database collection, and enter the following JSON search index definition:

```
{
  "analyzer": "lucene.english",
  "searchAnalyzer": "lucene.english",
  "mappings": {
    "dynamic": true,
    "fields": {
      "datetime": [
        {"type": "date"},
        {"type": "dateFacet"}
      ]
    }
  }
}
```

This definition indicates that the index should use the `lucene.english` analyzer. It includes an explicit mapping for the `datetime` field to ask for the field to be indexed in two ways to simultaneously support a date range filter and faceting from the same pipeline. The mapping indicates that all other document fields will be searchable with inferred data types.

## Defining the aggregation pipeline

Once you have set the sample data and inserted records, define a pipeline ready to perform the aggregation:

```
var pipeline = [
  // For 1 day 'fraud' enquiries group into periods of the day counting them
  {"$searchMeta": {
    "index": "default",
    "facet": {
      "operator": {
        "compound": {
          "must": [
            {"text": {
              "path": "summary",
              "query": "fraud",
            }},
          ],
          "filter": [
```

```
          {"range": {
            "path": "datetime",
            "gte": ISODate("2022-01-30"),
            "lt": ISODate("2022-01-31"),
          }},
        ],
      },
    },
  },
  "facets": {
    "fraudEnquiryPeriods": {
      "type": "date",
      "path": "datetime",
      "boundaries": [
        ISODate("2022-01-30T00:00:00.000Z"),
        ISODate("2022-01-30T06:00:00.000Z"),
        ISODate("2022-01-30T12:00:00.000Z"),
        ISODate("2022-01-30T18:00:00.000Z"),
        ISODate("2022-01-31T00:00:00.000Z"),
      ],
    }
  }
        }
      }},
    }
  ];
```

## Executing the aggregation pipeline

Now, execute the aggregation using the defined pipeline:

```
db.enquiries.aggregate(pipeline);
```

> **Note**
>
> At the time of writing, it is currently not possible to view the explain plan for a $searchMeta-based aggregation.

## Expected pipeline result

Once executed, the aggregation should show the pipeline matched six documents for a specific day on the text fraud, spread out over the four six-hour periods, as shown:

```
[
  {
    count: { lowerBound: Long("6") },
    facet: {
      fraudEnquiryPeriods: {
        buckets: [
          {
            _id: ISODate("2022-01-30T00:00:00.000Z"),
            count: Long("0")
          },
          {
            _id: ISODate("2022-01-30T06:00:00.000Z"),
            count: Long("3")
          },
          {
            _id: ISODate("2022-01-30T12:00:00.000Z"),
            count: Long("2")
          },
          {
            _id: ISODate("2022-01-30T18:00:00.000Z"),
            count: Long("1")
          }
        ]
      }
    }
  }
]
```

If you don't see any facet results and the value of count is 0, double-check that the system has finished generating your new full-text search index.

## Pipeline observations

- **Search metadata stage**: The $searchMeta stage is only available in aggregation pipelines run against an Atlas-based MongoDB database, which leverages Atlas Search. A $searchMeta stage must be the first stage of an aggregation pipeline, and under the covers, it performs a text search operation against an internally synchronized Lucene full-text index. However, it differs from the $search operator used in the previous example. Instead, you use $searchMeta to ask the system to return metadata about the text search you executed, such as the match count, rather than returning the search result records. The $searchMeta stage takes a facet option, which takes two sub-options, operator and facet, which you use to define the text search criteria and categorize the results in groups.

- **Date range filter**: The pipeline uses a $text operator to match descriptions containing the term fraud. Additionally, the search criteria includes a $range operator. The $range operator allows you to match records between two numbers or two dates. The example pipeline applies a date range, only including documents where each datetime field's value is 30-January-2022.

- **Facet boundaries**: The pipeline uses a facet *collector* to group metadata results by date range boundaries. Each boundary in the example defines a six-hour period of the same specific day for a document's datetime field. A single pipeline can declare multiple facets, so you need to give each facet a different name. The pipeline only defines one facet in this example, labeling it fraudEnquiryPeriods. When the pipeline executes, it returns the total count of matched documents and the count of matches in each facet grouping. There were no *fraud-related* inquiries between *midnight* and *6 A.M.*, indicating that perhaps the fraud department only requires *skeleton staffing* for such periods. In contrast, the period between *6 A.M.* and *midday* shows the highest number of fraud-related inquiries, suggesting the bank dedicates additional staff to those periods.

- **Faster facet counts**: A faceted index is a special type of Lucene index optimized to compute counts of dataset categories. An application can leverage the index to offload much of the work required to analyze facets ahead of time, thus avoiding some of the latency costs when invoking a faceted search at runtime. Therefore, use the Atlas faceted search capability if you are in a position to adopt Atlas Search, rather than using MongoDB's general-purpose faceted search capability described in *Chapter 9, Trend Analysis Examples*.

- **Combining a search operation with metadata**: In this example, a pipeline uses $searchMeta to obtain metadata from a search (counts and facets). What if you also want the actual search results from running $search similar to the previous example? You could invoke two operations from your client application, one to retrieve the search results and one to retrieve the metadata results. However, Atlas Search provides a way of obtaining both aspects within a single aggregation. Instead of using a $searchMeta stage, you use a $search stage. The pipeline automatically stores its metadata (see `https://www.mongodb.com/docs/atlas/atlas-search/facet/#search_meta-aggregation-variable`) in the $$SEARCH_META variable, ready for you to access it via subsequent stages in the same pipeline. For example:

```
{"$set": {"mymetadata": "$$SEARCH_META"}}
```

# Summary

In this chapter, you explored how to build aggregations using the Atlas full-text search capabilities to search for matches and perform analytics on unstructured textual data. The examples also directed you to additional resources in the *Appendix* of this book, which will help you create indexes for your full-text search deployment.

# Appendix

## Create an Atlas Search index

To complete the examples in *Chapter 13, Full-Text Search Examples*, you need to use a MongoDB Atlas cluster rather than a self-managed MongoDB deployment. The simplest way to provision an Atlas cluster is to create a free-tier cluster (see `https://www.mongodb.com/cloud/atlas`). Once created, you can use the following steps to create a search index:

1. First, in the Atlas (see `https://cloud.mongodb.com/`) console, for your database cluster, click the **Search** tab and then click **Create Search Index**:

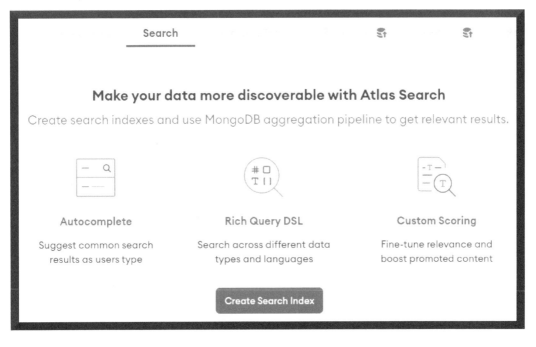

2.  Select **JSON Editor** and then click **Next**:

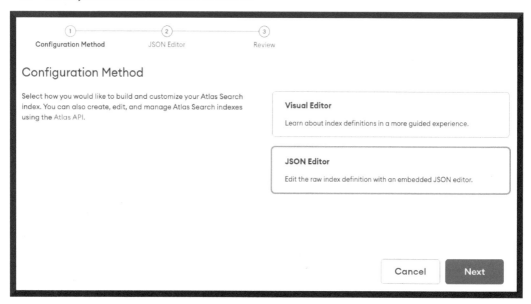

3.  Leave **Index Name** as **default**, select the **Database and Collection** you require, paste in your JSON index definition, and then click **Next**:

4.    On the review screen, click **Create Search Index** to finish:

5.    It may take a few minutes for the system to generate the text search index.

> **Note**
>
> It is also possible for you to automate creating a search index by using the Atlas Admin API (see `https://www.mongodb.com/docs/atlas/reference/api/fts-indexes-create-one/#examples`) in MongoDB version 4.2 and greater, or by using the `createSearchIndexes` command in MongoDB version 7.0 and greater.

# Afterword

And now you know everything there is to know about aggregations—at least, the essential knowledge.

I hope this book has been as helpful to you as it has been to all of us at MongoDB. I joined MongoDB in 2013, and one of the areas where I experienced the most difficulty was aggregations. The resource I turned to most frequently was Asya (*Principal Engineer, MongoDB, Inc.*), or Paul Done himself, and his numerous writings on the subject.

Here at MongoDB, we regularly use the aggregation framework to answer some of the most complex questions about our products. Aggregations provide analytical capabilities that are performant and scalable inside of MongoDB Atlas for millions of users. Knowing how to use the aggregation functionality provides our teams—product, analytics, data science, operations, and other business functions—with fast insights to power our decision making and priorities.

I would like to thank Paul Done, our author, for writing this book and enabling thousands of developers. Paul wrote this book in his spare time and not as part of his actual job. His commitment to MongoDB, our users, and to technical excellence is truly inspiring. So, thank you Paul for teaching us all to be better developers.

And if you are still reading this far, thank you for learning MongoDB. We appreciate you.


**Rachelle Palmer**

Director of Product

Developer Experience and Education

MongoDB, Inc.

# Index

www.packtpub.com

Subscribe to our online digital library for full access to over 7,000 books and videos, as well as industry-leading tools to help you plan your personal development and advance your career. For more information, please visit our website.

## Why subscribe?

- Spend less time on theory and more time coding with practical e-books and videos from over 4,000 industry professionals

- Improve your learning with Skill Plans built especially for you

- Get a free e-book or video every month

- Fully searchable for easy access to vital information

- Copy and paste, print, and bookmark content

Did you know that Packt offers e-book versions of every book published, with PDF and ePub files available? You can upgrade to the e-book version at www.packtpub.com and as a print book customer, you are entitled to a discount on the e-book copy. Get in touch with us at customercare@packtpub.com for more details.

At www.packtpub.com, you can also read a collection of free technical articles, sign up for a range of free newsletters, and receive exclusive discounts and offers on Packt books and e-books.

# Other books you may enjoy

If you enjoyed this book, you may be interested in this other book by Packt:

**MongoDB Fundamentals**

Amit Phaltankar, Juned Ahsan, Michael Harrison, and Liviu Nedov

ISBN: 978-1-83921-064-8

- Set up and use MongoDB Atlas in the cloud
- Insert, update, delete, and retrieve data from MongoDB
- Build aggregation pipelines to perform complex queries
- Optimize queries using indexes
- Monitor databases and manage user authorization
- Improve scalability and performance with sharding clusters
- Replicate clusters, back up your database, and restore data
- Create data-driven charts and reports from real-time data

# Packt is searching for authors like you

If you're interested in becoming an author for Packt, please visit `authors.packtpub.com` and apply today. We have worked with thousands of developers and tech professionals, just like you, to help them share their insight with the global tech community. You can make a general application, apply for a specific hot topic that we are recruiting an author for, or submit your own idea.

# Download a free PDF copy of this book

Thanks for purchasing this book!

Do you like to read on the go but are unable to carry your print books everywhere? Is your eBook purchase not compatible with the device of your choice?

Don't worry, now with every Packt book you get a DRM-free PDF version of that book at no cost.

Read anywhere, any place, on any device. Search, copy, and paste code from your favorite technical books directly into your application.

The perks don't stop there, you can get exclusive access to discounts, newsletters, and great free content in your inbox daily

Follow these simple steps to get the benefits:

1. Scan the QR code or visit the link below

https://packt.link/free-ebook/9781835080641

2. Submit your proof of purchase

3. That's it! We'll send your free PDF and other benefits to your email directly

Milton Keynes UK
Ingram Content Group UK Ltd.
UKHW050759200923
428987UK00003B/3